123:1 · January 2024

Transnational Queer Materialism
Rana M. Jaleel and Evren Savcı, Special Issue Editors

AGAINST the DAY

Rana M. Jaleel and Evren Savcı

Transnational Queer Materialism

As early as 2003, Turkey's authoritarian leader Recep Tayyip Erdoğan positioned himself and presumably his pious Sunni voter base as the "Negros (zenci)" of Turkey. In the Turkish republic today, "whiteness" also makes an appearance with talk of "white turks" throughout academic and activist work, popular media, and daily life.

In the early 1990s, the Serbo-Croatian-language paper *Danas* ran a lengthy article, "Europe Is Raped Again," by Professor Muradif Kulenović, which theorizes the wartime rape of women through the words of Black Panther Eldridge Cleaver, who calls rape a "dialogue between races" and the "'rebellion' of a black man against the white master via the 'desecration of his women'" (Žarkov 2007: 137, Jaleel 2021: 74–75).

In these examples, the sexual and racial histories of the United States and the transatlantic slave trade are brought to bear on political and economic problems that cannot be said to share those histories in any clean or uncomplicated way. In Turkey, the transatlantic slave trade historically overlapped with other iterations of slavery, including the East African Ottoman slave trade. Today, Turkish claims to Blackness and whiteness are mediated by the country's strategic and shifting relationships with the European Union, the United

The South Atlantic Quarterly 123:1, January 2024
DOI 10.1215/00382876-10920741 © 2024 Duke University Press

States, NATO, and Russia on issues such as climate, migration and refugee crises, security, counter-terrorism, and trade agreements. Claims to Blackness and designations of whiteness unfold in this geopolitical context. Meanwhile, in the former Yugoslavia, Kulenović's invocation of Cleaver's erstwhile take on rape[1] fed narratives that positioned Bosnian and Croat Muslims closer to whiteness, one threatened by Serbian ethno-religious nationalism. Through this maneuver, the economic fallout of the Cold War's end, the withdrawal of Soviet financial support for the unaligned nation, loses its explanatory power for the state's collapse. The conflict becomes "ethnic"— fueled by long-standing animosities between groups. The putative end of socialism and the global triumph of capitalism—the instabilities and global realignments that they wrought—slip from view.

The uses of Blackness in these peripheral European contexts do not come about simply because of the bad intentions or the racisms of those who invoke them. Nor can these uses of Blackness be blamed solely on the unhampered spread of a liberalism that depends on group-based identities of the sort supported by civil and human rights frameworks. These aren't imposed racial categories, policies, or analyses disseminated by state or international governing orders or the NGOs that enact them. Instead, in these examples Blackness and its many histories are taken up in distant locations and re-signified to make sense of and shape the world. In both contexts, Blackness is claimed or deployed to assert a certain kind of victimization and narrate real or perceived injury through particular frames. This has become a kind of global common sense. Erdoğan's "Black Turks" are pious citizens from rural backgrounds, belittled by secular (left) urban elites. On behalf of "Black Turks," Erdoğan continues to justify an authoritarian rule that criminalizes ethnic and religious minorities, queers, and dissident leftists. In the former Yugoslavia, Kulenović's racialization of rape relies on a notion of predatory, sexually savage Blackness that threatens the (would-be) white heart of Europe. We might think of these instances as part of what Ruth Wilson Gilmore (2022: 322) calls "a world movement of racial capitalist relations." From the breakup of the former Yugoslavia to the rise of global authoritarianism, seismic shifts in Cold War, Third World, or European projects create new narratives and relations of power. The "release," for instance, of China, South Africa, Brazil, and India from the old Third World project has created new relations of imperialisms and colonialisms that have in some ways, as Vijay Prashad (2014) writes, little to do with the US or Western Europe. And yet the complex of sex, race, and violence made evident by the turn to those particular racial categories (Black and white) and histories of rape and slavery have everything to do with US and Western European racial (and therefore gendered, sexual) legacies and the circuits of racial capitalism that encourage their travel.

This special issue begins with an interest in that kind of travel—of concepts and terms that people use to give themselves and their worlds social and political meaning. It brings broader scholarship and interest in racial capitalism—itself a transnational, historical formation—into necessary and explicit conversation with queer studies' decades-long attempts to grapple with the complex of sexuality, sex, and gender within the study of race and political economy, both in the US and outside of it. This framing is an effort to deepen racial capitalism's engagement with gender/sex/sexuality, and an invitation to consider racializations in and beyond the transatlantic slave trade. In the same breath, this framing seeks to tackle the thorny issues that the transnationalization of queer studies has engendered as it attempts to bring political economy, the study of race, and geopolitics to bear on the production, meanings, and lived experiences of nondominant genders and sexualities—analyses that so often occur through terminologies, categories, and thought systems produced elsewhere. At issue here are the analytic categories available to think through the political and economic transits of race—including words like *Black* and *white* and *queer* and *trans*—that so often result in a reading of race that universalizes formations that are particular to the US. When those words travel out of context, we are once again caught in the projections of US racial imaginaries that have now turned from historical particularity into generalizable theory and concept. This, as we discuss, is exacerbated by the use of *queer* as a metaphor without a fixed referent (Eng, Halberstam, and Muñoz 2005). Understanding this article's opening claims to Blackness, for example, as a way of "queering" or "transing" race through its "strange" deployment and travel—a position not unimaginable in a field that gave us queer drones[2]—would participate in the closed circle of US epistemes just as it attempts to move beyond them and account for the rest of the world. The transits of Blackness and US racial politics in non-US geopolitical contexts are not easily tracked by scholarship on racial capitalism and queer of color critique that erases the specificity of US racial, gender, and sexual formations and presumes their facile portability. Nonetheless, these frameworks often set the theoretical ground that is then applied to non-US contexts.[3] This occurs at times, as we discuss, through the use of postcolonial theorists like Frantz Fanon, when these thinkers are uprooted from critical contexts and used to make sense of US racial and colonial violence before they get a ticket to travel the world again, this time embedded within would-be universal abstractions of Blackness, queerness, or transness.[4]

The appropriations of Blackness in the peripheries of Europe, as well as appropriations of postcolonial theorists by the US academy, each serve—purposefully or inadvertently—the production and reproduction of various racial, ethno-religious, political, and economic orders.[5] On the edges of Europe, and in the former Yugoslavia, for example, the use of Blackness to frame war rape as ethno-religiously motivated maintains the notion of discrete ethno-religious identities not only as conflict motivators but as indexing social positions that correspond to particular political views. This framing of the conflict as "ethno-religious" ultimately led to the enshrining of these identities within post-conflict agreements and the establishment, for example, of a tripartite inter-ethnic presidency in the constitution of Bosnia and Herzegovina. Here, the appropriation of US Blackness to make sense of conflict known for mass war rape taps into the heart of state formation, providing a cognizable framework for a world struggling to adjust to the putative end of the Cold War (Jaleel 2021: 85). And because this and the Turkish claim to Blackness are attempts to produce and reproduce racial, ethno-religious, political, and economic orders, they require an analysis of gender/sex. How can queer critique and analyses of racial capitalism account for narrations of injury that depend on an unmoored travel of Blackness?

Beginning with the global circuits of racial terminological travel helps us re-envision the production, meanings, and possibilities of queer and trans study and racial capitalism. To do so, we focus on particular strands of queer analysis: (1) those that concern "queers/trans of color" as subjects or (2) deploy some iteration of queer of color critique as a method or analytic. Queer of color critique is an epistemological intervention and a "method for analyzing cultural formations as registries of the intersections of race, political economy, gender, and sexuality . . . [one that situates] those formations within analyses of racial capitalism and the racial state" (Ferguson 2018: 1). Grace Kyungwon Hong and Roderick Ferguson (2011: 2) further define queer of color critique as "emerging from women of color feminism rather than deriving from a white Euro-American gay, lesbian, and queer theory tradition." Scholars like M. Jacqui Alexander (2006), Martin Manalansan (2003), Gayatri Gopinath (2005), and others continue to participate in this tradition, one that does not view queer of color (as identity or critique) as a universal category but one that depends on situated analyses of the operations of racial capitalism. But some uses of queer and trans of color critique can inadvertently reinforce US racial epistemologies—and the gender/sex systems that animate them—as such critique moves beyond analyses of US empire to take up new subjects, objects, and relations of study. As queer or trans is simultaneously an analytic, an identity, and a subject position, it can attach to subjects and objects not necessarily sexualized or gendered as nonnormative.[6] The normative/nonnormative divide can also result in a lumping effect that privileges the distinction between normative and nonnormative over other or more subtle operations of power (Cohen 1997). In the process, this flexibility risks homogenizing what it seeks to name and liberate.

For queer /trans of color, both as a term claimed by individuals and affixed to groups and populations, while also deployed as an analytic, the stakes are compounded by the openness of "of color"—especially when posed against an undifferentiated "whiteness"—and the many histories, legacies, and theorizations of racialization and colonialism that reside therein.[7] Meanwhile, racial capitalism recognizes that "capital can only be capital when it is accumulating, and it can only accumulate by producing and moving through relations of severe inequality among human groups" (Melamed 2015: 77). As such, the "racial" of racial capitalism describes a process integral to how accumulation and dispossession work through capitalism—it is not an analytic that exists solely for describing how Black or other minoritized people experience targeted suffering. And yet the political, economic, and governance work of gender/sex systems are not always at the forefront of racial capitalist analyses. This omission compounds the ways that the "racial" of racial capitalism so often becomes synonymous with a monolithic account of US Blackness and Black experience—a move often critiqued by Africanist scholarship.[8] This also ironically runs counter to Cedric J. Robinson's (2000) approach in *Black Marxism*, which popularized the term *racial capitalism* by describing European racialisms within feudal Europe as preceding the advent of capitalism. What remains to be theorized is a transnational queer approach to historical materialism—one capable of keeping queer of color critique firmly attached to its historical roots in the global study of racial capitalism.

Here, we take up the narrations and values produced by the travels and transits of words like queer of color, like race, like racial capitalism to both co-mobilize and re-theorize queer of color critique and the content and contours of global racial capitalism. From this perspective, queer of color critique and racial capitalism are not only sites from which to critique but entwined objects of critique themselves that are crucial to the circulation of racial terms. With and beyond the story of US empire and the transatlantic slave trade—from peripheral European engagements with Africa to the circulation of caste in Africa via Indian Ocean worlds—in this special issue we examine some of the histories and present modes of capitalist accumulation that are relevant to telling global stories of race and capitalism, which are entwined with other categories such as caste and religion. A queer/trans lens keeps our attention trained as well on the arrangements and estrangements of the sex/gender systems that power them. So positioned, we enter ongoing debates on the geopolitics of queer studies, the import of queer materialism, and theorizations of racial capitalism by asking (1) what is the "racial" of racial capitalism?, and (2) what is the "of color" in trans/queer of color critique? The questions form a method for thinking global racial capitalism and queer/trans of color study together—what we call *transnational queer materialism*.

In what follows, we outline some of the key debates and omissions in trans/queer studies—particularly certain trans theorizations of Blackness—and racial capitalism to demonstrate the utility of a transnational queer materialist approach. Transnational queer materialism offers "a historiographic approach to queer of color critique: an inquiry into the formation of queer approaches to political economy as part of a broader question of how the reproduction of the terms of freedom and justice, particularly sexual ones, are produced, reproduced, and thwarted" (Jaleel 2022). A transnational queer materialist approach is not about what *is* queer or trans or *who* is queer or trans, but *how* queer/trans as an analytic and field is able to be reproduced or interrupted—the material conditions, infrastructures, feelings, and concepts that make queer/trans subjects, objects, and relations possible. This means that "of color" cannot stand in for the "racial oppression" of minoritized groups in the way that theorizations of racial capitalism can enable when it is reduced to accounts of racialized, especially Black, suffering. The sort of historiography on offer by transnational queer materialism would instead, to apply it to the article's opening examples, use an analytic to account for how race is mobilized to support and reproduce specific, geopolitical ethnoreligious claims to power. In some ways, transnational queer materialism requires paradoxically broadening the scope of queer (of color) inquiry in order to narrow it. In other words, it must look globally in order to more precisely ground a queer and trans studies that is no longer solely about US sexual and gender politics. Transnational queer materialism is also a check against the universal and automatic situating of some bodies as always already queer or trans because they fall outside of a colonial whiteness and the frames of intelligibility dictated by it, resulting in the automatic "queering" or "transing" of entire geographies and populations.

The story, then, that transnational queer materialism tells about Blackness, Erdoğan, and the former Yugoslavia is one that narrates Blackness as intimately tethered to global governance and geopolitics. This story emphasizes how free-range notions of queer, trans, and Black obscure the role of nation-states and their political systems as key players in the creation, maintenance, reproduction, and reconfiguration of racialized gender/sex and the meaning and import of queer critique. In this way, transnational queer materialism pushes against approaches to queerness/transness and Blackness that portray these categories as functionally undifferentiated and/or perpetually victimized no matter their location in space or in time.[9] The maintenance of monolithic abstractions like queerness, transness, whiteness, and Blackness risk repeating the gestures transnational feminists have warned against, where "fantasized similarity" supports "an elision of material difference" (Grewal and Kaplan 1996: 6).

In an age of rising global authoritarianisms and appropriations of Blackness as injury, transnational queer materialism invites us to reconsider the operations of liberalism and the meanings of reform. Global instability, the uneven development of liberal democratic governance as well as rising right-wing populism and authoritarianism, and the relationships between people, their needs, and their histories can frustrate any easy assessment or dismissal of what in the US context David Eng (2010) has called "queer liberalism." Beginning here, with the differences between political orders around the globe, opens the door to a transnational queer materialist critique. This focus on geographies, governance, and geopolitics in turn puts pressure on the categories that comprise queer of color critique—queer, of color—and on the presumed contours of racial capitalism and queer materialist inquiry. In the process, queer and trans of color are reconnected to the historical material conditions of sexuality, indigeneity, and raciality—and the many histories and loci of power that drive them. Beginning here, lets us reimagine the question that drives so much left scholarship: how to best respond to proliferating global emergencies, how to best be against the injustices of what Randall Williams (2010) calls a "divided world"—when this "we" is itself divergent and interconnected, critical but also unable to definitively apprehend the many forces of history.

Queer/Black/Trans at the Limits of Empire

From Judith Butler's "Against Proper Objects" (1994) to the 2005 special issue of *Social Text*, "What's Queer about Queer Studies Now?" to *Social Text's*

2020 issue "Left of Queer," scholars have repeatedly emphasized the contingency of the term *queer* as a way to assess, if not defend, its political relevance and contemplate its potential obsolescence (Eng and Puar 2020). The insistence that *queer* not prescribe proper subjects, objects, or relations of inquiry—a dedication, in other words, to "subjectless" and "objectless" critique—has resulted in the explicit move away from sexuality as queer studies' "proper object" to a queer studies that runs, as the authors of "What's Queer about Queer Studies Now?" put it, toward "historical emergency." In the aftermath, queer might now contend with race and geopolitics, with various Marxisms and postcolonial inheritances—all of these were once, perhaps, not proper objects. But do improper objects remain? *Queer* is after all a term whose less-than-liberatory possibilities have been theorized through homonormativity (Duggan 2003) and homonationalisms (Puar 2007)—as put in bad service by governments and populations to police behavior, shore up borders, or otherwise assemble and control.[10] Better yet, how does queer come to be put in bad service conceptually, in bad relation?

To try to answer this question, we use a transnational queer materialist approach to identify certain epistemic tendencies across some iterations of largely US-based queer/trans studies, Black studies, and especially work occurring at the nexus of the two. Black, trans, and queer studies share the dilemma central to any work that involves "identity" politics: namely "the challenge of calling an object into being without owning or being owned by the call of identity or identification, of recognition or acknowledgment" (Best 2018: 16). Both Black studies and queer/trans studies are concerned with the question of violence and how to understand the systematic production of anti-Black violence and anti-trans/queer violence, respectively, and as co-constitutive phenomena. Approaches to these tense and mobile questions are as varied as their interdisciplinary commitments, methods, and sites of intervention. Here, we are not intending to present a definitive "state of the field" of Black or trans/queer studies. This is a much less ambitious attempt to identify how certain lines of thought or theoretical tendencies might benefit from a closer engagement with transnational queer materialism. Among these tendencies, we note (1) in queer studies in particular, the unmarked travel of US racial categories and rubrics; (2) the decontextualized use of postcolonial theorists like Frantz Fanon to shore up theorizing by US scholars of queer/transness and Blackness; (3) a kind of "queer liberalism overwhelm" in which the failures of US-style democratic governance and the nation-state are extrapolated as universal grounds for analysis; and (4) a romance with ungovernability and fugitivity that uncritically extends these rubrics beyond largely US-based experiences of slavery. Acknowledging these tendencies moves us closer to accounting for claims of Blackness without Black people taking place on the outskirts of Europe, where Blackness becomes metaphor and simile that depends on the free travel of US racial histories. This travel relies on and in turn reinforces the circulation of racial capitalism as a term that is functionally synonymous with US racial binaries (Black/white) and US histories of slavery even as it dematerializes these histories.

Many modes and kinds of travels of theory and history have contributed to the need for transnational queer materialist critique. These include transits between disciplines and methods as queer moves out of psychoanalytic and literary studies; the global travel of queer of color critique; and the travel of US racial categories under the term racial capitalism. At times, disciplinary transits, namely US queer studies' early roots in literary studies and psychoanalytic theory, have limited the utility of the field to grapple with the geopolitics of racialized gender. In those fields, some queer theorists were invested in radical breaks thought to be initiated by gay sex or queerness writ large. These include psychic oppositionality in the case of Leo Bersani, where sex is a scene of "shattering," but also the strains of queer negativity or antisocial orientations that were often theorized from the closed and fictional worlds of literary texts and other cultural productions, as in Lee Edelman's (2004) *No Future*, where queerness is not tied to individual identity or a collective impulse but is a figural position that opposes sociality itself, given its presumptive investments with reproductive futurity. In this view, queer abjection is the destruction of the social order and against a politics of hope—and not simply because it denounces social life, but, as Lauren Berlant and Lee Edelman (2014: xii) clarify, because it upends "social relations that appear . . . irreparable."

José Estaban Muñoz (2006: 825) responds to Edelman's antirelationality, antisociality, and abandonment of reparative social politics in forceful terms: "the antirelational in queer studies was the gay white man's last stand" and thus for Muñoz a final attempt to keep sexuality as a single node of analysis, separate from race, class, and other forms of social difference. As such, Muñoz (2009: 95) rejects Edelman's critique of reproductive futurity emblematized by the child; the heteronormative fixation on the child "is only the stuff of some kids. Racialized kids, queer kids, are not the sovereign princes of futurity." These theoretical and methodological inheritances— the investments in rupture and stark figural claims— can follow *queer* and *trans* to, in particular, the interdisciplinary field of American Studies, where

US empire and US theorizations of racial capitalism set the stage for the kinds of "historical emergency" to which *queer* or *trans* now attend: one overdetermined by US racial histories mistaken for universal ones. This transit to American studies privileged the study of US empire, which has at times stood in for transnational queer materialism as a way to address the world beyond US borders, if not beyond its imperial reach. As Anjali Arondekar and Geeta Patel (2016: 156–57) query, "What would it mean to imagine an analytic of race that would take the transatlantic trade to the Indian Ocean and not produce African subjects in the same trajectory of slavery?" To ask these questions is not in any way to dismiss US-focused projects but to put pressure on their component parts: which and whose "global" histories become relevant, whose concepts and categories carry the day, and what assumptions about race (or more broadly, "difference") and political economy move through such inquiries and their attendant methods?

While the focus on US empire brought political economic analysis to bear on examinations of sex and sexuality, the corresponding study of racial capitalism on offer is nonetheless limited by the field's focus on US empire and the racial logics that pertain to it. Chandan Reddy's (2005: 113) excellent "Asian Diasporas, Neoliberalism, and Family," for example, analyzes the gay Pakistani US asylum seeker "as formed in the contradiction between heteronormative social relations mandated for immigrants of color by the state's policies and the liberal state's ideology of universal sexual freedom as a mask for growing these social relations." The focus on the US state here means that Reddy's essay follows how Pakistan must remain a flat figuration—a historical void of a country, a projected geography against which the United States erects itself—and implicitly how the Pakistani asylum seeker's material circumstances, including his potential class and caste privileges pre-asylum, disappear with it. Transnational queer materialism would build on this work by fleshing out what would be abstractions (both Pakistan and the Pakistani gay asylum seeker). In the process, this fleshing out might perhaps tell us something about the complexities of "racial" and "capitalism" through the intersecting political and economic histories of nations and regions.

Efforts to think race and transness transnationally have at times also stumbled back into US racial categories without attention to other racializing histories. If the global uptake of LGBT+ and queer has raised many eyebrows, queer of color has had little comparable objection, if anything the term seems to unite "queers" and "trans" across geopolitics and geographies as long as they are not "white." In "Trans Necropolitics. A Transnational Reflection on Violence, Death, and the Trans of Color Afterlife," for example,

C. Riley Snorton and Jin Haritaworn (2013: 67) rightfully advocate for trans studies and related fields to "push our accounts of violence and anti-violence to beyond limited formulas such as 'race, gender, and class' in both their intersectional and post-identitarian formulations" and that "we must be wary of analogizing categories like, women, gay and trans, or even 'queer of color' and 'trans.' Yet in analyzing the circulation of Black trans women's death transnationally–including how the death of Tyra Hunter in Washington, DC, and the hate crime discourse boosted certain forms of transgender inclusion in Germany—Snorton and Haritaworn (2013: 66) argue that "the lives of trans people of color in the global North and West are celebrated and their deaths memorialized, in ways that serve the white citizenry and mask necropolitical violence waged against gender variant people from the global South and East." But what racial orders and historical relations are captured and missed by the term *trans of color* as it goes to Europe, especially when it is opposed to the free-floating signifier of an undifferentiated "whiteness"? [11] Homogenous categories of "Turks" and "Muslims," argued to be the ultimate victims of trans-friendly legislation in Germany, erase the various ethnic, class, and religious differences within and between them.

If the work of "queer" is to respond to "historical emergencies," then "queer" uses of US Blackness and racializing logics by political actors in the peripheries of Europe are a five-alarm fire that can't assuaged by queer studies as usual. Building on these observations, we might put some pressure on what counts as a "historical emergency" subject to queer/trans critique and ask when is an improper object a historical emergency? Is the Turkish "Negro" and white Turk a historical emergency of this sort? Is Kulenović's attempt to portray war rape through a Black Panther's take on rape a historical emergency subject to queer of color critique? We think so because these historical emergencies can interrupt the replication of queer analytics that ignore global racial capitalisms and value making beyond the legacies of the US experience of race. The two examples that open our essay illustrate this point.

While there are actual Afro-Turks in the Republic, including those who trace their lineage to the East African slave trade of the Ottoman empire, Erdoğan's use of the term *zenci* (negro), and at other times *siyah Türk* (Black Turk), does not refer to them. His usage instead dislocates Blackness from its multiple historical contexts, estranging Blackness from broader global discourses about raciality. In Erdoğan's mouth, Blackness becomes a metaphor for oppression due to systematic and historic discrimination that justifies, if not requires, righteous revolt against the political order and demands a right-ing of historical wrongs. In a 2003 interview with the *New York Times* shortly after assuming the Turkish prime ministry, Erdoğan claimed that there are white Turks in Turkey, and that there are Black Turks. He, "your brother Erdoğan," was one of the Black Turks. In 2013, Erdogan, now the Turkish president, ordered the police forces to attack the Gezi Park protests with tear gas, water cannons, and plastic bullets while nonetheless positioning himself and his Sunni voter base as the oppressed yet again through the metaphor of Blackness: "According to them we do not understand (anything) from politics. According to them we do not understand anything from arts, theater, cinema, painting, poetry. . . . According to them we do not understand anything from aesthetics, architecture. According to them we are uneducated, ignorant, lower-strata/subaltern, people who need to be content with what they receive . . . in other words a "negro" group."[12] In this context, Erdoğan appropriates Blackness in order to evoke the oppression of pious Muslims in Turkey, including himself, due to the historical discrimination against pious Muslim women with headscarves. Such a claim to Blackness masquerades as a devout stand against secularizing forces imagined to be aligned with ominous "foreign powers," even as "your brother Erdoğan" brutalizes any political protest against his rule from all classes and religious backgrounds—including Muslim-minority Alevi youth—who were disproportionately murdered in the violent police repression of the uprisings over plans to demolish a public park and to replace it with a shopping mall (Savcı 2021).

Erdoğan makes a case for his own Blackness by "invisiblizing" his government's violent marginalization of various ethnic and religious minorities while nonetheless attempting in another context to *claim whiteness*. In the course of Turkey's growing investment in diplomatic ties with Africa south of the Sahara, Erdoğan and his cabinet position themselves as "white" in order to "lend credibility and validity to their promises of know-how transfer, technological advancement, industrialization, modernization and development in individual African countries"—but they distinguish themselves from colonial whiteness (Güner 2021). During and after President Erdoğan and his cabinet members' various trips to Africa, pro-government media have reported statements by African leaders and simple civilians regarding the "different kind of Whiteness" of Turks. The Turkish government's "nice (read noncolonialist) white guy" act in Africa unfolds within the history of the East African slave trade to the Ottoman empire and contemporary Turkey's large arms sales to African countries, not to mention the close to $80 billion worth of construction projects built by Turkish companies in addition to the "humanitarian aid" provided (Güner 2021).

Erdoğan invoked the same distance from white colonizers in speeches that rhetorically condemn "Europe" for its hypocritical "democracy." In those speeches, Erdoğan lambasted Europe's refusal to accept Syrian refugees, omitting the financial compensation Turkey received from the EU to contain three and a half million refugees within its borders and deny them passage to Europe. Also omitted were the dismal living conditions of the refugees stationed in Turkey. Instead of racializing Islam wholesale, transnational queer materialism pays attention to the things that fracture that category, like sect, like class, like gender and sexuality. "The figure of the Muslim" as terroristic might make sense in the US, but in the context of Turkey, we are faced with a Sunni government that has dubbed most Kurds, LGBT activists, and academics for peace terrorists simply because they opposed the war waged on the Kurdish territories (Savcı 2021). Erdoğan's claims to Blackness as injury on behalf of pious Sunnis serve to mask his regime's racialized violence against Kurdish citizens.

Meanwhile, in the former Yugoslavia, Kulenović's explanation of war rape through US feminist theory and histories of US Blackness supported a narrative of "ethnic" conflict that tapped into long-standing, global Euro-American racial projects of state formation and management (Jaleel 2021: 74). As Piro Rexhepi (2023: 14) explains, "The nineteenth century geopolitical mapping of the geographic, temporal, and racial borders of Europe that produced the Ottomans as an intrusion in the Balkans charged newly formed countries such as Greece, Bulgaria, Romania, and Serbia, and later the kingdom of Serbs, Croats, and Slovenes, with the re-Europeanization of the post-Ottoman spatial and social relations." Such racial imaginaries, forged on the outskirts of Europe, where it rubs elbows with Africa, the Middle East, and Asia, are thus activated through demands to consolidate white power through statecraft. As Rexhepi (2023: 14–15) continues, the notion of the Balkans as "the borderland battlefield" where white Christianity was besieged by its many Others was not just a "European concern." Instead, "these were joint Euro-American visions of what the eugenist David Starr Jordan considered 'the racial unity' of all white people." These visions of whiteness at the very edges of Europe were preserved not only through the racialization of various (and perversely sexualized) minorities in the region, including Jews, Muslims, and Roma, but by promoting ethno-nationalisms as the motivation for the many wars and territorial skirmishes to follow.

During the dissolution of the former Yugoslavia, as many scholars of the region have noted, international media, law, and policy understood Croat and Bosnian Muslims as victims of mass rape and Serbian aggression. In the process, they relied on an association of these particular Muslims with a secular, cosmopolitan whiteness (Atanasoski 2013: 180–81)—the kind that, at least at that time, must be defended—while ignoring the significantly more complicated political and racial history of a region plagued by invasion, partition, and division. This history included—to give one brief, evocative example—the establishment of the Independent State of Croatia as a satellite Nazi state after the 1941 invasion of Yugoslavia by Hungarian, Italian, and German forces. Yet the former Yugoslavia and other "second world" (former state-socialist) countries are absent from most US-based analyses of racial capitalism. Such formulations of racial capitalism then miss how ethnoreligious categories of difference are shored up through a geopolitical defense of whiteness (Rexhepi 2023)—even as politically, the former Yugoslavia has been associated with the Brown and Black Global South through its participation in the NonAligned Movement, which Josip Broz Tito, leader of the former Yugoslavia, co-founded with then leaders of Egypt and India, Gamal Nasser and Jawaharlal Nehru. As Catherine Baker (2018: 1–2) explains,

> These entanglements, moreover, have created conditions for shifting, ambiguous identifications with symbolic histories and geographies of race. They include not only identifications with "Europe" as a space of modernity, civilisation and (critical race studies would insist) whiteness, but also analogies drawn between "Balkanness" and "blackness" in imagined solidarity, as well as the race-blind anti-colonialism of Yugoslav Non-Alignment (which, under Tito, cast the leader of this European country as a model of national liberation for the Global South).

This omission of robust analysis of how global racial categories have shaped and continue to shape the historical and contemporary politics of the region have furthered the impression—one that was until fairly recently characteristic of even much of the scholarly literature—that race is not relevant to Southeastern Europe. As Baker (2018: 5) writes, "Even studies deconstructing or decentring ethnicity beyond realist frameworks of 'ethnic war' still hold their ethnicity and nationhood conversation largely outside race."[13] This perception has persisted despite the racialization of the persecuted Roma within white/Black racial binaries. The term *gypsy* (*cigan* in Bosnian/Croatian/Serbian) is associated with having dark skin while the term *white gypsy* (*beli cigan/rom* in Bosnian/Croatian/Serbian) is not—a distinction that, as Sunnie Rucker-Chang (2019) notes, signals larger regional relationships to Europe and elsewhere. The obfuscation of the racial politics of the region are compounded by another omission: the absence of the "second world" from the lion's share of transnational and international feminist research, narratives, and discussions of gender and sexual justice (Suchland 2011). This, too, limits how regional racial geopolitics are thought to operate.

As these examples suggest, any global analysis of Blackness must contend with a complex of historical particularities. As such, a transnational queer materialist approach is at odds with strands of Black studies that refuse futurity, political engagement, or solidarity, but ultimately ground that refusal in very specific historical, geopolitical, and economic conceptions of Blackness. Such analysis, typified by the work of Frank Wilderson (2020), risks disavowing the geopolitics of social difference through a narrowing of race to a particular perspective on US-based histories of the transatlantic slave trade. These strands of Black Studies—often gathered under the term *Afropessimism*—frame the systematic production of anti-Black violence as an undifferentiated global commitment, one distinct from other orders of oppression, one where, as Wilderson (2020) puts it, "The spectacle of Black death is essential to the mental health of the world." For Wilderson, Blackness is "coterminous with slaveness," and people of color are invariably "junior partners" in the enslavement of Black people because the very definition of freedom is "the freedom not to be Black" (Mitchell 2020: 113). Some might argue that Erdoğan's claim to be a Black Turk and the turn to Eldridge Cleaver to explain rape in the Balkans might prove the point—that unfreedom and injury are synonymous with Blackness and that these appropriations show this to be common knowledge capable of being leveraged for opportunistic political ends. But the material history of Blackness—as an analytic, as a designation—nonetheless matters. Blackness has never been monolithic.

The invocation of a uniform Blackness, we argue, renders it a queer/trans site of social reproduction—the notion of a uniform Blackness up for the claiming functions as an appraising line between groups—one that attempts to shape what ethno-religious orders and what populations within those orders will be valued. In turn, the appropriation of Blackness shows how the racialized production of gender/sex acquires meaning and value for political actors in Turkey and the former Yugoslavia, through their attempts to reproduce certain ethno-religious social and political orders. In Wilderson's account of Blackness, as Nick Mitchell (2020: 122) eloquently writes, so much needs "to disappear, to be forgotten, assumed, overlooked, or silenced, in order for its sense of Black solidarity to appear." Wilderson's (2020) contention tells us little about what is happening to Blackness as a concept, much less Black people, when Blackness is claimed outside of the US by those in European peripheries. It tells us little about the relationships, for example, between those claims to Blackness and Black people within their borders, namely Afro Turkish and Afro Albanian population, who trace their ancestry to a different system of slavery: the Ottoman system, where slave status was not determined primarily by race. Blackness in the Afropessimistic tradition can be presented as a transparent claim—something obvious, something identifiable across the globe—in part because the social and geopolitical operations of gender/sex as mechanisms of racial capitalism and as animators of US queer and trans possibility fall from view. But even some work that stakes its critical acumen at the intersection of racialized gender/sex—that operates under the influence of queer/trans materialist traditions or in favor of a transnational global Blackness as a way to theorize the live connections between seemingly disparate struggles—can fall into the trap of reproducing oppression as solidarity. In the process, such work abandons historical social distinctions between groups that might offer other ways of thinking power, violence, and liberation.

Recent work in trans studies, notably Eric Stanley's (2021: 5) *Atmospheres of Violence: Structuring Antagonism and the Trans/Queer Ungovernable*, follows this track, adding gender/sex analysis to a foundational and unyielding anti-Blackness so that "anti-trans/queer violence is foundational to, and not an aberration of, modernity." For Stanley (2021), efforts to denounce the "poison" (115) of democracy and the dangers of the (US) state, liberalism, and representational democracy transmute trans/queer to "a nonidentity where force is made to live" (26), so that Blackness and trans/queerness are made virtually interchangeable through a relationship to violence. This move—posed, unlike Wilderson's, toward solidarity forged through "the" state's anti-Black and anti-trans/queer foundational settler colonial violence—nonetheless reduces Blackness and trans/queerness to univocal, transhistorical, global death and inhumanity. In turn, it produces a concept of trans/queer that cannot adequately theorize the metaphorical borrowing of Blackness in places like Turkey or the Balkans. Instead, violence across race, across sex/gender, across time, and across geopolitics merges to figure fugitivity and ungovernability as privileged responses to the particular failures of the US state and liberal democracy. This happens in ways that elide the difference between using abstraction to intervene at the level of metaphysics and using that abstraction to prescribe a general orientation or approach to governance—to mistake abstract critique for political praxis. This results, paradoxically, in the obliteration of postcolonial politics—all the messiness of anticolonial engagements with states and the international order of them—even as postcolonial theory is mobilized to prove a transhistorical point about

Blackness and trans/queerness. This leaves the metaphorical appropriation of Blackness in the service of ethnoreligious politics, for example, outside the bounds of its analysis as such actors universalize what should remain particular historical framings of Blackness.

Ungovernability and "the" State in an Age of Global Authoritarianisms

Special issue contributor Rahul Rao (2020: 2) has noted that "queer theory's determination to stand askew to the progressive march of time has been shaped by its geopolitical provenance in the contemporary United States and its opposition to what David Eng has described as 'queer liberalism.'" While, for example, much queer scholarship has rightly focused on the global dissemination of liberal LGBTQ+ rights discourses through transnational NGOs, the conservative counters to these operations often fall from the frame. Kristopher Velasco and Sebastian Cabal Rojas's forthcoming work, for example, interrogates the meaningfulness of accepting liberalism as a done deal when in 2013 transnational anti-LGBTQ+ spending came to around $57 million compared to $2.5 million in "pro-LGBT" funding. These uneven investments are further exacerbated by a notion of time that keeps queer "progress" firmly in Western temporal frames and scholarly inquiries that presume that "we" have our liberal rights in hand. Together, this geopolitical notion of queer progress over time and the reality of conservative funding investments obscure, as Rao (2020: 2) writes, "the shadow of struggles around the decriminalisation of queer sex in places where it seemed . . . that people had not got what they wanted, or had only just got what they wanted, or felt implicated in the fact of others not having what they wanted." And it directs attention away from how, increasingly, global politics is marked by widespread neoliberal authoritarianisms and sectarianisms organized through racial and sexual management, restriction, and outright violence (bombings, shootings, targeting of gay and trans people and places) even as, increasingly in the US, fascism arrives through liberal processes themselves.[14] Such critiques of liberalism are also made possible by the collapse of social liberalism into economic liberalism, forgetting that many early proponents of economic liberalism themselves were not politically liberal and in fact understood decolonialization and democracy in postcolonial nation-states to be a threat to the global liberal economy (Hong 2020; Slobodian 2018).

The intensification of global authoritarianisms sheds a certain light on US-based Black/queer/trans work that pivots on a generalized anti-state political analysis and practice that range from broad condemnations of "liberalism" to calls by trans theorists like Stanley (2021) to become "ungovernable." Justified critiques of particular states or "the state" as a primary unit of political organization become secondary to the idea of the possibility of a radical break, another shattering, the promise of a way to be always otherwise. Broad critiques of "liberalism," "reformist" politics, the failures of representational democracy, and "the" law can perversely ignore the complexity of postcolonial struggles over state power and control, even as postcolonial theorists, particularly Black postcolonial theorists like Frantz Fanon (1964), are summoned in these same projects as evidence of attention to colonialisms—and even as they are marshaled to speak for all erstwhile colonial subjects. Here, Fanon's (1964: 44) elaboration of Kantian humanism—his claim that "universality resides in [the] decision to recognize and accept the reciprocal relativism of different cultures, once the colonial status is irreversibly excluded"—is instructive. He and other postcolonial thinkers in this way insist that any breed of universal humanism—understood as something unstable, something changeable—worth entertaining would begin with a rejection of colonialism, so that the idea of "humanity" remains contentless and "no one people or set of ideas" become "the hallmark of what it means to be 'men'"[15] (Cornell 2000: 77). Blackness and transness as analytics might rightly traverse the international order of states when they travel to intervene at a high level of abstraction—against, for example, humanisms that purport to be universal but instead smuggle in a particular genre of Man (Wynter 2003). But when theorists like Fanon are stripped from their historical context—in this case, the Algerian war against French colonialism, which itself occurs in the context of a global Cold War—and put to use for queer and trans studies in the US, there is a risk of homogenizing state power and the interplay of power between states through a "reciprocal relativism" of colonialisms, which, like states themselves, do not have the same structurations or histories. Such abstraction allows Stanley (2021: 24) to rely on "the racialized phenomenology of Blackness under colonization that Fanon illustrates" as something "to [be] read against and with a continuum of anti-trans/queer racialized violence in the settler colony that is the United States." As such, Fanon's theorizations of Blackness can inadvertently feed US academic left theoretical production that ignores how Fanon's understanding of Blackness is inextricably tied to material politics of the Algerian Revolution against French settler colonialism. Such US uses of Fanon also ignore his commitment to political praxis (versus abstract theory) and his caution against a flattening of Blackness and racism even in the context of France at the time (Davis 2022). Thus, in this analysis, the transnational solidarity

Stanley so movingly seeks can only be forged through a curated archive of violence, one that links state-sponsored terrors and extra-state violence across times and geographies. The unrelenting emphasis on Black/trans/ queer death justifies a rejection of "the" state and its processes—not only as a mode of political organization, but also almost entirely as a site of political engagement. As Stanley (2021: 118) writes, "If the attempt to fashion a more perfect democracy is also the order under which its deadly force expands, then ungovernability becomes an abolitionist way of life."

Fugitivity is the break from bondage, being on the run, living outside of what would define you. But it is also an ontological escape or bursting of the confines of a Blackness defined only by law, racialisms, and racisms: Black is, in this sense, ungovernable, in excess, to use the familiar parlance—"anoriginal lawlessness." "To become black," as Amaryah Shaye (2014) writes, "is to refuse being made a something—to be and become nothing. Not because nothing is an absence or lack of life, but precisely because nothing is the abundance and multiplicity out of which life is formed." And there are so many things to burst—the skin and the state and law and culture—the wrap of governance, that many layered thing. To be clear, we are not suggesting that metaphysical accounts of trans or Black do not matter, but we caution against their uncritical overextension. A free-floating Fanon, and other sorts of Black travel in this vein, can paradoxically limit political possibility when they come solely to denote an anarchic position to "the" state and turn away from the complexity of international politics and transnational social movements and their engagements with institutional governance across local, state, regional, and international orders. If, then, fugitivity and ungovernability are an ongoing refusal to accept standards from elsewhere (Moten 2018), and there are many elsewheres, then what ungovernability entails cannot be a one-size-fits-all agitation. Such a totalizing approach obscures how global racial capitalism often operates beyond the terms and categories of difference relevant to the US. Stanley's use of ungovernability and fugitivity replicates some of the more totalizing moves of queer antisociality but transmutes them through a critique of democracy and liberalism into an undifferentiated antistate analysis. This occurs in part by way of a Fanon pinned to the categories and categorical content (race as Blackness, Blackness as trans/queer) that, for Stanley, give US liberal democracy social and political meaning.

These sorts of racial travels also prevent analyses of the different ways gender/sex (in concert with religious difference and the reproduction of ethno-religious difference) structures racial formations, including Blackness, in various times and sites. For queer and trans studies, this means that subject-less and objectless critique—especially the movement of queer and trans study beyond US gender and sexuality—can facilitate these problems. This occurs when subjectless and objectless critique are not expressly interrogated as forms for *reproducing* the dominant geopolitical coordinates of transness and queerness, when they are set *within* an abstracted idea of racial capitalism instead of authorizing a corresponding interrogation of it and the relationships between states, institutions, and peoples that make it possible. What sex or race or more specifically Blackness and transness are or can be—as lived experiences and as analytics or concepts—can't be detached from the when, how, where, and why of their formulation.[16] Such histories are potential sites from which to rework humanism, "genres of the human" (Wynter 2003), or theories of universalism more broadly. How, for example, might caste systems in India and in Africa (such as those in Senegal,) complicate the relationships between Blackness, status, and "the" state?[17] Or as roundtable contributor Sahin Acikgoz discusses, how does including the Ottoman slave trade, where religion and race were both critical to enslavement in ways that do not always allow us to distinguish clearly between the two, shift the way we theorize the "racial" in racial capitalism? Thinking Indian Oceans slavery and trade systems alongside transatlantic ones emphasizes multi-state and extra-state systems of trade and travel whose racial politics do not fall easily into a false choice of for or against "the" state or "liberalism." Finally, it is unclear what being anarchic or fugitive entails as a political praxis against a nonexistent state, when, as Achille Mbembe (2003: 32) describes, "many African states can no longer claim monopoly on violence"—where urban militias and private armies without state loyalty rule the day or where there are simply no institutions to save or passively kill the citizens or populations that would be under their purview. It is also unclear what a theory and practice of ungovernability under extreme conditions of state neglect (including US state neglect—think the lead laden water in Flint, Michigan) would entail. If the harm that people suffer through is not the result of a cruelly optimistic attachment to liberal democracy and the state form, what then?

Recent feminist theorizations have used transnational left politics to reimagine the political possibilities of the state form. Lisa Duggan (2023: 246) had this to say in the aftermath of global Leftist infighting after the 2021 election in Ecuador, where some anti-extractivist indigenous groups withheld support for Left candidates who had come into political prominence on the crest of the Pink Tide but nonetheless implemented extractivist economic policy that jeopardized the very existence of indigenous people:

The Eurocentrism of left binary thinking is strangling the political imagination of the left in the Global North. A deep engagement with the history of racial colonialism, with decolonial theory and practice, and with Indigenous ways of thinking and living, accompanied by eco-socialist, feminist, and queer strains within and alongside them, can help lead us out of the impasses of the entrenched binaries, the unwavering attachment to individual European male thinkers, the enmeshment in European histories, the dependence on extractivist economies.

Part of what Duggan recognizes here is the need for histories of governance, politics, and organizing that do not presume an all-or-nothing approach or rehearse a static vision of the state, where politics is framed as a choice between engagement or disengagement with state power and institutions. Instead, following Noura Ekrat's and Veronica Gago's work in Palestine and Argentina, respectively, Duggan (2023: 247) suggests "putting care for people and land into the center of political focus" in order "to connect and create new socialities, new institutions, and new conceptions of power on our way to reimagining the state."

Conclusion: Thinking Transnational Queer Materialism

While Wilderson (2020) and Stanley (2021) cannot address variegated mobilizations of Blackness in the US and around the globe, the Black Radical tradition offers another way to frame Blackness, injury, and its complex relationship to contemporary forms of violence and liberatory struggle against it. Transnational queer materialism builds on Black study and Blackness in the Black Radical tradition that describes a global Blackness attuned to historical context and political economies. In *Black Marxism: The Making of the Black Radical Tradition*, Cedric J. Robinson (2000) famously criticizes Marx and Engels's short-shrifting of the effects of racial ideology on class consciousness and for universalizing the English working class as the prototype of proletarian revolt. As Robinson (2000: i) writes, "Marxism's internationalism was not global; its materialism was exposed as an insufficient explanator of cultural and social forces; and its economic determinism too often politically compromised freedom struggles beyond or outside of the metropole." Robinson instead emphasizes unfree labor resistance across the globe, where the ideological motivations for revolt exceeded the mode of production. Focusing particularly on enslaved African peoples' refusal to surrender the substance of African cultures—the "critical mixes and admixtures of language and thought, of cosmology and metaphysics, of habits, beliefs and morality" (121–22)—to Western notions of freedom, Robinson identifies Black historical consciousness as a wholesale rejection of the very terms of what Western life had on offer. The Black radical tradition is for Robinson (169) "a revolutionary consciousness that proceeded from the whole historical experience of Black people and not merely from the social formations of capitalist slavery or the relations of the production of colonialism"—a consciousness that always existed in the Black masses, one that was always discoverable, never invented, by the Black intelligentsia. The Black Radical Tradition, then, explodes the categorical assignations of meaning that *proletariat* and *Black* and *slave* and *freedom*—and even *intellectual* and *author*—might be thought to hold, singularly and in relation. This dissolution, however conceptual, is nonetheless tethered to (1) a historical and geographically specific set of actions and locations in time: the slave trade involving the African continent, particularly (but not exclusively) the transatlantic slave trade; (2) a theory of capitalism activated by the kidnapping, trafficking, and sale of the peoples of Africa; and (3) the lived experience of those Africans forcibly removed from their homes—the memories and cultural transmission of those other ways of life as what gives rise to the Black Radical Tradition. This is not to deny or endorse critiques of various aspects of Robinson's (2000) project but to emphasize *Black Marxism*'s dedication to historical and material specificity within a project premised on refusing–even shattering—the categories and frameworks that make racial, economic, and social structurings cohere and make intuitive sense. Here, Blackness achieves its oppositional form through grounded historical context.

If queer is to have any remaining utility, we must understand how its reproduction is tied to analyses of race and geopolitics. Queer/trans critique cannot passively permit the study of racial capitalism to become, contra Robinson, about how Black people or other groups suffer instead of how capitalism works to spread and consolidate through the production of difference. As Ruth Wilson Gilmore (2022: 321) has remarked, "If we have learned anything from . . . *Black Marxism*, it's that capitalism and racial practice co-developed because the racial practice was already there [internal to feudal Europe] and it had nothing to do with Black people." When certain US histories of Blackness become synonymous with racial capitalism, they cloak the many forms of Blackness in the US and across the globe. In particular, the reduction of racial capitalism to Blackness as injury provides no analytic framework that can speak to how Blackness is valued, how it gets summoned in European peripheries to reproduce ethno-religious orders. Transnational queer materialism connects racial capitalism more fully to global histories of sexuality and gender—which are always histories of racial, ethno-religious, indigenous management. It "queers" racial capitalism by illuminating some of the invisible terms of its reproduction. Transnational queer materialism thus requires queer and queer of color to account for what analyses of racial capitalism let those terms move through the world, just as it insists that racial capitalism account for the gender/sex systems that power it.

Returning to our opening examples, how would transnational queer materialism respond to the "historical emergencies" of peripheral European claims to Blackness in order to name an injury—moments where Blackness becomes a metaphor that alleges wrongdoing that demands redress and even justifies state-backed violence in the pursuit of such relief? In the Turkish case, this would require, as a first step, that Islam is not treated as radical alterity to liberal capitalist relations (Savcı 2021). Arif Dirlik (2013) suggests that since the 1980s the search for alternatives to capitalism has increasingly focused on cultural difference, with Islam rising as a key alternative. In fact, when queer studies analyzes the Islamic non-West, capitalism is often completely absent from discussions and modernity's central defining feature shifts from capitalism to secularity. As a result Islam is doubly removed from the political economy and rendered as cultural twice over (Savcı 2021). Attention to transnational queer materialism would counter the relegation of the Islamic non-West to a capitalist alternative by remembering the historical investment of the US in moderate Islamic regimes in the Middle East during and after the Cold War. Transnational queer materialism would, for example, understand US involvement in the region in the 1980s as a strategy to fight the spread of "godless" communism on one hand and the radicalization of Islam following the Iranian model on the other—both of which challenged US imperialism and capitalism—as actively shaping the political meaning of Islam.

Transnational queer materialism would also consider how the imbrications of race and religion happen, too, outside of state strictures—beyond both legal and institutional orderings and state-sponsored violence. Revisiting Eastern Europe surfaces another complicated set of claims around Africa, Islam, and whiteness. The 2018–2019 Albanian student protests, which spanned the Albanian public university system, were a series of street protests, online activism, and general disruption in opposition to proposed tuition hikes. A 2019 live report of the protest included a news commenter reading aloud a homemade student protest sign, one that had been popular since the strike's inception. It read, "European prices, African Salaries, Arian Race, Taliban Standards, Miserable Albania." The broadcast commented that the sign signaled "the strength and sentiment of rage and disappointment that the students were delivering home" (Tudor and Rexhepi 2021: 197). Piro Rexhepi, in dialogue with Alyosxa Tudor (2021), however, interprets the sign as part of a story of coloniality and racial capitalism. In short, "How can an Arian race be given African salaries, Taliban standards, and yet pay European prices while not being part of the European market? Or in short, why are Albanians being robbed of their 'Arian' race privilege?" (197). The sign is therefore an example of how "race functions as capital that the post-socialist subject can claim, trade, and negotiate in the racial capitalist marketplace of the European Union" (197).

But to put a finer point on it, it is race ("Arian"), region (Africa and the shadow of Blackness so once again race and religion), religion (Taliban-style Islam so again race shot through with sexual savagery), and capitalism (the vision of a prosperous European modernity) that all collide in the crude space of a handmade sign. The complicated maneuvers of "race" in the racial capitalism of Eastern Europe have led, moreover, to heated debates about the meaning of "racialization' vis-à-vis white Eastern European "migratised positions," where white Eastern Europeans have claimed racisms against themselves—and demanded to be included in European discussions of racism—in ways that can overwrite postcolonial experiences and theorizations of race and racisms. These complicated debates "between the posts" of post-socialism (where state-sponsored socialism is narrowly construed here as a European phenomena) and postcolonialism (Chari and Verderi 2009) have led some to comment that the "fight for the inclusion of . . . white migratised positions into the definitions of racism, the frustration and the feelings of being left out are not mainly directed against the dominant group but come with envying the perceived recognition of Black and anti-racist interventions" (Tudor and Rexhepi 2021: 193).

It is clear that a general, abstracted stand "against oppression" that demands white Eastern European inclusion can paper over histories of European empire and colonialisms within the margins of Europe by appropriating the form of anti-racist critique through a proximal association with Africa and the Asiatic to protest the economic and political violence of Europe proper (Tudor and Rexhepi 2021). A transnational queer materialist reading of this situation might also consider the interplay between the specific racisms up for discussion in Eastern Europe—the ones that white migratised people might efface and claim to face—as part of the broader global travel of racial categories and imaginaries. If, for example, Albania as one of two Muslim-majority states in Europe is simultaneously "a poorhouse of Europe," a "defective democracy," and the "North Korea of Europe," the turn to this more complicated geopolitical imaginary and interrogation of the racial categories in use might help clarify the definitional stakes of racism, religion, and geopolitics in the region and beyond it. This would not only involve Albania's relationship to Euro-American economic and social policy but also consider its historical connections to coloniality and the global circuits of Islam.

Transnational queer/trans materialism questions the abstraction and separation of race and religion, of Blackness as metaphor, and Muslim as a static figuration, by returning them to the material conditions, infrastructures, feelings, and concepts that made them possible. Today, Blackness can be claimed by those jockeying for geopolitical power in ways that conceptually mirror some scholarship that reduces racial capitalism to a one-note tale of universal and unvariegated Black oppression. So much falls from the frame: class, caste politics, the many systems of slavery, other empires and colonial racial systems—and the list goes on. In a world without a singular "imperial" center (Grewal and Kaplan 1994), neat categories of "oppressors" and "oppressed" do not exist. Transnational queer materialism remembers this. As Grace Hong and Roderick Ferguson (2011: 11) have emphasized, women of color feminism and queer of color critique are "not a multiculturalist celebration, not an excuse for presuming a commonality among all racialized peoples, but a cleareyed appraisal of the dividing line between valued and devalued, which can cut within, as well as across, racial groupings."

Through what we call transnational queer materialism, we have considered once again how to appraise that dividing line—across and within racial groupings, across and within geographies, and across and within epistemes of racialized gender that do not only describe discrete categories, peoples, or populations, but that also, crucially, organize ways of being and living. When Blackness becomes abstracted and synonymous with unvariegated injury—within the US and as it travels, authorized by a certain US history, that American passport—the claims made in its name are never transparent or innocent. They are instead attempts to bend the world, to reproduce, if not reorder, specific racial, ethno-religious, gendered, and sexual positionings and, at times, game geopolitical and economic power. This is a historical hijacking of Blackness—one that finds its odd reflection in the flat-figured "others" of US empire— from "the" Muslim to an empty, oppositional "whiteness." This is history evacuated of its contradictions and its mess— what transnational queer materialisms sets itself against.

Notes

We would like to thank Michael Hardt and the *SAQ* team; Kathryn Lofton and the Yale Humanities Dean's Office and the Department of Gender, Sexuality, and Women's Studies at UC Davis for funding workshops on each university's campus; CLAGS for hosting a discussion of our Introduction in their Queer of Color/Trans of Color Conversations series; Yale WGSS Colloquium and Working Group for reading an early draft; our brilliant authors; our students in WGSS 745 and CST 206 for discussing many of these ideas with us; and Neda Atanasoski, Grace Hong, and Greta LaFleur for critical feedback on drafts.

1   Eldridge Cleaver (1967: 33–34) describes his once-held view on the rape of white women as an insurrectionary act and the circumstances that led him to retract the claim.

2   In an award-winning *International Feminist Journal of Politics* article entitled "Drone Disorientations," Cara Dagget (2015: 362) discusses how unmanned weapons "queer the experience of killing in war."

3   As Anjali Arondekar and Geeta Patel (2016: 156–57) write, "The pervasive understanding of race as understood primarily through the history of the transatlantic slave trade, [is] such that this idea of race could be said to constitute the background against which all representations of racial formation take place."

4   For other work on queer geopolitics and terminological travel, see Arondekar and Patel (2016) and Mikdashi and Puar (2016).

5   We follow Michelle Murphy (2011: 23–23), whose concept of "distributed reproduction" stretches beyond family making to consider "reproductive politics—and the question of what is reproduction—as a struggle over ontology" that requires "tracking the dispersion of sexed living being into its infrastructural and political economic milieu."

6   See Amy Villarejo's (2005) discussion of "queer of color" about potential issues that arise from theorizing the nonnormative as both a symptom of racial capitalism and a site of agential resistance to it.

7   Indigenous studies scholars have also debated the practice of reading some bodies, regions, and subjects as de facto queer. In a response to Audra Simpson's discussion of the state as a white, straight heteropatriarchy, Byrd (2020: 113) notes: "[Simpson] suggests a nonnormative, nonstraightness for all Indigenous bodies and their flesh that resists settler governance. . . . The nondifferentiation of a possible queer or gender nonconforming Indigenous body who does not or cannot reproduce is collapsed into the materiality of the Indigenous woman as already queer."

8   See Pierre (2019), who explores in part how diasporic models of Blackness can obscure the complicated histories of race and exchange in modern Africa. See also Clarke and Thomas (2020).

9   As Stuart Hall (1987: 45) writes, "'Black' has always been an unstable identity, psychically, culturally, and politically" as well as "a narrative, a story, a history . . . something constructed, told, spoken, not simply found."

10 Such "liberal" uses of queer and queer theory have been critiqued by a number of scholars, including Kadji Amin (2016). In response, Amin offers attachment genealogy as a method that "engage[s] queer's multiple pasts . . . in order to differently animate queer's dense affective histories" (174). Beyond the question of whose attachments and histories matter in the making of queer studies is the question of what methods we use to make those histories and recognize those attachments. Given the travel of theory and the travel of US histories of Blackness, where, when, and how global political economies explicitly

fit into the recognition and narration of such queer histories, attachments, and desires remains an open question. We respond to it with transnational queer materialism.

11   In contrast, Fatima El-Tayeb's (2011: xiv) *European Others: Queering Ethnicity in Postnational Europe* discusses "processes of ethnicization in postwar Europe that closely interact and overlap with longer-term, in part precapitalist processes of racialization," including the ambiguity of the "whiteness" of Eastern and Southern Europeans migrants and various differences within immigrant and minority groups.

12   For a lengthier discussion of Erdoğan's use of Black Turks and its political genealogy, see Michael Ferguson (2013).

13   See Rucker-Chang (2018) for an exploration of the movement of US civil rights discourses to Roma populations in the European "South." See also Miglena S. Todorova (2018) on how the 20th twentieth-century travel of US Black women and feminists to socialist countries influenced understandings of racism, imperialism, patriarchy, and capitalism in the US and abroad.

14   For a broader discussion of the authoritarian turn see Bassi and LaFleur (2022).

15   Cornell (2000: 77) reads reciprocal relativism as "an appeal to universality . . . perfectly consistent" with "Kant's own insistence that a concept of humanity as an idea coherent with moral freedom must remain contentless at least on the abstract level of philosophy."

16   If, for example, the state does not hold together civil life but is in fact itself held together by civil life, as Marx and Engels ([1845] 1975, 121) suggest, then attention to the various forms civil life take would in turn tell us something about the various historical workings of states over time. Stanley uses Marx and Engels's analysis to suggest that "as anarchists like Kuwasi Balagoon saw in nationalism, and Frantz Fanon discerned in his analysis of colonialism, the state is fashioned from singularities, yet [possessing a] structure [that] maintains the racialized, gendered, and classed demands that enable its appearance as an intelligible force." Building on Marx and Engels's account of civil life and the state, Stanley, however, then draws from Balagoon and Fanon to conclude that, "categories most viciously subjected to violence have persisted since the moment of settler contact and chattel slavery, yet the tools administering this cruelty are ever adapting, which is among the reasons for their endurance" (8). We agree that the tools are ever adapting—but so too are the categories and their relations and contents.

17   For example, Shobana Shankar (2022) builds on the work of the Senegalese scientist Cheikh Anta Diop, to argue that the "association between caste and race was made and remade in different historical moments by Africans and Asians because they are experiences of power, not merely abstract categories." See also Shankar (2021). See also Hazel V. Carby (2021, n.p.): "After the Abolition Act of 1833, the British repurposed slave ships to transport more than a million indentured labourers from India to work on plantations in their colonies around the globe, resulting in the complex entanglements of caste and race in British Guiana, Jamaica, and Trinidad."

References

Alexander, M. Jacqui. 2006. *Pedagogies of Crossing.* Durham, NC: Duke University Press.

Amin, Kadji. 2016. "Haunted by the 1990s: Queer Theory's Affective Histories." *Women's Studies Quarterly* 44, nos. 3–4: 173–89.

Arondekar, Anjali, and Geeta Patel. 2016. "Area Impossible: Notes Towards an Introduction." *GLQ* 22, no. 2: 151–71.

Atanasoski, Neda. 2013. *Humanitarian Violence: The US Deployment of Diversity.* Minneapolis: University of Minnesota Press.

Baker, Catherine. 2018. *Race and the Yugoslav Region.* Manchester, UK: Manchester University Press.

Bassi, Serena, and Greta LaFleur. 2022 "Introduction: TERFs, Gender-Critical Movements, and Postfascist Feminisms." *TSQ* 9, no. 3: 311–33.

Berlant, Lauren, and Lee Edelman. 2014. *Sex, the Unbearable.* Durham, NC: Duke University Press.

Best, Stephen. 2018. *None Like Us: Blackness, Belonging, and Aesthetic Life.* Durham, NC: Duke University Press.

Butler, Judith. 1994. "Against Proper Objects." *differences* 6, nos. 2–3: 1–26.

Byrd, Jodi A. 2020. "What's Normative Got to Do with It? Towards a Queer Relationality." *Social Text* 38, no. 4: 105–23.

Carby, Hazel V. 2021. "The Limits of Caste." Review of *Caste: The Origins of Our Discontents,* by Isabel Wilkerson. *London Review of Books* 43, no. 2. https://www.lrb.co.uk/the-paper /v43/no2/hazel-v.-carby/the-limits-of-caste.

Chari, Sharad, and Katherine Verdery. 2009. "Thinking between the Posts: Postcolonialism, Postsocialism, and Ethnography after the Cold War." *Comparative Studies in Society and History* 51, no. 1: 6–34.

Clarke, Kamari Maxine, and Deborah A. Thomas, eds. 2020. *Globalization and Race: Transformations in the Cultural Production of Blackness.* Durham, NC: Duke University Press.

Cleaver, Eldridge. 1967. *Soul on Ice.* New York: McGraw-Hill.

Cohen, Cathy J. 1997. "Punks, Buldaggers, and Welfare Queens: The Radical Potential of Queer Politics?" *GLQ* 3, no. 4: 437–65.

Cornell, Drucilla. 2000. *Just Cause: Freedom, Identity, and Rights.* New York: Rowman & Littlefield.

Dagget, Cara. 2015. "Drone Disorientations: How Unmanned Weapons Queer the Experience of Killing in War." *International Feminist Journal of Politics* 17, no. 3: 361–79.

Davis, Muriam Haleh. 2022. "The U.S. Academy and the Provincialization of Fanon." *Los Angeles Review of Books,* November 9. https://lareviewofbooks.org/article/the-us-academy -and-the-provincialization-of-fanon/.

Dirlik, Arif. 2013. "Thinking Modernity Historically: Is 'Alternative Modernity' the Answer?" *Asian Review of World Histories* 1, no. 1: 5–44.

Duggan, Lisa. 2003. *The Twilight of Equality? Neoliberalism, Cultural Politics, and the Attack on Democracy.* Boston: Beacon Press.

Duggan, Lisa. 2023. "Reimagining the State." *WSQ: Women's Studies Quarterly* 51, no. 12: 243–48.

Edelman, Lee. 2004. *No Future: Queer Theory and the Death Drive.* Durham, NC: Duke University Press.

El-Tayeb, Fatima. 2011. *European Others: Queering Ethnicity in Postnational Europe.* Minneapolis: University of Minnesota Press.

Eng, David. 2010. *The Feeling of Kinship: Queer Liberalism and the Racialization of Intimacy.* Durham, NC: Duke University Press.

Eng, David L., Judith Halberstam, and José Esteban Muñoz. 2005. "Introduction: What's Queer about Queer Studies Now?" *Social Text* 23, nos. 3–4: 1–17.

Fanon, Frantz. 1964. *Towards the African Revolution.* Translated by Hakkon Chevalier. New York: Grove Press.

Ferguson, Michael. 2013. "White Turks, Black Turks and Negroes: The Politics of Polarization." *Jadaliyya* (blog), June 29. https://www.jadaliyya.com/Details/28868.

Ferguson, Roderick A. 2018. "Queer of Color Critique." In *Oxford Research Encyclopedia of Literature*, edited by Paula Rabinowitz. https://doi.org/10.1093/acrefore/9780190201098.013.33.

Gilmore, Ruth Wilson. 2022. "Racial Capitalism Now: A Conversation with Michael Dawson and Ruth Wilson Gilmore." In *Colonial Racial Capitalism*, edited by Koshy, Susan, Lisa Marie Kacho, Jodi A. Byrd, and Brian Jordan Patterson, 311-332. Durham, NC: Duke University Press.

Gopinath, Gayatri. 2005. *Impossible Desires: Queer Diasporas and South Asian Public Cultures.* Durham, NC: Duke University Press

Grewal, Inderpal, and Caren Kaplan. 1994. *Scattered Hegemonies: Postmodernity and Transnational Feminist Practices.* Minneapolis: University of Minnesota Press.

Grewal, Inderpal, and Caren Kaplan. 1996. "Warrior Marks: Global Womanism's Neo-Colonial Discourse in a Multicultural Context." *Camera Obscura* 13, no. 3: 4–33.

Güner, Ezgi. 2021. "Rethinking Whiteness in Turkey through the AKP's Foreign Policy in Africa South of the Sahara." *Middle East Report* 299. https://merip.org/2021/08/rethinking-whiteness-in-turkey-through-the-akps-foreign-policy-in-africa-south-of-the-sahara/

Hall, Stuart. 1987. "Minimal Selves." In *The Real Me: Postmodernism and the Question of Identity*, edited by Lisa Appignanesi, 44–46. London: Institute for Contemporary Arts.

Hong, Christine. 2020. *A Violent Peace: Race, US Militarism, and Cultures of Democratization in Cold War Asia and the Pacific.* Palo Alto, CA: Stanford University Press.

Hong, Grace Kyungwon, and Roderick Ferguson. 2011. *Strange Affinities.* Durham, NC: Duke University Press.

Jaleel, Rana M. 2022. "Rethinking Racial Slavery and Queer of Color Critique." Paper presented at the American Studies Annual Conference. Paper on file with author.

Jaleel, Rana M. 2021. *The Work of Rape.* Durham, NC: Duke University Press.

Manalansan, Martin. 2003. *Global Divas.* Durham, NC: Duke University Press.

Marx, Karl, and Friedrich Engels. (1845) 1975. "The Holy Family." In *Collected Works*, 4:78–143. New York: International.

Mbembe, Achille. 2003. "Necropolitics." *Public Culture* 15, no. 1: 11–40.

Melamed, Jodi. 2015. "Racial Capitalism." *Critical Ethnic Studies* 1, no. 1: 76–85.

Mikdashi, Maya, and Jasbir K. Puar. 2016. "Queer Theory and Permanent War." *GLQ* 22, no. 2: 215–22.

Mitchell, Nick. 2020. "The View from Nowhere: On Frank Wilderson's Afropessimism." *Spectre* 1, no. 2: 110–22.

Moten, Fred. 2018. *Stolen Life.* Durham, NC: Duke University Press.

Muñoz, José Esteban. 2006. "Thinking beyond Antirelationality and Antiutopianism in Queer Critique." *PMLA* 121, no. 3: 825–26.

Muñoz, José Esteban. 2009. *Cruising Utopia: The Then and There of Queer Futurity.* New York: NYU Press.

Murphy, Michelle. 2011. "Distributed Reproduction." In *Corpus: An Interdisciplinary Reader on Bodies and Knowledge*, edited by Monica Casper and Paisley Currah, 21–38. New York: Palgrave Macmillan.

Pierre, Jemima. 2019. *The Predicament of Blackness: Postcolonial Ghana and the Politics of Race.* Chicago: University of Chicago Press.

Prashad, Vijay. 2014. *The Poorer Nations: A Possible History of the Global South.* New York: Verso.

Puar, Jasbir K. 2007. *Terrorist Assemblages: Homonationalism in Queer Times.* Durham, NC: Duke University Press.

Rao, Rahul. 2020. *Out of Time: The Queer Politics of Postcoloniality.* Oxford, UK: Oxford University Press.

Reddy, Chandan. 2005. "Asian Diasporas, Neoliberalism, and the Family: Reviewing the Case for Homosexual Asylum in the Context of Family Rights." *Social Text* 23, nos. 3–4: 101–19.

Rexhepi, Peri. 2023. *White Enclosures: Racial Capitalism and Coloniality Along the Balkan Route.* Durham, NC: Duke University Press.

Robinson, Cedric J. 2000. *Black Marxism: The Making of the Black Radical Tradition.* Chapel Hill: University of North Carolina Press.

Rucker-Chang, Sunnie. 2018. "Challenging Americanism and Europeanism: African-Americans and Roma in the American South and European Union 'South.'" *Journal of Transatlantic Studies* 16, no. 2: 181–99.

Rucker-Chang, Sunnie. 2019. "Mapping Blackness in Yugoslavia and Post-Yugoslav Space." *Black Perspectives* (blog), July 17. https://www.aaihs.org/mapping-blackness-in-yugoslavia-and-post-yugoslav-space/.

Savcı, Evren. 2021. *Queer in Translation: Sexual Politics under Neoliberal Islam.* Durham, NC: Duke University Press.

Shankar, Shobana. 2021. *An Uneasy Embrace: Africa, India, and the Spectre of Race.* Oxford, UK: Oxford University Press.

Shankar, Shobana. 2022. "Blackness as Solidarity/ Identification Against Casteism and Racism in 'South India.'" *The Funambulist*, December 14. https://thefunambulist.net/magazine/article/blackness-as-solidarity-identification-against-casteism-and-racism-in-south-india.

Shaye, Amaryah. 2014. "Refusing to Reconcile, Part 2." *Women in Theology* (blog), February 16. https://womenintheology.org/2014/02/16/refusing-to-reconcile-part-2/.

Slobodian, Quinn. 2018. *Globalists: The End of Empire and the Birth of Neoliberalism.* Cambridge, MA: Harvard University Press.

Snorton, C. Riley, and Jin Haritaworn. "Trans Necropolitics: A Transnational Reflection on Violence, Death, and the Trans of Color Afterlife." In *The Transgender Studies Reader 2*, edited by Susan Stryker and Aren Z. Aizura, 66–76. New York: Routledge.

Stanley, Eric. 2021. *Atmospheres of Violence: Structuring Antagonism and the Trans/Queer Ungovernable.* Durham, NC: Duke University Press.

Suchland, Jennifer. 2011. "Is Postsocialism Transnational?" *Signs: Journal of Women in Culture and Society* 36, no. 4: 837–62.

Todorova, Miglena S. 2018 "Race and Women of Color in Socialist/Postsocialist Transnational Feminisms in Central and Southeastern Europe." *Meridians* 16, no. 1: 114–41.

Tudor, Alyosxa, and Piro Rexhepi. 2021. "Connecting the 'Posts' to Confront Racial Capitalism's Coloniality." In *Postcolonial and Postsocialist Dialogues: Intersections, Opacities, Challenges in Feminist Theorizing and Practice*, edited by Redi Koobak, Madina Tlostanova, and Suruchi Thapar-Björkert, 193–208. New York: Routledge.

Velasco, Kristopher, and Sebastian Cabal Rojas. "Fighting in the Rearguard: U.S. Anti-LGBTQ+ Organizations' Foreign Spending after Marriage Equality." Forthcoming.

Villarejo, Amy. 2005. "Tarrying with the Normative: Queer Theory and *Black History*." *Social Text* 23, nos. 3–4: 69–84.

Wilderson, Frank. 2020. *Afropessimism*. New York: W. W. Norton & Company, Inc.

Williams, Randall. 2010. *The Divided World: Human Rights and its Violence*. Minneapolis: University of Minnesota Press.

Wynter, Sylvia. 2003. "Unsettling the Coloniality of Being/Power/Truth/Freedom: Towards the Human, after Man, Its Overrepresentation—An Argument." *CR: The New Centennial Review* 3, no. 3: 257–337.

Žarkov, Dubravka. 2007. *The Body of War: Media, Ethnicity, and Gender in the Break-up of Yugoslavia*. Durham, NC: Duke University Press.

Neda Atanasoski and Rana M. Jaleel

Reproducing Racial Capitalism:
Sexual Slavery and Islam at
the Edges of Queer of Color Critique

Slavery has a rape problem. If we follow the work of Black feminist historians of the transatlantic slave trade, slavery *is* a rape problem. Saidiya Hartman (2022), Hannah Rosen (2009), and Jennifer Morgan (2004), for example, have placed reproductive labor and sexual violence at the heart of the transatlantic slave trade. In an allied scholarly tradition, queer of color critique—including foundational work by Roderick Ferguson (2005), Grace Hong (2015), and Chandan Reddy (2011)—also insists on the centrality of sex, gender, and violence to the operations of racial capitalism, even if queer of color critique has remained largely silent on the issue of sexual violation. In their own and overlapping traditions, the collective interventions of Black feminist historiographies of slavery and queer of color critique have each enhanced contemporary theorizations of racial capitalism and the transatlantic slave trade. Such insights have galvanized research in US histories of slavery and in gender studies more broadly. And this work raises further questions. What does the shock of this work, its groundbreaking status, tell us about the historical, geopolitical, and racial imaginaries of slavery elsewhere, beyond the transatlantic trade in peoples? How do those other, often neglected or effaced slaveries, particularly those involving the

The South Atlantic Quarterly 123:1, January 2024
DOI 10.1215/00382876-10920723 © 2024 Duke University Press

Ottoman and East African slave trade, in turn shape how we understand the transatlantic slave trade and its legacies?

We ask these questions in relation to contemporary debates about human trafficking, sex trafficking, and the slave trade, in which the fanciful specter and imaginary of the Ottoman empire and its system of slavery—as well as other "Oriental" slave systems—emerge as templates for imagining the place of sex in slavery. Meanwhile, Black feminist scholarship on social reproduction and chattel slavery is largely *not* the touchstone for contemporary understandings of sexual enslavement. In this way, the questions posed above raise issues not only for human trafficking debates, but also for how we conceptualize the "racial" in racial capitalism and the "queer" and "of color" in queer of color critique. Racial capitalism, a term popularized by Cedric Robinson (2000) in *Black Marxism*, recognizes that, as Jodi Melamed (2015: 77) writes, "capital can only be capital when it is accumulating, and it can only accumulate by producing and moving through relations of severe inequality among human groups." As such, the "racial" of racial capitalism describes a process of group differentiation integral to how accumulation, extraction, and dispossession work through capitalism—it is not an analytic that exists solely for describing how minoritized people experience targeted suffering. Our approach to racial capitalism furthers this understanding by considering the racializing effects of sexual expropriation across systems of slavery. We use the concept of sexual expropriation to name something beyond the individualized antagonisms of coerced sex and beyond what law understands as violations of bodily autonomy in order to bring the operations of sex, racial capitalism, and labor into closer analytic communion. Importantly, we do not presuppose or argue for clean divisions between or neat categorical assessments of slavery, human trafficking, prostitution, sexual enslavement, or rape, focusing instead on the how their recognition or submersion, legally and popularly, produces certain epistemologies about sex and race that in turn order what can and cannot be known. Specifically, tracking sexual expropriation and its many names (rape, human trafficking, white slavery) lets us bring the Ottoman slave system into ongoing conversations in Black feminisms on the afterlives of the transatlantic slave trade, queer of color critique, and Asian American studies' treatments of sexual slavery and empire that concern themselves primarily with East Asia.

Even as Ottoman and Muslim slavery has been linked to sexualized slavery, it has been delinked from many contemporary discussions of racial slavery and racial capitalism. For instance, in her talk, "Still Missing in

Action," the prominent legal scholar Patricia Viseur Sellers (Bhor, Boldis, Danhouser 2020: n.p.) argues for reanimating the prohibition of the slave trade in international law by invoking Ottoman harem slavery as an example of sexualized and gendered slavery. For Sellers, the history of Ottoman slavery as a system of sexual violation paves the way for understanding some instances of contemporary wartime rape and human trafficking as modern forms of slavery and slave trade. *Voices of Promise*, a student-run human rights blog, describes the evidence that Sellers' marshals to make her claim. Sellers, they write, emphasizes that "while Muslim men cannot have more than four wives under Islamic law, they may have unlimited concubines, and the East African Slave Trade supplied the Ottoman empire's demand for concubines. Additionally, boys and men were enslaved as eunuchs, who were used to guard harems and were traded many times as gifts, perpetuating their enslavement. Male reproductive organs were sometimes removed during the trade to bypass Islamic law forbidding Muslims to conduct castrations" (Bhor, Boldis, Danhouser 2020: n.p.). Cedric Robinson (2000), too, demarcates Muslim systems of slavery from the transatlantic slave trade which, as we will discuss, affects the narration of racial capitalism.

In what follows, we examine how the Ottoman slave system figures (even if inaccurately) as a prehistory of present-day human trafficking (as sex trafficking). We further explore how the juridical and historical separation of this system from that of transatlantic slavery produces a particular notion of race within racial capitalism due to a reliance on the epistemological primacy of US-based analyses of slavery. To do so, we track the reverberations of the racialized partitioning of sex slavery from slavery in the Americas in late nineteenth and early twentieth century "white slavery" moral panics into the 1990s, when human trafficking returns as a foremost human rights issue as the Cold War's putative end transformed the political and economic global order. In the early twentieth century, the hysteria around European women and girls becoming white slaves was not just related to the abolition of the transatlantic slave trade, but also to the Ottoman empire's system of enslavement, the specter of Islam in the white heart of Europe, and the colonial project of international law, which crosses oceans to link the transatlantic and Ottoman slave trade to the sex slavery of Asiatic domestic households. Following the shifting terms of recognition of sexual expropriation as empires and economic systems rise and fall, we argue, allows us to bridge related, but often disciplinarily distinct bodies of work on slavery, sexual enslavement, human trafficking, gendered labor, and race that themselves so often engage specific geographic imaginaries.[1]

Centering rape and coercive or compelled reproduction—sexual expropriation—as a method for assessing the political economy of slaveries, including the transatlantic slave trade, complicates the historical coordinates of Robinson's *Black Marxism* and its resulting portrait of racial capitalism, which requires a separation between the "Muslim" slave trade and the transatlantic one. Our positioning—one that historicizes how modes of sexual expropriation function alongside necessary and robust scholarship detailing various historical systems of enslavement—extends and deepens the notion of "the afterlives of slavery" (Hartman 2008: 6) and the racial, gendered, and sexed legacies that shape how we discuss the complex of race, sex, labor, and violence today.

Black Marxism, Queer of Color Critique, and the Ottoman Empire

The 2022 film *Three Thousand Years of Longing*, which received a standing ovation at the Cannes film festival, portrays the improbable encounter of a white British scholar of narrative structure, Alithea Binnie (played by Tilda Swinton) with a Djinn. Alithea purchases a bottle at a Turkish bazaar only to accidentally release the Black Djinn (played by Idris Elba) when she returns to her luxurious hotel room. Taken aback, Alithea initially refuses to make a wish, certain that all wishes lead to bad outcomes. The Djinn, who needs her to make wishes in order for him to be free, pleads for her cooperation. As he stalls for time, he tells Alithea a story of his imprisonment and three thousand years of "longing"—longing for freedom from his entrapment in a bottle. The Djinn's enslavement spans Ottoman imperial history. After being initially imprisoned in the bottle by King Solomon and cast away into the Red Sea, the Djinn is first found by a Gülten, a slave and concubine in Suleiman the Magnificent's palace. Her first wish is for Mustafa, Suleiman's son, to fall in love with her—a dangerous wish for which she is killed due to the jousting for power that occurs in the Sultan's harem. Thus, the Djinn remains enslaved. In the centuries that follow, several other Sultans and concubines fail or refuse to free the Djinn. The Djinn's final story, set in more recent times, is about the wishes of the third wife of a polygamous wealthy and elderly Muslim merchant, a teenage girl named Zephir. She comes close to freeing the Djinn, but in the end wishes she had never met him and prolongs his unfreedom. It is thus up to Alithea to free the Djinn. After wishing for the Djinn to have love (with her) and health, she wishes, as her third and final wish, that he be free. The backdrop of the Ottoman empire—its premodern mysticism, the space of the harem, polygamy, racialized slavery and illiberal rule—structure the film's fantasy of proper (white) love and freedom that can only come to fruition in present-day London.

Eunuchs, harems, and enslavement converge in this vision of premodern Oriental excesses that figure contemporary debates around sexualized slavery. This is in part because in the film, Ottoman slavery itself represents a story of family and romance, outside of capitalist relations. In contrast, queer of color critique, following Roderick A. Ferguson, locates gendered, racial, and sexual pathology and excess as produced by racial capitalist relations. In *Aberrations in Black*, Ferguson (2004: 11) argues that "Queer of color analysis can build on the idea that capital produces emergent social formations that exceed the racialized boundaries of gender and sexual ideals . . . and must challenge the idea that those social formations represent the pathologies of modern society." But what is portrayed as outside capitalist relations—in this case, the resurrection of Ottoman harem slavery and its sexual excesses in not just this film, but also in contemporary political and juridical considerations of human trafficking—remains thus far undertheorized by queer of color critique. Here, we think about an approach that considers modes of imperial rule and enslavement that were contemporaneous to but distinct from the transatlantic slave as crucial for reimagining the parameters and utility of queer of color critique—an analytic for rethinking the gendered and sexual coordinates of racial capitalism. As such, we employ "a historiographic approach to queer of color critique: an inquiry into the formation of queer approaches to political economy as part of a broader question of how the reproduction of the terms of freedom and justice, particularly sexual ones, are produced, reproduced, and thwarted" (Jaleel 2022). We examine how Ottoman and Muslim slavery is represented in *Black Marxism* and in contemporary human tracking and slavery debates and cultural productions to consider how representations of the Ottoman slave trade surface in each of these projects. By doing so, we link the genealogy of the exceptionalizing of sex slavery as a part of a moral (rather than financial) economy to representations of Ottoman slavery as separate from the transatlantic system.

In *Black Marxism*, Cedric Robinson (2000) tracks the origins of racial thinking and economic development in Europe to distinguish modern capitalist expansion (as racial capitalism) from prior imperial and economic modes. Robinson references slavery in Islamic societies as a counterpoint to the history of the transatlantic slave trade. He writes, "Muslim slavery was characteristically associated with unlimited potential for social mobility and much less racialism, it is not surprising to find whole dynasties in Muslim history founded by slaves (e.g., the Egyptian Mamelukes) or the emergence to prominence of Africans as soldiers, poets, philosophers, writers, and statesmen" (95). For Robinson, it is Islamic teachings and beliefs that engender this system of slavery that allows for upward mobility: "The Koran encouraged manumission as an act of piety, in many instances the punishment for criminal acts was less harsh for the slave than the freeman, slaves might purchase their freedom and might assume second-rank offices in state administration and the religious hierarchy" (95). Furthermore, Robinson notes that Sunni, Shia, and Maliki schools each limited the rights of masters and articulated the rights of slaves. Different juridical orders thus account for distinctions in slave systems.

Europe was once besieged by the Ottoman empire, under threat and invaded, and these incursions ultimately shaped its relationship to Blackness. As Robison (2000: 99–100) writes, "Islam once represented a more powerful civilization . . . [and] one closely identified in the European mind with African and Black peoples." As such, Europe's battle against and victory over Muslim empires, like the Ottoman one, become linked to Islamophobia, cast racially, and tethered to the emergence of the figure of "the Negro" and the trade in African slaves. In freeing itself from Muslim occupation, Europe opened the door for the expansion of its own outward facing colonial projects, which went hand in hand with the slave system. As Robinson (99) explains, "in freeing itself from Muslim colonization, Europe once again had a vigorous bourgeoisie and the state institutions to begin the construction of its own extra-European colonialism. From the fifteenth century on, that colonialism would encompass the lands of Asian, African, and New World peoples and engulf a substantial fraction of those peoples into the European traditions of slave labor and exploitation."

While it is important to note, as Robinson does, that the Ottoman encroachment onto Christian Europe and the fear of being subdued by Islam led to an Islamophobia that set the stage for the figure of "the Negro," we further mark how the cleaving of Ottoman slavery from transatlantic chattel slavery inadvertently marginalizes, or makes secondary, gendered and reproductive slave labor. Emphasizing slave status (or the possibility of upward mobility) as a break between the forms of slavery, regardless of whether or not this is accurate, obscures how gender and sexual violation are at the core of both systems. International legal scholar Jean Allain describes the scope of the Oriental Slave Trade, a trade parallel to the transatlantic one and one that includes "Muslim" or Ottoman slavery, in expressly gendered terms:

The Oriental Slave Trade (as opposed to the western-oriented, capitalist-driven trade) generally *enslaved two women for every man, for the purpose of work as domestic servants or concubines in north Africa and western Asia.* This trade, like that of the Atlantic, focused on the enslavement of inhabitants of sub-Saharan Africa. The main means of transportation was not ocean-going caravels, but camel caravans crossing the North African desert and small dhows sailing the Indian Ocean, the Persian Gulf, and the Red Sea. It is estimated that this trade involved seven million slaves, of which three million were transported during the nineteenth century (emphasis added). (2007a: 647)

Here, and in contradistinction to Black feminist historiographers' observations, Allain divorces the reproductive labor of the household from "capitalist-driven" forms of slavery. While British and US abolitionists largely ignored this slave trade, when it did emerge in the Euro-American imaginary it was often through a counterfactual focus on victims of the Oriental slave trade as white women. As Black feminist historians have shown, the literal making of "property" through forced reproduction, whether legally codified in doctrines like *Partus sequitur ventrem* (that which is born and "follows the womb" into slavery) or not, and the use of sexual violence to generate property and police categories of citizenship and civic life is central to understanding slavery and its aftermaths (Morgan 2018; Rosen 2009).[2] Yet when the transatlantic slave trade is put in broader historical context and understood as part of a complex of slave trade systems, past historical inattention to the gendered and sexual dimensions of enslavement—as the theft of reproductive labor, as the expropriation of sexual services or "sexual slavery"—can't solely be explained as a lack of concern for "women's experience" or the "ungendering" of Black people by the transatlantic slave trade.

White Slavery/Sex Slavery: Whiteness and Property

We extend Black feminist historiography's careful focus on slavery's gendered and racial reproduction to broader geopolitical and historical contexts. These other contexts help to explain why the gendered aspects of transatlantic slavery and its dependence on sexual expropriation were not always integrated into the discussion of its horrors. The split between sexual slavery as moral economy and chattel slavery as a racialized and coercive practice of unfree labor in political discourses at the turn of the twentieth century helped produce this omission.[3] Within this historical context, the legacy of the Ottoman slave trade, its place in broader "Oriental" or Asiatic slave trade systems, and its relationships between race and sexual expropriation includes the complex gendered racialization of religious difference that often goes ignored or unaccounted for in Euro-American legal traditions that, as we discuss, can function in the service of colonial expansion.

To illustrate the centrality of the Ottoman slave system to international human trafficking and slavery debates, we discuss late nineteenth and early twentieth century international and legal discourses around white slavery, which serve as the juridical and political precedent for contemporary accounts of human trafficking and other forms of "modern" slavery. While the League of Nations International Convention to Combat the Traffic in Women and Children, ratified in 1921, replaced *white slavery* with the racially neutral term *traffic* to describe the traffic in women and girls, the geopolitical and racial logics of the "white" slave nonetheless persist. In the following discussion, and as we'll elaborate, we understand *whiteness* to signal the vulnerability attached to the legal category of women and girls (later *gender*). This framework not only illuminates white slavery's continuing connection to human trafficking, but also emphasizes the instability of racialization and its connection to shifts in geopolitics and global economies. Focusing on sexual expropriation across historically and geopolitically distinct yet interrelated contexts of slavery, lets us track the racialized scripts of "bad sex" from Euro-American abolitionist uproar over the Barbary Coast, the Ottoman empire, and the broader Oriental/Asiatic slave trade to juridical discussions of human and sex trafficking at the twentieth century's beginning and end. The campaign against white slavery, as Laura Hyun Yi Kang (2020: 51) writes, shows how "beginning in the nineteenth century, the work of anti-trafficking has always been scored by a racializing and racist fault line between white and nonwhite women, which has betrayed its internationalist and globalist claims." Kang (51) emphasizes that "beyond being expressions of the racialist and racist worldview of individual anti-trafficking subjects, these conceptual, methodological, and rhetorical habits enact the paradoxical hyper-visibility and unknowability of the 'traffic in women.'" The unknowability of the "traffic in women" is abetted, we argue, by ignoring the sexual expropriation of those who fall out of the category's facile embrace. Crucially, the Black ungendered harem guard, "the eunuch," who maintains racialized boundaries in the households of the sixteenth century Ottoman elite, is not a figure at the center of juridical and political accounts of sex slavery. Rather, it is the "white" harem concubine and Oriental/Muslim patriarch that become one prominent racial and gendered foundation of the moral economy of anti-sex slavery and sex trafficking today.[4]

The moral economy of sex trafficking begins with accounts of "white slavery" that emerge contemporaneously with, although also distinct from, the abolition movement centered on the transatlantic slave trade and chattel slavery in the Americas. In the nineteenth century and early twentieth centuries, white slavery as a concept circulated to describe both prostitution and the enslavement practices of the Muslim world. In his 1847 lecture to the Boston Mercantile Library Association, and as part of a strategy to condemn slavery in the United States, Massachusetts senator and well-known white abolitionist Charles Sumner spoke of "white slavery" in the Barbary States (Ottoman North Africa, of which Algiers was the capital). As part of a broad abolitionist strategy to move white audiences to identify with the enslaved, in the lecture, Sumner emphasized the presence of European concubines in harems:

> It is notorious that, in Algiers, [the dynamics of slavery] exerted a most pernicious influence on master as well as slave. The slave was crushed and degraded, his intelligence abased, even his love of freedom extinguished. The master, accustomed from childhood to revolting inequalities of condition, was exalted into a mood of unconscious arrogance and self-confidence, inconsistent with the virtues of a pure and upright character. Unlimited power is apt to stretch towards license; and the wives and daughters of Christian slaves were often pressed to be the concubines of their Algerine masters. (Sumner 1847: 58).

In a footnote to this statement, Sumner (58) writes, "Among the concubines of a prince of Morocco were two slaves of the age of fifteen, one of English, and the other of French extraction. [In] Lemprière's Tour, there is an account of the fate of 'one Mrs. Shaw, an Irish woman,' in words hardly polite enough to be quoted. She was swept into the harem of Muley Ishmael, who 'forced her to turn Moor'; but soon after, having taken a dislike to her, he gave her to a soldier."

The cruelty of the "Moors" with unlimited power is, as Lyndsey Beutin (2023: 3) notes, a trope in Euro-American discussions of slavery: "The figure of the Arab slave trader [is] often positioned within American and British rhetoric as coming before 1619 and after 1807 and as being more barbaric and less caring than plantation owners in the American South." For Beutin (3), this dichotomy drives a pervasive "anti-Blackness" where "the benevolence of nineteenth-century American and British abolition, the pretransatlantic slave trade within Africa, and the brutality and threat of Arab culture" function as "rhetorical alibis for white historical innocence when the history of transatlantic slavery and its relevance to ongoing racial violence comes up in public conversation." However, as in many discussions of race that take the US experience of the transatlantic slave trade as their theoretical coordinates, both whiteness and Blackness carry the hidden baggage of US racial schemas. The figure of the Arab slave trader is tied to a history of not only transatlantic, but Ottoman and other "Oriental" systems of slavery, which in turn requires an account of religious clashes that were so central to the formation and defense of Europe as a white, non-Muslim space. As Ottoman historian Madeline Zilfi (2010: 98) writes, "Islamic regimes like the Ottoman empire defined liability to enslavement not in terms of race, color, or ethnicity but in accordance with the conjoined attributes of geography and religion." The specter of forced conversion of Christians to Islam and of rape and the turning into property of primarily Christian daughters and wives (not just women in general) were central to American and British abolitionist uproar. By disconnecting Ottoman slavery from overlapping transatlantic slave histories, the crucial connections between religion, race, gender, and racial capitalism are lost both historically and in more contemporary considerations of slavery and the "new" slave trade (that is, human trafficking, and especially sex trafficking/slavery). In this way, a thin portrait of anti-Blackness as the sole way to understand slavery writ large can emerge. Decontextualized from a transnational context, this limited version of anti-Blackness reinforces US racial histories and analytic frameworks that so often turn on the binary of Black and white.

Turning from the Muslim slavers to the French, English, and Irish enslaved European women that figure in Sumner's lecture, it is clear that the gendered articulations of whiteness as vulnerability to sexual slavery emerge in part through a relation to the threat of Islam. Crucially, European slaves were a minority among the different slaves in the Ottoman empire (the vast majority of whom were African domestic slaves) (Zilfi 2010). Nevertheless, the existence of white (European) slaves is the foundation for the moral outrage that resonated in the US and Western Europe. We can thus observe that the Ottoman empire played an important role in the broader landscape of juridical and political debates around abolition, since Blackness, whiteness and Islam work in concert and in tension to articulate slavery as a moral rather than economic concern. It is the gender and race of the slaves (rather than the labor they are performing) that is at the core of the concern. This complex of Islam, sexual impropriety, and Blackness tells us something about the construction of Europe as a white space and the role of whiteness in colonial property claims.

In the US context, legal theorist Cheryl Harris (1993) made the groundbreaking argument that self-possession is tied to the status of whiteness as property in the US, and that this status is enshrined and perpetuated in US law. We might think about the property interest in whiteness that Harris describes as subject to shift as the meaning of property shifts across different historical epochs and regimes of accumulation. In a word, whiteness is never fully transparent or stable. In the early twentieth century, the moral panic around "white slavery" reached a peak in the United States, which translated its own racial logics onto the moral economy surrounding sex slavery. In 1910, the Mann Act, also known as the White Slave Traffic Act, passed as one of the main pieces of Progressive era legislation in the United States. The act criminalized moving women and children across state lines "for the purpose of prostitution or debauchery, or for any other immoral purpose." Crucially, the act criminalized not just "sexual slavery" or prostitution, but also a variety of consensual non-normative sexual acts, including adultery and same-sex sex. The 2004 PBS documentary *Unforgivable Blackness*, about the life of the Black heavyweight champion Jack Johnson, who was convicted under the Mann Act for sexual relations with white women, describes discourses of white slavery as a hysteria and moral panic that, though about sex, were also very much about race. Race and sex became the sites where "the rapid changes that the Industrial Revolution had brought to American society," including "urbanization, immigration, the changing role of women, and evolving social mores" were worked through (PBS 2004). In particular, fears that "unfettered immigration provided an endless supply of both foreign prostitutes and foreign men who lured American girls into immorality" were stoked by "muckraking journalists," who "fueled the hysteria with sensationalized stories of innocent girls kidnapped off the streets by foreigners, drugged, smuggled across the country, and forced to work in brothels" (PBS 2004). In the midst of this cultural frenzy, one such muckraker, George Kibber Turner, borrowing a term from the nineteenth-century labor movement, summed up the moment by naming prostitution "white slavery'" (PBS 2004). In the US context, then, the "whiteness" of white slaves wasn't intended solely to convey the race of prostitutes and sex trafficked women and children, but rather to describe the vulnerability of women and girls to racialized sexual appetites of nonwhite men (especially Black and Asian) within the context of industrialized capitalism. The conflation of whiteness with innocence, at the same time, cleaves sex slavery from racial slavery and its association with labor to depict immoral sexual relations.

　　Whiteness, its relation to property and the meaning of property, changes not only as capitalism shifts, but as particular histories and geographies other than the US, including other histories of race, sex, religion, and slavery are engaged. Thinking whiteness globally, outside of US juridical and property regimes, shows in part how the US Black/white binary relies on the excision of religion and racialized sex, occluding the historical entanglements of Islamophobia and anti-Blackness. The fantasies and fears around white concubinage and forced conversion to Islam that fall under the umbrella of sex slavery are the historical backdrop for contemporary local, national, regional, and international laws on human trafficking that draw a sharp distinction between *sex trafficking* (a term that encompasses, but is broader, than "sexual" slavery) and *labor trafficking*. Thus "bad" (coerced, but also immoral, improper, non-normative and non-nuclear) sex is placed in a category separate from labor, whether coerced or free, paid or unpaid. As the Ottoman slave trade is cut cleanly from the transatlantic one through its association with sexual barbarity, only a thin version of anti-Blackness, one that follows race through US racial categories and experiences, can emerge.

Writing about the 1904 International Agreement for the Suppression of the "White Slave Traffic" (which had been in negotiation since 1902), Jean Allain (2007: 6) describes, on the one hand, European delegates' dissatisfaction with the term *white* to describe sexual degradation. At the same time, he argues that "the racialised element of the term 'white' slave traffic . . . was not happenstance and was evident throughout the deliberation of the 1902 International Conference [on White Slave Traffic]"—a conference that while billed "international" was nonetheless "an affair of the kingdoms of Europe and, save Switzerland, their aristocratic representatives" (8). The conference's Report of the Legislative Commission, for example, made clear to all present the harm white slavery presented specifically to "women of European stock," who were "led astray" or enticed into prostitution in the classic scenario of a woman out of place: "The victim procured in a northern country, conveyed across a central country, has been delivered up in a southern country" (Allain 2007: 8–9). French jurist Louis Renault's summary of the conference evinced "the undercurrent of racialised thinking which permeated the era," as he noted that "the draft [proposal] developed between European delegates naturally was aimed at the White Slave trade, but it is worth remarking that the trade is not only fixed on women of a certain colour. In that, a not inconsequential traffic in yellow women is practiced between Japan and different countries" (8).

In the late nineteenth and early twentieth centuries, Ottoman administrators responded to the colonial project of abolition by themselves insisting on the distinction of their system of slavery from that of the transatlantic slave trade. Ottomans came to view the development of international law and abolition of the slave trade as a threat to their own notions of family and the private sphere. Bilal Ali Kotil (2023) argues that in the nineteenth century, as the European abolitionist movement gained traction in international law, it infringed on Ottoman sovereignty through its interference with the elite domestic arrangements of wealthy Ottoman families. In those ruling families, domestic slaves were integral to the household structure and the perpetuation of the Ottoman patriarchy. For the wealthy, slave labor was necessary not only to sustain a large household, but to provide charity beyond the household to the needy and the poor. As Kotil (2023: 64–65) notes, "Without slave labour, the image of the compassionate and humanitarian patriarch would not have been possible." In this way, Kotil shows that Ottoman social reproduction (as patriarchal benevolence) hinged on the domestic slave system and was not strictly a "private" affair. At the same time, Kotil (73) notes that during international conventions focused on the abolition of slavery, Ottoman officials took great pains to argue that domestic servitude (not slavery) in elite Ottoman households was completely distinct from the enslavement of Africans in the context of the Americas.

British moral outrage at ongoing Ottoman practices of slavery, which fueled Ottoman responses to changing international laws, were not actually about morality. European historical fears of Islam, coupled with increasingly more robust calls to end slavery, opened the door to greatly expanding European colonization of Africa. According to Allain (2007a: 347), when Great Britain outlawed the slave trade in 1807 and became the main global proponent of abolition, its focus was solely on the transatlantic slave trade and ignored the parallel "Oriental slave trade" in East Africa. "It was only when the Atlantic Slave Trade ended and European States *undertook to conquer the whole of the African continent* that Great Britain showed any great zeal in promoting the suppression of the Oriental Slave Trade [emphasis added]" (Allain 2007a: 347). Moreover, As Kotil (2023: 68) writes, "To counter the influence of Islam and avoid possible hindrances to the expansion of the European trade and missionary works, the European discourse on Islam in the late nineteenth century sought to define it by marking a difference between the urban legal Islam of the Arab-Swahili traders and Sufi networks, and the folk Islam of the African inhabitants." William Ponty, governor-general of French West Africa (1908–15), for example, urged the protection of "Islam noir" from the influences of "Islam arabe" (cited in Kotil 2023: 68). By the 1870s, the European anti-slavery movement was "linked fatefully" to European conquest and colonization in Africa (68). By taking up the work of anti-slavery activists, Europe turned opposition to slavery into a mandate for conquest (68). As "morality" became the provenance of white abolitionists, projections of racial slavery were cast back upon the Ottoman empire. Thus in 1888, when

Cardinal Lavigerie, the archbishop of Carthage and Algiers, stated that "'slave-hunting is a right and almost a duty for Muslims' and Muslims 'believe and teach that the black is not part of the human family' and are instead 'between humans and animals,'" he was using moral abolitionist arguments to open the door for European rule in Africa (cited in Kotil: 63).

That the struggle for imperial domination over Africa plays out in the language of morality, but also of private family relations, may indicate why sex slavery emerges as an ongoing "modern" slavery while racialized chattel slavery is written, at least in dominant US history, as being aberrant to proper free market capitalism. This formulation runs counter to Robinson's (2000) demonstration of all capitalism being rooted in racial capitalism and slavery that begins within feudal Europe's own internal racialisms and fears of Ottoman incursion. By rendering sex slavery a moral rather than economic concern—or more pointedly, a moral concern that masks conquest and extraction—US-European control over territory and resources, enacted through emerging systems of international law and subsequently, as we'll discuss, capitalism itself—can be posited as the modernizing solution to bad sexual relations.

From White Slavery to Human Trafficking: Capitalist Arrangements of Sex, Capital, and Labor in the Post-Cold War

In the above debates, not just "race," but the complex interplay of race, sex, religion, and gendered vulnerability shape how international law addresses slavery in both past and present anti-trafficking and sex slavery initiatives. The significance of the Ottoman empire to international debates about slavery and the slave trade cannot be underestimated, although they have been largely erased from present-day considerations of antitrafficking movements except as examples of sensationally bad sexual practice. From this perspective, whiteness as property is contoured by the fear of becoming property of sexually savage (Brown or Black) men–from the Irish Mrs. Shaw in the harem of Ishmael to today's endless parade of Asian sex slaves shackled to dirty beds.[5] As the prehistory of human trafficking—where whiteness is a negotiation between gendered vulnerability and Islamic or Oriental-style patriarchy—we can thus track whiteness in contemporary human trafficking and slavery debates as continually renegotiated and reproduced at the intersections of political liberalism and illiberalism.

We see this genealogy, for instance, in Patricia Viseur Sellers and Jocelyn Getken Kestenbaum's[6] (2020) example of modern-day slave and sex trafficking, as they argue for the reanimation of international law's prohibition against the slave trade. They write, "It is undisputed that ISIS fighters enslaved Yazidi women, girls, and boys. Buttressed by a political ideology of gender inequality and religious superiority, ISIS arranged for its fighters to 'buy, sell, or give as a gift female captives' who were 'war spoils.' The policy intentionally reduced into slavery 'non-believing' women and children and deemed them Caliphate property. The female slaves were called 'sabaya.' ISIS often presented Yazidi women and girls 'as a package' until girls reached the age of nine and, thereafter, sold them separately" (Viseur Sellers and Getken Kestenbaum 2020: 8–9). This is the reemergence of Charles Sumner's late nineteenth century appeals to liberal modernity (written as freedom) over and against ethno-religious patriarchal brutality. The sexualized specter of the Ottoman slave trade connects, facilitates, and contours such attention to race, labor, sex, and slavery and positions present-day US and Europe as leading the resolution to the racialized sexual violence and enslavement happening elsewhere.

To be clear, this continuity from white slavery to human trafficking does not occur through an unchanging idea of slavery, a stable definition of forced sex, or an abiding social desire to end exploitation. The extension of white slavery through human trafficking is instead tied to the geopolitical upendings occasioned by the Cold War's end and the relationships between international law and capitalism that emerge as the US and the Global North turn to international law to manage the contradictions of gender, sex, and race of the moment. Renewed popular and legal interest in human trafficking and slavery only converged as the twentieth century gave way to the twenty first. At that time, as Allain (2012) notes, the first international judgments on slavery appeared since 1905.[7] The new interest in slavery occurred as "sex slavery" in the former Yugoslavia and the wave of global labor migrations spurred by the ascent of global capitalism in the aftermath of the Cold War led to the passage of the first anti-trafficking instruments in roughly sixty years, when the United Nations General Assembly adopted the 2000 Protocol to Prevent, Suppress, and Punish Trafficking in Persons, Especially Women and Children, as a supplement to the United Nations Convention Against Transnational Organized Crime. Given that the Balkans were historically the location where white Christian Europe sought to stave off the Ottoman empire, and that Serbia and Bosnia were both a part of the Ottoman empire, and later part of a worker self-managed state socialist nation, we might observe that as a reinvigorated international law takes up bad sex as a global problem, the multiple histories of capitalism, colonialism, and slavery converge.

The associations between sexual slavery, the laws of war, and human trafficking are linked not only by law, but by public and expert perception as well. As Siddarth Kara (2009) remarked, "Abolitionists [of human trafficking] must also not forget that powerful macroeconomic forces unleashed during the process of economic globalization in the post-Cold War era have been more responsible than any other force for the unforgivable rise in contemporary slavery." Subsequently, slavery cases reappeared on the international legal scene. In an interview about the rise of "modern slavery," Kevin Bales, noted and much criticized anti-human trafficking advocate and researcher, described the relationship between law and human trafficking in this way: "When Yugoslavia broke up and the rule of law broke down, a lot of us were shocked at the incredible speed with which enslavement and human trafficking and even the sale of people on auction blocks just mushroomed. You might say that on Monday law broke down and by Tuesday you had slavery" (Butler 2007).

As the risks and dangers previously organized through state socialisms and the threat of the Soviet Union turned to one marked by what Western media and politicians labeled sectarian violence and ethno-religious clashes, the ostensible spread of global mass sexualized violence became an issue of overwhelming concern in liberal feminist political and legal circles (Atanasoski 2013; Jaleel 2021). This narrative of violence and sex as essentially bad group behavior in need of institutional governance strips, as many have remarked, the economic fallout of the Cold War's end and its attendant geopolitical upendings of national and international organizations of power of their explanatory potential for conflict (Atanasoski 2013; Jaleel 2021). That narrative of sex and violence also reinvigorated international law, whose authority had waned in the latter half of the twentieth century in the wake of decolonization but ascended once again as a way to manage risk as one global superpower emerged. With the erstwhile end of the communist threat, new systems of international law emerged as newly authoritative sites of justice.[8]

Conclusion

It is worth recalling that Cedric Robinson distinguishes slave systems through juridical frameworks; transatlantic slavery becomes an ownership/property regime, while the chance for mobility in the Ottoman system is, in contradistinction, not dependent on the mercy of benevolent transatlantic master, but coded within Islamic slave jurisprudence. Robinson's formulation of slavery as a result obscures operations of gendered and racialized sexual conquest that were also—as Zilfi, Morgan, and others attest—central to the project of Ottoman slavery and also the transatlantic slave trade. Both systems were also central to early developments in and consolidations of international law that, as we discussed, morally authorized European imperial expansion and, by the beginning of the twenty-first century, positioned capitalism as a solution to slave trafficking rather than its driving engine. Today, the structure of law continues to abet a narrow conception of race in the service of nation-states' political ambitions. Rather than link the operations of race, sex, and capital, as women of color and queer of color scholarship has urged in approaches to slavery, empire, and their aftermaths, contemporary human trafficking law and jurisprudence separate race/labor and sex from each other—and largely ignore capital flows altogether—in their accounts of justice.

Queer of color critique is an engagement with Marxist thinking but not an uncritical adoption of it. For Marx, the prostitute was a symptom of alienation wrought by capitalism—a symptom of dissolution and exploitation in a world where everything is for sale. Roderick A. Ferguson (2004) takes issue with Marxist and revolutionary thought and the continual pathologization of the prostitute—someone who is pressured into an economy, whose sexual services can be bought and sold—as the ultimate form of alienation under capitalism. Ferguson (11) reframes the (in his example, drag-queen) prostitute to be a site of potential social rupture that does not capitulate to aberrant racialized gender/sex as social pathology, arguing that we must "locate her within a national culture that disavows the configuration of her own racial, gender, class, and sexual particularity and a mode of production that fosters her own formation." Yet this intervention already builds on a theory of racial capitalism that separates understandings of sexual slavery from racial slavery. This separation, as we have argued, does not fully show how racial and sexual formations emerge through transnational maneuvers of geopolitical and racialized world orderings that shape the meanings and potentials of queerness, queer of color thought, and queer study. If we consider how sexual expropriation works across not only the sale of sex but across other iterations of gendered and sexual value extraction via sexual slavery, rape, and human trafficking—and how these terms converge and disperse at different historical moments, especially as global economic and governance systems shift—then a more complex account of what Ferguson names "the normative investments of nation-states and capital" can emerge.

In the process of separating sexual slavery from racial slavery, and the delinking of what were interlinked geopolitical and historical contexts of simultaneous and parallel slave trades, the U.S. and Western Europe become sites where "race" matters while the "Oriental" world remains perpetually sexually deviant. Connections between struggles across the globe are separated by imagined frameworks of racial and sexual difference that erase material histories of different and interconnected systems of gendered and sexual enslavement. One such unexpected and submerged connection can be found in how Yugoslavia's "state socialism identified with the decolonising Global South more than eastern Europe through Non-Aligned ideology, and where Aimé Césaire, the theorist of Négritude, could identify a Dalmatian shore, Martinska, in anti-colonial solidarity with his own Martinique" (Baker 2018: 4). These non-Western histories of enslavement, colonialism, and anti-capitalism fall from the frame through the separation of bad sex from global histories of racial capitalism.

Notes

1   Human trafficking encompasses both labor trafficking and sex trafficking, which is at times considered synonymous with prostitution. See Halley 2008 for a detailed account of shifting legal approaches to sex trafficking.

2   In spite of the association of the Ottoman slave trade with gendered, sexual slavery in today's imaginaries, Ottoman historian Madeline Zilfi (2010: 24) writes that "the significance of gender in the history of Ottoman slavery has been seriously neglected." Particularly, Zilfi (24) notes that "the received narrative has treated female slavery as a minor addendum to the elite male and ethnic story"—one where "the scholarly interest in women's experience of slavery has, for the most part, been confined to polygyny and concubinage." Further, that scholarly interest has essentially been a numbers game— "how many men were polygynous? How many wives or concubines did men have? What percentage of men had large harems?" Meanwhile, "the matter of coerced female sexual uſage . . . haſ generally been unproblematized and ſevered from other ſocial iſſueſ and processes" (24). Zilfi's observation that sexual coercion remains undertheorized within Ottoman slave historiography even as scholarly attention has spectacularized the concubine and the harem mistress has a strong resonance with how Ottoman slavery appears as one history of sex slavery in the Western world. "Coerced female sexual usage" in the Ottoman world is simply a stand-alone fact—one that becomes, as we discuss in the next section–part of the sexualized threat to white Europe that ignores the Ottoman production of eunuch harem guards, who were, at various points during the Ottoman empire, seized from Africa and/or Europe (Hathaway 2017). This, we argue, is deeply imbricated with the well-worn discourses around sex slavery that narrow gender politics to the mistreatment of women by illiberal (ethno-religious and patriarchal) cultures.

3   We can see how interpreting contemporary human trafficking through a history US slavery and its civil rights traditions produces racialized geographies of labor as distinct from sexual expropriation, as if sexualized violence could not be present and could not generate value, when people are put to work. For example, Louis CdeBaca, the Obama Administration's U.S. Ambassador-at-Large to Monitor and Combat Human Traffick-

ing in Persons, explains the trajectory of slavery and human trafficking as follows: "In the wake of the Civil Rights Movement, there was a perception that the problem of slavery, of sharecropping, was a thing of the past . . . And, quietly, the abusers were bringing in immigrants to replace the African American community . . . The involuntary servitude and slavery program had been a little bit on the back burner during the '70s and '80s because of the gains of the Civil Rights Movement . . . And, then, by the '80s and '90s, we were starting to see—whether it was Guatemalans, or Mexicans or others—suffering often in the same farms in the American South picking tomatoes, cucumbers, onions" (Martin, "Underground Trade Part Seven: n.p.).

4   In a different context, Julietta Hua has written about the production of "culpable" patriarchal orientalized cultures that are produced through contemporary anti-trafficking campaigns (Hua 2011).

5   For more information on Asian women and the imaginaries of human trafficking, please see Kang (2020).

6   For an account of how legal feminists attempted to influence the development of international law and how they theorized gender-based violence, from war rape to human trafficking, see Halley 2008.

7   As Allain (2012: n.p.) writes, "As the twentieth century drew to a close, the international legal regime related to slavery and servitude existed for all intents and purposes in name only . . . As a result, though the twentieth century saw only one international judgment linked to slavery—the 1905 Muscat Dhows case—the first decade of the twenty-first century would see decisions related to slavery by the International Criminal Tribunal for the former Yugoslavia (2002 Kunarac et al), the European Court of Human Rights (2005 Siliadin and 2010 Rantsev), the ECOWAS Community Court of Justice (2008 Mani Koraou v Niger) and the Special Court for Sierra Leone (2008 Brima)." Dhows, like judgments that would follow it, evinced the complex entanglements between geopolitics, state power, and anti-slavery campaigns. In Dhows, British efforts to suppress the Indian Oceans slave trade also conveniently extended British dominance and influence over Africa and the high seas.

8   These included the establishment of the ad hoc tribunals to adjudicate serious violations of international humanitarian law, specifically for the former Yugoslavia and Rwanda, in 1993 and 1994, respectively. The ad hoc tribunals paved the way for the eventual adoption of the Rome Treaty in 1998, which established a permanent International Criminal Court capable of addressing what had before been the purview of ad hoc tribunals, which only had authority over particular geographies and only for delimited time spans associated with isolated conflict.

References

Allain, Jean. 2007a. "The Nineteenth Century Law of the Sea and the British Abolition of the Slave Trade. *British Yearbook of International Law*, 78, no. 1: 342–388. https://doi.org /10.1093/bybil/78.1.342

Allain, Jean. 2007b. "White Slave Traffic in International Law." *Journal of Trafficking and Human Exploitation* 1, no. 1: 1–40.

Allain, Jean, ed. 2012. *The Legal Understanding of Slavery: From the Historical to the Contemporary*. Oxford, UK: Oxford University Press. Kindle.

Atanasoski, Neda. 2013. *Humanitarian Violence: The US Deployment of Diversity*. Minneapolis: University of Minnesota Press.

Baker, Catherine. 2018. *Race and the Yugoslav Region*. Manchester, UK: Manchester University Press.

Beutin, Lyndsey P. 2023. *Trafficking in Antiblackness: Modern-Day Slavery, White Indemnity, and Racial Justice*. Durham, NC: Duke University Press.

Bhor, Ilina, Eszter Boldis, and Leigh Marie Dannhauser. 2020. "Still Missing in Action: The International Crime of the Slave Trade." https://www.promisehumanrights.blog/blog/2020/11/still-missing-in-action-the-international-crime-of-the-slave-trade

Butler, Bill. 2007. "On Abolishing Slavery–Again." *Vision*. https://www.vision.org/interview-kevin-bales-abolishing-slavery-again-576

Ferguson, Roderick A. 2004. *Aberrations in Black: Toward a Queer of Color Critique*. Minneapolis: University of Minnesota Press.

Halley, Janet. 2008. "Rape at Rome: Feminist Interventions in the Criminalization of Sex-Related Violence in Positive International Criminal Law." *Michigan Journal of International Law* 30: 1–123.

Harris, Cheryl I. 1993. "Whiteness as Property." Harvard Law Review 106, no. 8: 1707–91. https://doi.org/10.2307/1341787.

Hartman, Saidiya. 2022. *Scenes of Subjection: Terror, Slavery, and Self-Making in Nineteenth-century America*. New York: W. W. Norton & Company.

Hartman, Saidiya. 2008. *Lose Your Mother: A Journey along the Atlantic Slave Route*. New York, NY: Macmillan.

Hathaway, Jane. 2017. "The Chief Eunuch of the Ottoman Imperial Harem: An Expanding Sphere of Influence Amid Institutional, Social, and Economic Change." https://www.ias.edu/ideas/2017/hathaway-chief-eunuch.

Hong, Grace. 2015. *Death Beyond Disavowal: The Impossible Politics of Difference*. Minneapolis: University of Minnesota Press.

Hua, Julietta. 2011. *Trafficking Women's Human Rights*. Minneapolis: University of Minnesota Press.

International Criminal Court. 2023. "Short Biography Ms. Patricia Viseur Sellers." Retrieved May 1 2023. https://www.icc-cpi.int/sites/default/files/itemsDocuments/otp/bios/Bio-Patricia-Sellers-(IOP).pdf

Jaleel, Rana M. 2022. "Rethinking Racial Slavery and Queer of Color Critique." Paper presented at the American Studies Annual Conference. Paper on file with author.

Jaleel, Rana M. 2021. *The Work of Rape*. Durham: Duke University Press.

Kang, Laura Hyun Yi. 2020. *Traffic in Asian Women*. Durham: Duke University Press.

Kara, Siddarth. 2009. "Interviews with Siddarth Kara." Columbia University Press (blog). http://www.cupblog.org/?p=488.

Kotil, Bilal Ali. 2023. "Extraterritorial Slaves: Late Ottoman Paternalism and the International Debate on Slavery." *The International History Review*, 45, no. 1: 63–80, https://doi.org/10.1080/07075332.2022.2118806.

Martin, Phillip. 2014. "Underground Trade Part Seven: Why Human Trafficking is Called Modern Day Slavery." *Huffington Post*. January 23, http://www.huffingtonpost.com/phillip-martin/underground-trade-part-se_b_2929373.html.

Melamed, Jodi. 2015. "Racial Capitalism." *Critical Ethnic Studies* 1, no. 1: 76–85.

Morgan, Jennifer. 2004. *Laboring Women: Reproduction and Gender in New World Slavery*. Philadelphia: University of Pennsylvania Press.

Morgan, Jennifer L. 2018. *Partus sequitur ventrem*: Law, Race, and Reproduction in Colonial Slavery. *Small Axe* 22, no. 1 (55): 1–17.

PBS. 2004. "The Mann Act." https://www.pbs.org/kenburns/unforgivable-blackness/mann-act.

Reddy, Chandan. 2015. Freedom with Violence: Race, Sexuality, and the U.S. State. Durham: Duke University Press.

Robinson, Cedric J. 2000. *Black Marxism: The Making of the Black Radical Tradition*. Chapel Hill, NC: University of North Carolina Press.

Rosen, Hannah. 2009. *Terror in the Heart of Freedom: Citizenship, Sexual Violence, and the Meaning of Race in the Postemancipation South*. Chapel Hill: University of North Carolina Press.

Sellers, Patricia Viseur and Jocelyn Getken Kestenbaum. 2020. "Missing in Action: The International Crime of the Slave Trade." 18 *Journal of International Criminal Justice*, Cardozo Legal Studies Research Paper No. 607.

Sumner, Charles. 1847. "White Slavery in the Barbary States." https://hdl.handle.net/2027/uc1.31175035150096.

Spillers, Hortense J. 1987. "Mama's Baby, Papa's Maybe: An American Grammar Book." *diacritics* 17, no. 2: 65–81.

Zilfi, Madeline. 2010. *Women and Slavery in the Late Ottoman Empire: The Design of Difference*. Cambridge, UK: Cambridge University Press, 2010.

Petrus Liu

Homonormativity's Racial Capitalism:
On the Differential Allocation of Grievability

From the start, the conflicts between Taiwan and China have been a product of racial capitalism in Cold War Asia. Since US House Speaker Nancy Pelosi's highly publicized visit to Taiwan in August 2022, however, there has been an increasing alignment between Taiwan's public opinion and an American ideology that reinterprets these conflicts as the result of China's unwillingness to accept democracy. Taiwan's vibrant LGBT culture plays an indispensable role in this narrative. Having legalized same-sex marriage in 2019, Taiwan has been the poster child of East Asian democratization and queer human rights in the international media, while China, despite its rapid economic growth, appears willfully resistant to such changes. China's political *illiberalism* stands in stark contrast to its economic *liberalism*, which has since 1978 introduced a series of market reforms to reintegrate the formerly socialist country into the world of financial capitalism. In more recent times the illiberal character of China has become even more pronounced with reports on its human rights abuses in Xinjiang and its stance on the ongoing Russia-Ukraine War.

By contrast, what has received virtually no media attention is the role of the United States

The South Atlantic Quarterly 123:1, January 2024
DOI 10.1215/00382876-10920669   © 2024 Duke University Press

itself in the ongoing conflicts in Asia. As an imperialist power, the United States has a vested interest in Taiwan's geostrategic value in the East Asian regime of capital accumulation. The United States continues to collect protection money from Taiwan in the form of billions of dollars of arms sales annually. Since Trump started a trade war with China in 2018, the so-called China threat has become the focus of US bipartisan concern, with Taiwan being further reduced to a pawn in US maneuvers to provoke China. Erasing a long history of US (neo-)colonial expansion into the Asia Pacific, the media portrays Taiwan as a hapless queer democracy—led by an unmarried woman president—in need of white saviors to fend off aggression from Chinese savages. In such instances, Taiwan's homonormative nationalism lends support to a racializing discourse against the Chinese, while the actual object of historical analysis—the combined and uneven development of East Asian capitalism—remains obscured from view.[1] Against this backdrop, the task of queer theory has never been more urgent. Rather than developing empiricist descriptions of LGBT lives, queer theory offers an interventionist strategy for rendering visible racial capitalism's effects on the contraction of the space of thought—what can be heard in contemporary conversations.

What would happen to the story of queer emancipation in Asia if, instead of marriage equality, we began with an analysis of the differential allocation of grievability across racialized populations under Taiwan's historical transformation into the Pax Americana's military outpost and vehicle of capital accumulation? In this essay, I consider memoirs of survivors of the Chinese Civil War as articulating an unintelligible order of queer kinship. I argue that their life stories reveal a queer racialization of Chineseness in a division system created during the Cold War. Weaving together progressive critiques of the marriage equality movement from within Taiwan and the fragmented life stories of war veterans, my essay contributes to the ongoing discussion of racial capitalism. As Singh (2022: 27) has noted in an insightful essay, contemporary discussions of racial capitalism have departed from its original usage in Cedric Robinson's *Black Marxism* to reflect on a wider range of topics from the impact of mass incarceration and subprime lending to the politics of #blacklivesmatter, while retaining Robinson's insight that capitalism is systematically built on "group-differentiated vulnerabilities as a valuable resource, even as a site . . . for new forms of social discipline and value extraction." My work further extends this analysis to interrogate the narrative of homonational emergence, which converts queerness from a radical vantage point into a congealed ontological category, as a form of "social discipline" and "value extraction" in capital's self-reproduction. With a rereading of quotidian lives that are lived, lost, and erased from public mourning under Cold War racial capitalism, I offer a conception of queerness as a critical analytic of the differential regulation and allocation of grievability.

The goals of this essay are twofold. On the one hand, the broadest aim of this essay is to augment the geographical focus of current theories of racial capitalism. Because East Asian racial capitalism and its entanglements with queer politics do not correspond to the historical experience of the trans-Atlantic slave trade, an examination of this archive is eminently useful for expanding the notion of race. Joining a growing body of literature on non-anglophone relations of race, racism, and racialization in less studied regions of the world, I offer an account of the morphology of racialized modes of identification and subjection in Taiwan. For reasons that will become clear in the body of the essay, I theorize these relations as "Blue versus Green" (as opposed to Black versus white). On the other hand, this essay also endeavors, through a queer Marxist lens, to situate emerging organizations of sexuality within the contradictions of racial capitalism. Contemporary queer theory has deepened our understanding of capitalism's dependency on gender-nonconforming bodies.[2] In this framework, the differentiation of human subjects along axes of race, gender, and sexuality is no longer considered anterior to the accumulation of capital. Rather, such differentiations and enclosures are necessitated and reproduced by capital in its quest to produce value. The best work in the studies of racial capitalism takes seriously the concept of capital as self-expanding value in spaces defined by racial and national exclusions, as opposed to reading it as a mere multiplication or intersectionality of identities. Melamed (2015: 77) captures this sense when she suggests that capital "can only accumulate by producing and moving through relations of severe inequality among human groups. . . . These antinomies of accumulation require loss, disposability, and the unequal differentiation of human value, and racism enshrines the inequalities that capitalism requires." Gilmore (2002: 16) characterizes racism as "a practice of [capitalist] abstraction, a death-dealing displacement of difference into hierarchies that organize relations within and between the planet's sovereign political territories." But racial differentiations are not the only integral component capital requires to harness human labor power. By attending to homonormativity's hidden basis in the racializing logic of US-led capitalism in Taiwan, I offer an account of the insidious mechanism whereby capital reproduces itself through the triangulation, rather than mere differentiation, of racialized and sexuality-based subjects.

Taiwan's Queer Democracy

Two tumultuous years after the 2017 Judicial Yuan Interpretation No. 748, a landmark decision that ruled the definition of marriage in Taiwan's current Civil Code a violation of the constitution of the Republic of China (Taiwan), on May 24, 2019, Taiwan became the first country in Asia to legalize same-sex marriage. During this period, demonstrations for and against LGBT rights, as well as a controversial referendum on this topic, drew countless citizens across gender, class, and regional divides into a historic debate under the riveted gaze of the international media. Prior to the legalization of same-sex marriage, Taiwan had already developed a reputation as a uniquely democratic and gay-friendly country in East Asia, particularly in comparison to other Chinese-speaking societies such as the People's Republic of China (PRC) and Singapore, both of which are known for having limited freedom of speech.[3] Dubbed in the Western media as "the San Francisco of the East," Taiwan is internationally known for its vibrant LGBT consumer culture and civil society.[4] As early as 1958, a lesbian couple had already filed a petition to register partnership, an effort that was repeated (performatively, as a symbolic protest) by the LGBT rights activist Chi Chia-wei in 1986.[5] Since 2003, LGBT pride parades have been held annually in Taipei city. Unsurprisingly, the island republic has been a popular destination for gender and sexual nonconforming minorities from Singapore, Malaysia, and mainland China. Since the Umbrella Movement in 2014, Taiwan has further become a sanctuary for LGBT emigrants from Hong Kong, a trend that has seen intensification since the 2019 Anti-Extradition Bill Movement.

On the surface, Taiwan's queer democracy is simply a story of the global liberalization of sexual cultures that has nothing to do with either race or capitalism. In what follows, I will argue the opposite—that the rise of homonormative politics in Taiwan was dialectically predicated on a specific form of racialization under US-led Cold War capitalism in Asia. After the conclusion of the Pacific War, Taiwan became a ward of American imperialism and a bulwark against Communism in East Asia. With lavish military and financial aid, the United States consciously cultivated Taiwan's developmental state and labor-intensive manufacturing industries in the capitalist supply chain. As Taiwan became incorporated into US-led capitalism in

Asia, it also developed a distinct form of racial thinking, one that separated the inhabitants into *bensheng* (authentically Taiwanese, literally "from the local province") and *waisheng* (Chinese or settler-colonial, literally "from outer provinces") populations.

After Taiwan's lifting of martial law in 1987 and concomitant democratization, the distinction between *bensheng* and *waisheng* became formally politicized by political parties—a Green faction under the leadership of the Democratic Progressive Party (DPP) promoting a distinct Taiwanese identity and Taiwanese independence, and a Blue faction under the leadership of the Kuomingtang Party (KMT) favoring a pan-Chinese identity and closer economic ties with the PRC. Instead of a traditional division between Left and Right along social values or religious views, the political landscape in Taiwan since then has been completely dominated by the racializing logics of the two parties. With DPP victories in the 2000 presidential elections, the island began a systematic process of "de-Sinicization" (*qu Zhongguo hua*) following the surge of nativist consciousness.[6] Since then, the advancement of a limited version of LGBT rights, which culminated in the 2019 legalization of same-sex marriage, has been a key instrument Taiwan uses to discipline mainland China and curry favor with American supporters. Under this discursive regime, *waisheng* or "Chinese" has become a stigmatized category of identity in Taiwan. Increasingly, identifying oneself as Chinese in Taiwan is immediately interpreted as supporting the present PRC government's aggression against Taiwan or whitewashing the KMT's past atrocities against the *bensheng* populations. The jingoistic rhetoric of the PRC's "One-China Principle," under which it regards Taiwan as a renegade province it is planning to reunify by any means necessary, produced a rigidified defensive posture and a heightened nationalism, one that racialized Taiwan's own *waisheng* populations into the imagined enemy of a postcolonial people's right to statehood. In turn, this racializing discourse also precludes an analysis of Taiwan's complicities in and material dependency on the capitalist order of things established by the United States.

The Communist threat played a pivotal role in the endless accumulation of capital during the Cold War (Harvey 2003: 39). For this reason, a critique of racial capitalism must begin with a reckoning of this history. At its founding in 1949, the PRC was an agrarian economy with over 100 million rural households working in small-scale farming and animal husbandry. Under the doctrine of New Democracy, the Chinese Communist Party sought to advance industrialization under state capitalism (Ren 2011: 104).

The outbreak of the Korean War in 1950 provided the conditions for China's primitive accumulation and first wave of industrialization. In exchange for getting involved in the war, China was offered aid in the form of technology transfer and a transplant of military heavy industry from the Soviet Union (Wen 2021: 12). With the infusion of Soviet capital, the Chinese state was able to accomplish primitive accumulation and proceed into industrial expansion and structural adjustment. During the Cold War, China was encircled by hostile states. Its economic modernization was interrupted until the Sino-American rapprochement of the 1970s brought about a second wave of industrialization. The deterioration of Sino-Soviet relations, which culminated in two bloody border clashes in 1969—with Soviet leaders reportedly considering a preemptive nuclear strike against their former Communist ally—spurred China to improve its relations with the United States (Chen 2001: 240).

The geopolitics of the Cold War transformed China from a vanguard state of world revolution to a center of capital accumulation. The mending of Sino-American relations marked a turning point in Mao Zedong's thinking from a revolution-driven agenda to development-oriented goals. Mao's successor, Deng Xiaoping, formalized the derevolutionization process with the introduction of the reform and opening policies at the Third Plenary Session of the Chinese Communist Party's Eleventh Central Committee in 1978, replacing the Maoist slogans of "class struggles" and "permanent revolution" with his famous saying, "Black cat or white cat, so long as it catches mice, it is a good cat" (1962: 323). Deng understood that cooperation with Washington was necessary for China to gain access to the US-dominated world market. Thus, having repudiated the socialism it had built in the 1950s and 1960s, China entered the international capitalist system.

On the American side, Washington saw China's opening as a golden opportunity to expand the reach of its capitalist market and to contain the expansion of Soviet power, but it would not concede on the issue of arms sales to Taiwan. It has become a well-established thesis in contemporary Marxism that capital accumulates most efficiently by grounding immobilized, racialized, and gendered subjects in territorially splintered spaces. The system of multiple nation-states supports the need for multiple capitals to be geographically segregated for competitive purposes while providing an ideological basis, nationalism, to bind each working class to its specific state and hence to capital.[7] A divided Asia allowed the United States access to cheap labor and markets without the protection of a strong unified state. Ironically, Washington's geostrategic decision to keep Taiwan as a protectorate ultimately facilitated the PRC's own capitalist transformations. Throughout the Cold War era, Washington extended tremendous amounts of financial and military aid to Japan and the Four East Asian Tigers, allies it considered too important to fail in the containment of Communism. With the infusion of US capital and the opening of the Western market, Taiwan and much of the rest of East Asia jumpstarted the capitalist-industrial takeoff that laid the endogenous foundation for China's own capitalist boom. The story of East Asian capitalism is therefore indissociable from the history of US Cold War efforts to create subordinate and prosperous bulwarks against Communism in East Asia (Hung 2016: 53). However, compared to its flourishing lesbian and gay communities, the history of Taiwan's role as a client state in the expansion of America's capitalist interests has not received similar media attention or scholarly treatment. A crucial phase of capital accumulation in Asia, the Cold War continues to structure the ethnic tensions underlying the "social apartheid" that keeps the manufacturing workforce in China's rural regions immobilized and the influx of capital from Taiwan and Hong Kong afloat. While the United States continues to profit from the installment of racial capitalism in East Asia, this system's consequences have been rewritten as emergent ethnic identities in Taiwan's pluralistic society, and Taiwan itself as a democratic, queer-friendly nation struggling to liberate itself from Beijing's imperial ambitions.

Homonormative Politics and the Marriage Equality Movement in Taiwan Reexamined

I suggest that a historical investigation of homonormativity, rather than Taiwan's LGBT legal and cultural victories, should be the proper starting point for our analysis. Taiwan's homonormative politics signifies the deepening of a racial capitalism that seeks to maximize certain social subjects' security, protection, and welfare while others fall into the domain of the unintelligible. The euphoric narrative of Taiwan's LGBT progress rests on an amnesia of a long history of violence against gender- and sexual minorities. Contrary to media reports, queer lives in Taiwan continue to be regulated by complex and insidious mechanisms that exclude them from democratic participation. Elsewhere, I have discussed some of the most egregious examples of queer precarity and human rights violations in Taiwan in the past three decades despite the normalization of homosexuality. These include Vice-President Lu Hsiu-lien's political campaign to create an "AIDS-village" to quarantine people living with HIV, a police raid of a gay sauna that forced the patrons to simulate sex while having their pictures taken, and the legal prosecution of radical feminist scholar Josephine Chuen-juei Ho for "spreading pornographic and obscene images" in violation of the country's criminal law (Liu 2015: 138–69).

The emphasis on the acquisition of legal rights institutes a formalist understanding of queerness that disconnects it from the substantive experiences of minoritized subjects. The formal right to marriage does not protect individuals from harassment based on gender presentation. Nor does it protect them from the persistent hold of Chinese procreative familialism, the maldistribution of life chances, or the gendered division of labor. As these structural inequalities fall outside the domain of the law—or are supported by it—we must take care not to confuse a culture of silent tolerance with an affirmative program that nourishes all gender expressions.[8] The marriage equality movement reduces the richness, radicality, and pluralism of what we call *queer* to the middle-class, family-oriented couple basking in domestic bliss. In its search for recognition and legitimacy from the state, homonormative politics naturalizes monogamy and domesticity as cultural ideals for all queers. Instead of challenging the state's custodianship of morals, the marriage equality movement in Taiwan succumbed to it.

The legalization of same-sex marriage has paradoxically resulted in the further stigmatization and alienation of those who do not conform to homonormative understandings of proper desire. For many polyamorous queers, sex workers, cross-dressers, people living with HIV, nonbinary people, and transgender people, the right to obtain a marriage license is a social ritual they must refuse. The rise of homonormative politics separates good queers (monogamous, responsible) from bad ones (polyamorous, socially non-reproductive) while creating an illusion that, with the legalization of same-sex marriage, *all* queers have become accepted and visible (Huang 2011). Under the slogan of "ai zui da" ("#LoveIsLove #LoveWins")—endorsed by a wide range of public figures from celebrity singers A-mei and Jolin to President Tsai Ing-wen in her tweets—mainstream LGBT organizations created a desexualized, nonthreatening image of the queer body that prepared its assimilation into Taiwan's civic culture.[9]

The narrative of Taiwan as the model of East Asian democratization and LGBT human rights flattens the polyphonic history of queer struggles into a singular desire for marriage and social acceptance. The idea that marriage should be the benchmark for measuring progress is itself a product of homonormative politics, one that rewrites Taiwan's queer history as advances brought about by mainstream LGBT organizations such as Tongzhi Hotline alone. In reality, not every queer activist organization in Taiwan has identified legalized marriage as a common goal, and the landscape of social protests in Taiwan has always been fractured between "state feminists" and "radical queers." Whereas state feminists generally support gender mainstreaming policies and "equality between genders" as a social value, radical queers combat a broader range of issues including the sex negativity of mainstream feminisms and the decoupling of gender from race and class (Ho 1994). In the years preceding the legalization of same-sex marriage, radical queer groups in Taiwan voiced their opposition to the plan, seeing it as an assimilationist tactic and proposing instead a full reconfiguration of marriage laws and customs. As they have argued, marriage, whether same-sex or heterosexual, enshrined economic and cultural rights in an idealized form of monogamous union between two individuals. The 2017 marriage law debates opened up an opportunity to reevaluate our social investment in this institution. However, this opportunity was lost. Instead of challenging the alignment of monogamous marriage, legitimate desire, and property rights, mainstream LGBT organizations embraced an oppressive and antiquarian ritual. Queer radicals launched a counter movement to abolish the institutions of marriage and family altogether (*huijia miehun*), though this side of the story was never reported by the international media.[10] The story of Taiwan's marriage equality movement is not a unilinear history of queer emancipation; it is, rather, the consolidation of bourgeois rights through the closing off of pluralistic possibilities. It erases the heterogeneity of queer communities and turns the desire for monogamous marriage into the necessary condition of lawfulness and legitimacy.

The narrative of queer progress implies that sexuality—because of Taiwan's Confucian culture, patriarchy, rural mentality, KMT autocracy, or any other factor—was repressed and needed to be liberated. As readers of Michel Foucault know so well, sexuality is organized by a technology of power that invites us to expose our sexuality. The legalization of same-sex marriage allows sexuality to become a new kind of truth. Through the performative act of marriage, one literally becomes a new kind of (legal) subject.[11] The marriage contract is an economic contract, one that binds sexuality to money in the organization of property rights, tax liabilities, social welfare, and inheritance. The marriage contract is also a symbolic contract that regulates queer subjects' desire for respectability and the distinction between proper and improper desire. But as numerous scholars from intersectional feminism to cross-solidarity projects have reminded us, we must resist the temptation to treat this performative act as a form of auto-constitution in a social vacuum.[12] Rather, the history of sexuality takes place within the history of racial capitalism. The case of Taiwan is particularly instructive.

Thinking Race Beyond the Black and White Binary: The Racial Politics of Blue and Green

As Jung (2021) has recently observed, Taiwan's increasing international isolation due to China's growing power has compelled the island republic to rearticulate the meaning of equality in the LGBT sense (marriage equality) within the postcolonial sense (independence). "Through the intimate entanglement of LGBT rights claims and sovereign aspirations, the marriage equality movement became a powerful emblem of the national vision that differentiated Taiwan from mainland China." In a different context, Chao (2000) argues that Taiwan's queer identity politics has reproduced an uncritical model of selfhood that has lent itself to nationalist appropriations in the service of Taiwan's autonomy and sovereignty, while Chang (2019) maintains that the legalization of same-sex marriage in Taiwan ought to be reevaluated in relation to the historical tensions between two kinds of regionalism that she terms "bloc Asia" and "Area Asia." As these observations show, it is imperative to situate Taiwan's sexual cultures within the logic of racial capitalism.

A distinctive feature of Taiwan's political culture, one that remains undertheorized in academic scholarship, is its lack of distinction between liberal and conservative bases. Support for and opposition to LGBT rights can be found across the entire political spectrum. Unlike in the United States, where it is possible to assign a particular stance on homosexuality or other economic and social issues to a left or right side of a spectrum, the political landscape in Taiwan is dominated by the issue of race. Neither the Blue nor the Green camp is right or left in the conventional sense or allied with environmental, labor, gender and sexual justice, pro-business, or religious organizations. As a result, it is extremely difficult to develop a meaningful and transformative form of queer activism. Any effort to foreground queer issues as "political" instantly gets eclipsed by or assimilated into the more pressing topic of reunification versus independence and its racializing logics. A compulsion to affirm or renounce one's racial identity as Chinese has taken over the citizens' imagination, monopolizing the terms of the political and of community.

How did Taiwan procure the most progressive legal rights for lesbians and gay men in Asia without ever developing a Left? As my analysis shows, the attainment of same-sex marriage rights was not the product of democratic struggles between the Left and the Right but the lack thereof. The fact that "merely cultural" issues such as homosexuality are considered to be of secondary importance ironically made it easier for mainstream society to cede limited rights to gay and lesbian marriage seekers who were "just like everybody else," while the historical incorporation of Taiwan into a regime of US-centered capitalism and commodity consumption made it more receptive to a Western style of sexual politics.[13] In recent years, the threat of China has made it even more urgent for political leaders in Taiwan to secure a global identity as sharing and embodying Western values of democracy and freedom. This political dilemma has incentivized Taiwanese intelligentsia to create an image of a liberal society in which lesbians and gay men are allowed to be legally married.

The reason for this occurrence is historical, and to understand it requires a more complex accounting of what democracy and democratization meant in the Taiwanese context. The creation of procedural democracy has not always succeeded in integrating the citizens into the decision-making process. Instead, what was democratized was the expression of racial identity as a wedge issue in electoral politics. Though racial conflict between *bensheng* and *waisheng* has always been a strong undercurrent in Taiwan, it did not fully emerge until after the lifting of martial law in 1987, when the DPP began to instrumentalize an "us-versus-them" rhetoric as a political strategy in its bid for power (Chen 2010: 55). In an influential interview (Hou et al. 2004) that appeared shortly following the 2004 presidential elections, four of Taiwan's most iconic cultural figures, including renowned filmmaker Hou Hsiao-Hsien and novelist Chu Tien-Hsin, spoke against the electoral manipulation of ethnic issues by both the Blue and Green camps. The interviewees, who were among the founding members of an organization called the Alliance for Ethnic Equality, expressed their concerns with a divisive identity politics playing on ethnic tensions. They critiqued Taiwan's procedural democracy, which has paradoxically sharpened tensions between racialized communities. In Hou's view, "so-called localization is simply Minnanization, excluding everything else. This is a programme of 'de-Sinicization,'" as some of its supporters term it, which continuously appears in each domain, and arouse strong repugnance" (21).[14] In the next two decades, the phenomenon of substituting ethnic tensions for substantive democracy has only intensified. Elected on the promise of de-Sinicization, DPP President

Chen Shui-bian promoted the view of Hokkien-speakers as authentically Taiwanese and hence the island's rightful inhabitants, against whom the Mandarin-speaking population became racialized as "Chinese" settler-colonizers. Neither identity includes Hakka, the third largest ethnic community with a distinct culture, or the Taiwanese Indigenous peoples, Austronesian speakers who are estimated to make up about 3% of Taiwan's current population.

Taiwan, whose official name today remains the Republic of China, was a product of overlapping imperialisms and capital accumulation in Cold War Asia. Following Qing China's defeat in the First Sino-Japanese War, Taiwan was ceded to the Empire of Japan by the Treaty of Shimonoseki in 1895. Japan began the Kominka Movement around 1935, an island-wide assimilation project to encourage the Taiwanese to see themselves as Japanese and adopt Japanese surnames (Ching 2001). After its defeat in WWII, Japan renounced all claims to Formosa and the Pescadores without specifying to whom they were surrendered. Conflicting interpretations of the legal documents continue to fuel contemporary debates over the sovereignty status of Taiwan.

After losing control of mainland China to the Communists in the Chinese Civil War in 1949, the Republic of China (ROC) government, along with two million soldiers and civilians, evacuated to Taiwan and made Taipei its temporary capital. After the outbreak of the Korean War on June 25, 1950, the United States began to use Taiwan as a military outpost in the Cold War crusade against Communism and sent the US Navy's Seventh Fleet into the Taiwan Strait to protect it from the advancing Communist army. Further interventions in the Chinese Civil War by the United States created the Sino-American Mutual Defense Treaty and the Formosa Resolution of 1955. Thus folded into an informal empire of "America's Asia," Taiwan became the protectorate of the US empire, an island fortress in the Pacific for it to project its power and contain the spread of Communism (Lye 2005). A divide-and-conquer tactic ensured the partition of East Asia to facilitate the accumulation of capital. Historically, the rise of East Asia depended on this creation of a "messy" but "capitalistically successful" system in the postwar period that "has left the United States in control of most of the guns, Japan and the Overseas Chinese in control of most of the money, and the PRC in control of most of the labor" (Arrighi 2002: 33–34).

During the 1996 Taiwan Strait missile crisis, proponents of independence demanded American military intervention to counter the threat of an attack by the PRC. In 2003, in the midst of international condemnation of the US invasion of Iraq, many advocated sending in Taiwanese troops to improve their combat experience and as a way to demand a quid pro quo from the Americans in the event of a Chinese attack in the future. With the slogan "Statehood for Taiwan—Save Taiwan—Say Yes to America," a radical group, Club 51, called for Taiwan to join the United States as its fifty-first state, which its members saw as the only path to "guarantee Taiwan's security, stability, prosperity, liberty, and democracy" (Chen 2010: 161–62).

As Anderson (2004: n.p.) has argued, Taiwan has always been "an outpost of the American empire, one of Washington's Asian trenches in the Cold War: a vital staging area for the US forces fighting in Vietnam, CIA activities in South-East Asia and Tibet, and a strategic base for nuclear weapons targeting China"; hence, "the peculiarity of the Taiwanese case lies in the fact that the nation claiming independence is itself completely dependent on a foreign power. The separation from the mainland that has formed its distinctive experience for the past century has always been a function of empire, not a revolt against it."

After the ROC's expulsion from the United Nations in 1971, the Formosa Incident in 1979, and the lifting of martial law in 1987, Taiwan's political culture gradually shifted from claiming to be the seat of the legitimate government of the whole of China to emphasizing its distinction from Communist-ruled mainland China. Rapid industrialization and economic growth achieved in this period—known as the Taiwan Economic Miracle—created the material conditions for the blossoming of lesbian and gay fiction, commercial venues, activism, and academic discourses in the 1990s. The connections between lesbian and gay culture and the development of capitalism in Taiwan have been observed by numerous scholars. Liou (2005), for example, notes that the oft-celebrated culture of lesbian and gay activism in the 1990s developed in tandem with other "postmodern" discourses in elite university circles introduced by capitalist globalization; as such, queer culture remained irrelevant and illegible to the quotidian lives of citizens outside Taiwan's metropolitan centers. Focusing on the example of *G&L*, a popular lifestyle magazine that first appeared in 1996 catering to young Chinese-reading gays and lesbians and their "collective social desire for affirmation," Erni and Spires (2005: 232, 241) trace Taiwan's commodified queer existence under the "homoeconomics" of capitalism as the formation of a cultural identity shaped and imagined by acts of consumption: "In contrast with the economic life of gays and lesbians in the US . . . the development in Taiwan of a labor force autonomous from the family sphere provides partial economic autonomy for queers without cultural autonomy from family responsibilities."

Improper/Impossible Subjects of Taiwanese History: Glorious Citizen Memoirs

It is not my intention to dispute the importance of the legal advances made for and by Taiwan's LGBT minorities. However, I'd insist that the meaning of *queer* cannot be restricted to legally recognized categories of sexuality. In the following section I offer an account of a different kind of queer kinship—families dismembered by the Chinese Civil War—that gave rise to a new genre of writings I call *glorious citizen memoirs*.

"Glorious citizens" are war veterans who were born in mainland China and "snatched" by the retreating KMT army during the Chinese Civil War.[15] They were forced—enslaved, even—to fight against the Communists and have been living in Taiwan since then. Despite being called as such, glorious citizens are anything but glorious; they are among the most widely abused and disempowered social classes in Taiwan. Glorious citizens are seen as politically suspect because of their thick "mainland Chinese" accents, lack of education, old-fashioned values, and connections to families they have left behind in mainland China. What is more, they also constitute a queer class. When finally released from military service and allowed to be married, glorious citizens were typically already in their forties, penniless, and deprived of any educational and social capital. Some were already married on mainland China and had families with whom they could not reunite, and such baggage further subtracted from their suitability as marriage material for a new family in Taiwan. As a class of Taiwan's most undesirable bachelors on the marriage market, glorious citizens are emblematically queer subjects abandoned by the heteronormative system. Over the years, the Taiwanese media has no shortage of sensationalist news stories about glorious citizens falling prey to younger women who saw in their advanced age and declining health an opportunity to inherit their social security; other controversies involve distant relatives or previous wives from China showing up to lay claim on property after their passing (Chao 2004).

Since the early 2000s, a small number of glorious citizen memoirs have appeared in Chinese. Some were written by the survivors themselves.[16] Others were oral history projects compiled by scholars.[17] These received almost no mainstream attention and saw limited circulation. Of those works, the most unique, and the most compelling testimony, was the one written by Shyihuei Liu. Not able to find a commercial press to support this project, Liu self-published three memoirs: *Da biandong shidai de canghai yi su—Liu Xihui huiyi lu* [A small grain in the vast ocean of changing eras: A memoir] in 2013; *Xihui wenji—Canghai yisu de yubo dangyang* [Essays by Shyihuei—repercussions of a small grain] in 2018; and *Cong huangmiu de shidai dao diaogui de shidai* [From the era of absurdity to the era of paradox] in 2020. As has been noted in the writings of others with PTSD, Liu's writing exhibits signs of Sigmund Freud's repetition compulsion; the three memoirs essentially tell the same story over and over again.

In 1949, the KMT army under General Hu Lien passed through Liu's hometown of Mei, a Hakka-speaking village in Canton. Liu's father protested as Hu's soldiers raided the village for food and supplies and was shot in cold blood. After murdering his father in front of him, the army snatched Liu, then a seventeen-year-old boy, along with some three hundred other Mei villagers, and took them to Kinmen for their first battle against something called "Communism" before retreating further to Taiwan. Among the conscripted was Liu's uncle, who was offered a bag of rice by a rich merchant to take the place of his son at the last minute. Liu's uncle thought it was a sweet deal and happily accepted, not knowing that he would never see his family in China again or that he would die a penniless soldier in Taiwan.

Liu was trafficked as human cargo with almost no food and water for three days on the boat ride to Kinmen. Soon after they had arrived in Taiwan, another snatched soldier became deranged from the trauma and started attacking his comrades in the middle of the night. He sliced Liu's chest open with an axe, leaving him hospitalized for a full year. But Liu miraculously survived. Once the Cold War phase began, Liu and other frontline soldiers were reassigned to hard labor in construction work, building mansions for high-level KMT officials who wanted to convert Taiwan into a temporary military base from which to take back the mainland. Liu spent his spare time studying and took the Taiwanese GED exams and went to college. Later he was selected by the KMT government and sent on a fellowship to study in the United States. After earning a master's degree in aerospace engineering, Liu became a military scientist for the defense department. One of Liu's largest regrets is that, to ensure his own survival in the military, he had to write a fake essay claiming that he had voluntarily joined the KMT army because the Communists had murdered his father. In fact, the KMT army did. But Liu had to remain in the closet and did not have the courage to tell the world the truth until the publication of his first memoir.

Liu got married in Taiwan and has children. Liu mentions them in passing but shares no memories or stories about them; his life in Taiwan—spanning over seven decades from 1949 to the present—is a blank in these autobiographical texts. The focus of all three memoirs is the family he never had: the father he never got to know and the mother he left behind at the age of seventeen. After 1987, the Taiwanese government began to allow limited contact between Taiwanese and Chinese civilians, but as a member of the defense department Liu was not permitted to visit China. Secretly through a friend in Hong Kong, Liu sent money to his two younger brothers on the mainland and asked them to look after their mother, but this windfall of cash tore the younger brothers apart. They fought over who gets a bigger piece and started demanding more from Liu, whom they blamed for their poverty. They believed that having an elder brother in the Taiwanese military was the reason they could not rise through the ranks of the Communist party, and that their own lives would have been more prosperous if Liu had been killed in the war instead. In 1989, after being separated for forty years, Liu managed to have his mother come to visit him in Taiwan as a "mainland Chinese refugee." His mother was an illiterate and hardworking Hakka woman who survived the loss of her husband and her eldest son. She worked on the farm all her life, never traveled outside Mei County, and knew neither Mandarin nor how to use money—her sons and grandchildren managed the household finances. She had never seen or used any electronics and did not know what a television or refrigerator was, and the idea of flying frightened her. But she bravely accepted the mission and had her son drive her to Hong Kong, where she boarded the plane and flew to Taiwan alone. She brought two eggs from her own farm and guarded them with her life on the flight, refusing to eat or drink anything. After she arrived she made meals with those for Liu, just as she had done when he was a child.

Conclusion—Ungrievable Lives

Glorious citizen memoirs signify a form of failed racialization. Though considered Taiwanese nationals, those snatched soldiers from China have never received full cultural citizenship in Taiwan or found themselves fully integrated into the normative capitalist circuits of wage and contract. This failed racialization also marks their queer sociality in the configuration of family and the language of belonging. It would not do to write off their stories as accidental tragedies or an unfortunate turn of events. Instead, we need to recognize how these stories occurred as the consequence of a racial capitalism that transformed US imperialist interests into a Chinese civil war.

The recent legalization of same-sex marriage, like the February 28, 1947, massacre of the *bensheng* populations, has become a pillar of national history, a monument with which Taiwan's past is told and memorialized. Tributes to the victims of the February 28 incident allow them to be publicly mourned with politically consequential affect such as guilt, horror, and loss. But for glorious citizens like Liu and the families they have lost, no frame of remembrance or reparation is available. In 2014, Liu submitted a petition to the Tsai Ing-wen administration, asking the state to recognize the army's actions during the war and issue a formal apology. The state authorities responded by saying that the reported event occurred in China, which is outside of Taiwan's jurisdiction and belongs to the list of evil deeds committed by the Chinese (Liu 2018: 44). Since the current regime under DPP leadership disavows any affiliation with China, the atrocities against the snatched soldiers and their families have become a "stateless" war crime for which neither the PRC government nor the ROC government takes responsibility. The Taiwanese government, however, does not shy away from publicly condemning the June Fourth Incident, the 1989 massacre of Tiananmen Square protestors by the Communist Party, which also took place in mainland China. Glorious citizen memoirs raise the fundamental question of what counts as a grievable life—what is allowed to enter the domain of politics and what remains excluded. What constitutes the frame through which political rights and reparation might be secured? What might be their conditions and prices? One of Liu's own examples is the "Little White" incident. On June 24, 2016, a video of a Taiwanese soldier torturing a dog named "Little White" was leaked to the media. The event was quickly elevated to a national trauma of sorts—the incensed public demanded a thorough investigation, and both the president and the minister of defense issued public apologies expressing their shock, disbelief, and promises to reform the military's discipline and ethics. Resigned to the fact that the murder of his father would never receive the same kind of state-conferred recognition, Liu wrote in the third memoir that "one is better off being a dog in a time of peace than a human in a time of war" (2020: 147).

Without the support of family, social networks, economic or cultural capital, Liu is only one among many social pariahs and queer figures ostracized from the heteronormative script of family and kinship. With the rise of nationalist "Taiwanese-first" politics in the post-2000 era, those émigré survivors experienced a new bout of discrimination and disenfranchisement. Still, their stories cannot be heard because they do not fit into the dominant narrative of either homonationalism or Taiwanese independence. Glorious citizen memoirs are queer stories reminding us that certain social subjects remain unintelligible and unaccountable despite the extending of rights and protection to minorities in established categories of race, gender, and sexuality. This differential allocation of grievability means that we must contest the state's selective framing of violence and distinguish between securing rights for existing minorities and transforming the sphere of thought itself.

The United States uses the rhetoric of keeping Taiwan safe from China to consolidate its power in the East Asian regime of capital accumulation, while Taiwan justifies its attachment to an imperialist power through the discourse of democracy and freedom. Casting LGBT freedom as symbolizing Taiwanese national independence from China, a new homonormative politics fuels the imagination of the United States as a selfless freedom fighter rather than an agent of racial capitalism in the Asia Pacific. But freedom is not freedom when it is sought through the patronage of white saviors, and national self-determination is not self-determination if it remains tethered to an insufficient understanding of the combined and uneven development of racial capitalism. Just as free wage labor in Marx's writings simply means the workers' freedom to enter a predetermined and deeply exploitative relationship, the various forms of freedom examined here—the same-sex couple's freedom to obtain a marriage certificate, Taiwan's de facto independence guaranteed by its status as a client state of the US empire and its instrument of capital accumulation—reproduce forms of power and subjugation that become legible only through a materialist analysis of racial capitalism. Conversely, the conventional view of China as a politically illiberal (authoritarian) and economically liberal(ized) country also needs to be rethought in this light. A history of colonial dismemberment, underdevelopment, and Cold War containment continues to shape the Chinese state's worldview and foreign policy. Its oppressive policies, at least in the Chinese mindset, are not aggressive but defensive. They do not reflect a cultural penchant for authoritarianism; rather, they embody the contradictions of an asymmetric world created by capitalism.

The point is neither to turn the US into the sole culprit for all the problems in the world nor to exonerate the Chinese state for its violence against subjects within and outside its borders. Rather, the point is to retool the framework of racial capitalism to develop a historical understanding of the triangulation of racialized and queer subjects in transnational regimes of capital accumulation and dispossession outside the US, as my example of Taiwan has shown. The distinctive political culture and dilemmas of Taiwan created a deradicalized form of LGBT movement, against which various experiences of racialization fall into unintelligibility. Conversely, the creation of a sanitized, homonormative politics without the interrogation of racial capitalism resulted in the impoverishment of the category of queer, reducing it from a multiply constituted plurality and a critical stance to a sociological category of gay men and lesbians awaiting the state's conferring of rights. Reading the ungrievable lives of glorious citizens and the homonormative formation of new economic and political rights side by side, I propose a conception of queerness as social existence that falls outside the available categories and frame of intelligibility created by the nation-state as an apparatus of capital accumulation. How are bodies rendered unintelligible and ungrievable under conditions of global racial capitalism? How do we mobilize the notion of the queer to hear life stories of those who do not qualify as human? How do we attend to this history of race and queerness without relying on the analytic afforded by the singular experience of US politics? The examples of Taiwan's homonormative politics and glorious citizen memoirs show us that the study of queerness is inseparable from the history of racialized relations of property and production, militarized violence, and value extraction. By attending to these entanglements, we can begin to formulate a rematerialized queer response to global crises and a historical understanding of the incessant reconstitution of racial capitalism in familiar and unfamiliar territories.

Notes

I am grateful to the special issue editors, Rana M. Jaleel and Evren Savcı, for their astute feedback.

1   In Lisa Duggan's influential formulation, homonormativity refers to "a politics that does not contest dominant heteronormative assumptions and institutions but upholds and sustains them, while promising the possibility of a demobilized gay constituency and a privatized, depoliticized gay culture anchored in domesticity and consumption" (Duggan 2003: 50). Jasbir Puar (2007) pioneered the critique of homonormative nationalism (or homonationalism) that I am extending to the case of Taiwan.

2   See P. Liu (2023), esp. chapters 1 and 2, for an analysis of these scholarly currents.

3   For a comparison of the cases of China and Taiwan, see Jeffreys and Wang (2018). For an account of Singapore's criminalization of homosexuality (Section 377A) in the face of rapid changes in Asia, see Yue and Zubillaga-Pow (2012). Section 377A in Singapore was repealed in 2023. On the impact of Taiwan's marriage equality movement on LGBT activism and organizing in China, see Damm (2018).

4   For the phrase, see L. Wen (2014). On Taiwan as a queer beacon for Asia, see Kemp (2019).

5   For details of this history, see *Fountain Monthly* (2019).

6   For a detailed analysis of the Cold War origins of the concept of the "Sinophone," see Shi (2021).

7   Davidson (2012). Davidson distinguishes between Marxists who view the interstate system in a historically contingent relationship to capital accumulation, such as Robert Brenner, Benno Teschke, Hannes Lacher, and Ellen Meiksins Wood, and those who

emphasize overlapping autonomous logics, such as Giovanni Arrighi, Alex Callinicos, and David Harvey.

8   For a critique of the conflation of tolerance with progress, see Ding and J. Liu (2005).

9   Lee (2017) has argued that in Taiwan, the agendas of assimilationists and radicalists are always interwoven with each other.

10   Ding and Liu (2011) was an early manifesto of the *huijia miehun* movement to abolish the institution of marriage and family. In 2015, a special issue of the journal edited by Yin-Bin Ning (2015) offered a reassessment of *huijia meihun* in the context of Taiwan's marriage equality movement, with contributions from leftist, conservative, and religious scholars.

11   Sedgwick (1993) poses the question of why (heterosexual) marriage (I pronounce you husband and wife) should be the example that inspired the philosopher J. L. Austin to formulate the distinction between performative and constative utterances. For a thorough analysis and critique of same-sex marriage advocacy, see Spade and Willse (2015).

12   See, among others, Cohen (1999).

13   As Jasbir Puar (2017) has observed in the US context, the reproduction of gender normativity is integral to the process that converts previously socially maligned populations to a version of liberal acknowledgment, inclusion, and incorporation into the national economy of value extraction.

14   Minnan or Hokkien-Taiwanese is the dialect spoken by the *bensheng* population.

15   "Snatching" (*la fu* 拉伕) was the illegal conscription of civilians by force during the Chinese war. For an overview of current legal debates on the practice, see Tseng and Wu (2021).

16   Other than the three memoirs of Liu considered at length here, Ma (2012) is another powerful memoir that details his life from a conscripted foot solider to a college professor. Li (2009) is a military history written from author's experience as a survivor and first-person witness.

17   Chien-Yuan Tseng and Chang-Yi Lo have conducted oral history projects to restore the life stories of figures such as Chang Sheng-Hua. See Tseng and Lo (2017). Ronggen Cai's recently published *Lang yan wei jin* (2021) reconstructs the personal histories of three glorious citizens into "a history of Republican China never taught in the classroom" (the book's subtitle).

References in English

Anderson, Perry. 2024. "Stand-Off in Taiwan," *LRB* 26, no. 11: n.p.

Arrighi, Giovanni. 2002. "The Rise of East Asia and the Withering Away of the Interstate System." In *Marxism, Modernity, and Postcolonial Studies*, edited by Crystal Bartolovich and Neil Lazarus, 21–42. New York: Cambridge University Press.

Chang, Hsiao-hung. 2019. "Asia as Counter-method." *Prism* 16, no. 2: 456–71.

Chen, Jian. 2001. *Mao's China and the Cold War*. Chapel Hill: University of North Carolina Press.

Chen, Kuan-Hsing. 2010. *Asia as Method: Toward Deimperialization*. Durham, NC: Duke University Press.

Ching, Leo T. S. 2001. *Becoming Japanese: Colonial Taiwan and the Politics of Identity Formation*. Berkeley: University of California Press.

Cohen, Cathy J. 1999. "What Is This Movement Doing to My Politics?" *Social Text* 17, no. 4: 111–18.

Damm, Jens. 2018. "The Impact of the Taiwanese LGBTQ Movement in mainland China with a Specific Focus on the Case of the 'Chinese Lala Alliance' and 'Marriage Equality in Chinese Societies.'" In *Connecting Taiwan: Participation—Integration—Impacts*, edited by Carsten Storm, 146–65. London: Routledge.

Davidson, Neil. 2012. "The Necessity of Multiple Nation-States for Capital." *Rethinking Marxism* 24, no.1: 26–46.

Ding, Naifei, and Jen-peng Liu. 2005. "Reticent Poetics, Queer Politics." *Inter-Asia Cultural Studies* 6, no. 1: 30–55.

Duggan, Lisa. 2003. *The Twilight of Equality? Neoliberalism, Cultural Politics, and the Attack on Democracy*. Boston: Beacon.

Erni, John Nguyet, and Anthony Spires. 2005. "The Formation of a Queer-Imagined Community in Post-Martial Law Taiwan." In *Asia Media Studies: Politics of Subjectivities*, edited by John Nguyet Erni and Siew Keng Chua, 225–52. Oxford, UK: Blackwell.

Gilmore, Ruth Wilson. 2002. "Fatal Couplings of Power and Difference: Notes on Racism and Geography." *The Professional Geographer* 54, no. 1: 15–24.

Harvey, David. 2003. *The New Imperialism*. Oxford, UK: Oxford University Press.

Hou, Hsiao-Hsien, Chu Tien-hsin, Tang Nuo, and Hsia Chu-joe. 2004. "Tensions in Taiwan." Interview with Perry Anderson. *New Left Review* 28: 18–42.

Hung, Ho-fung. 2016. *The China Boom: Why China Will Not Rule the World*. New York: Columbia University Press.

Jeffreys, Elaine, and Pan Wang. 2018. "Pathways to Legalizing Same-Sex Marriage in China and Taiwan: Globalization and 'Chinese Values.'" In *Global Perspectives on Same-Sex Marriage: A Neo-Institutional Approach*, edited by B. Winter, M. Forest, and R. Sénac, 197–219. London: Palgrave.

Jung, Minwoo. 2021. "Imagining Sovereign Futures: The Marriage Equality Movement in Taiwan." *Social Movement Studies*. https://doi.10.1080/14742837.2021.2010528.

Kemp, Brandon. 2019. "Taiwan Offers Queer Lessons for Inclusivity in Asia." *Nikkei Asia*. https://asia.nikkei.com/Editor-s-Picks/Tea-Leaves/Taiwan-offers-queer-lessons-for-inclusivity-in-Asia.

Lee, Po-Han. 2017. "Queer Activism in Taiwan: An Emerging Rainbow Coalition from the Assemblage Perspective." *The Sociological Review* 65, no. 4: 682–98.

Liou, Liang-ya. 2005. "Queer Theory and Politics in Taiwan: The Cultural Translation and (Re)Production of Queerness in and beyond Taiwan Lesbian/Gay/Queer Activism." *NTU Studies in Language and Literature* no. 14: 123–54.

Liu, Petrus. 2015. *Queer Marxism in Two Chinas*. Durham, NC: Duke University Press.

Liu, Petrus. 2023. *The Specter of Materialism: Queer Theory and Marxism in the Age of the Beijing Consensus*. Durham, NC: Duke University Press.

Lye, Colleen. 2005. *America's Asia: Racial Form and American Literature, 1893–1945*. Princeton, NJ: Princeton University Press.

Melamed, Jodi. 2015. "Racial Capitalism." *Critical Ethnic Studies* 1, no. 1: 76–85.

Puar, Jasbir K. 2007. *Terrorist Assemblages: Homonationalism in Queer Times*. Durham, NC: Duke University Press.

Puar, Jasbir K. 2017. *The Right to Maim: Debility, Capacity, Disability*. Durham, NC: Duke University Press.

Robinson, Cedric. 1983. *Black Marxism and the Making of the Black Radical Tradition*. London: Zed.

Sedgwick, Eve Kosofsky. 1993. "Queer Performativity: Henry James's *The Art of the Novel*." *GLQ: A Journal of Lesbian and Gay Studies* 1, no. 1: 1–16.

Shi, Flair Donglai. 2021. "Reconsidering Sinophone Studies: The Chinese Cold War, Multiple Sinocentrisms, and Theoretical Generalisation." *International Journal of Taiwan Studies* 4, no. 2: 1–34.

Singh, Nikhil Pal. 2022. "Black Marxism and the Antinomies of Racial Capitalism." In *After Marx: Literature, Theory, and Value in the Twenty-First Century*, edited by Colleen Lye and Christopher Nealon, 23–39. New York: Cambridge University Press.

Spade, Dean, and Craig Willse. 2015. "Norms and Normalization." In *The Oxford Handbook of Feminist Theory*, edited by Lisa Disch and Mary Hawkesworth, 551–71. Oxford, UK: Oxford University Press.

Wen, Lii. 2014. "Taipei Gay Pride Parade Draws Tens of Thousands." *Taipei Times*, October 26. https://www.taipeitimes.com/News/front/archives/2014/10/26/2003602927.

Wen, Tiejun. 2021. *Ten Crises: The Political Economy of China's Development (1949–2020)*. Singapore: Palgrave.

Yue, Audrey, and Jun Zubillaga-Pow, eds. 2012. *Queer Singapore: Illiberal Citizenship and Mediated Cultures*. Hong Kong: Hong Kong University Press.

References in Chinese

Cai, Ronggen 蔡榮根. 2021. *Lang yan wei jin* 狼煙未燼 [Flames of War]. Kinmen: Kinmen wenhua ju.

Chao, Antonia趙彥寧. 2000. "Taiwan tongzhi yanjiu de huigu yu zhanwang—yige guanyu wenhua shengchan de fenxi"台灣同志研究的回顧與展望-一個關於文化研究的分析 [A reflection on Taiwan's queer studies: From a viewpoint of cultural production and reproduction]. *Taiwan shehui yanjiu jikan* 台灣社會研究季刊 [Taiwan: A radical quarterly in social studies] 38: 207–44.

Chao, Antonia趙彥寧. 2004. "Gongmin shenfen, xiandai guojia yu qingmi shenghuo: Yi lao danshen yu dalu xinniang de hunying wei yanjiu anli" 公民身分、現代國家與親密生活:以老單身榮民與「大陸新娘」 的婚姻為研究案例 [The modern state, citizenship, and the intimate life: A case study of Taiwan's glorious citizens and their mainland wives]. *Taiwan shehui xue*台灣社會學 [Sociology in Taiwan] 8: 1–41.

Deng, Xiaoping 邓小平. 1962. "Zenme huifu nongye shengchan" 怎么恢复农业生产 [How to restore agricultural production]. In *Deng Xiaoping wenxuan*邓小平文选 [Collected works of Deng Xiaoping], 1:322–27.

Ding, Naifei 丁乃非, and Jen-peng Liu 劉人鵬, eds. 2011. *Zhiyi hunying jiating lianxuti*置疑婚姻家庭連續體 [Querying the marriage-family continuum]. Taipei: Shenlou.

Fountain Monthly 新活水. 2019. Special issue on "Taiwan tongzhi qunxiang yu he an zhi guang" 台灣同志群像與黑暗之光 [Love Is Equal: A special issue on the images and hopes of LGBT communities in Taiwan].

Ho, Josephine Chuen-juei何春蕤. 1994. *Haoshuang nüren* 豪爽女人 [The gallant woman]. Taipei: Crown.

Huang, Tao-ming 黃道明. 2011. "Aidao wuse qingchun: Fanchang nüxing zhuyi zhi lanqing zhengzhi yu aishang xiandai 'xing'" 哀悼無色青春:反娼女性主義之濫情政治與哀傷現

代「性」[Mourning the monogamous ideal: Anti-prostitution feminism, conjugal sentimentality and the formation of melancholic sexual modernity in Taiwan]. *Taiwan shehui yanjiu jikan* 台灣社會研究季刊 [Taiwan: A radical quarterly in social studies] 85: 5–50.

Li, Rongchang 李隆昌. 2009. Shidai jianzheng 時代見證 [Bearing witness to history]. Taipei: Quankai.

Liu, Shyihuei 劉錫輝. 2013. *Da biandong shidai de canghai yi su—Liu Xihui huiyi lu* 大變動時代的滄海一粟—劉錫輝回憶錄 [A small grain in the vast ocean of changing eras: A memoir]. Taipei: Bokesi.

Liu, Shyihuei 劉錫輝. 2018. *Xihui wenji—Canghai yisu de yubo dangyang* 錫輝文集—滄海一粟的餘波盪漾 [Essays by Shyihuei—repercussions of a small grain]. Taipei: Shiyiwen chubanshe.

Liu, Shyihuei 劉錫輝. 2020. *Cong huangmiu de shidai dao diaogui de shidai* 從荒謬的年代到弔詭的年代 [From the era of absurdity to the era of paradox]. Taipei: Showwe.

Ma, Chungliamg James 馬忠良. 2012. *Cong erdeng bing dao jiaoshou—Ma Zhongliang huiyilu* 從二等兵到教授—馬忠良回憶錄 [From foot soldier to college professor: A memoir]. Taipei: Xinrui.

Ning, Yin-Bin 甯應斌, ed. 2015. "Tongxing hunying mianmian guan" 同性戀婚姻面面觀 [Special issue on same-sex marriage]. *Yingyong lunli pinglun* 應用倫理評論 [Applied ethics review] 58.

Ren, Lixin 任立新. 2011. *Mao Zedong xin minzhu zhuyi jingji sixiang yanjiu* 毛泽东新民主主义经济思想研究 [Studies of Mao Zedong's New Democracy economic thought]. Beijing: Zhongguo shehui kexue.

Tseng, Chien-Yuan 曾建元, and Jing-Yuan Wu 吳靖媛. 2021. "Guo gong nei zhan houqi che Tai guo jun lafu xingwei zhi falü pingjia" 國共內戰後期撤臺國軍拉伕行為之法律評價 [A legal evaluation of forced recruitment of the National Army's retreat to Taiwan during late Chinese civil war]. *Zhonghua xingzheng xuebao* 中華行政學報 [The journal of Chinese public administration] 28: 79–104.

Tseng, Chien-Yuan 曾建元, and Chang-Yi Lo 駱長毅. 2017. "Jiangxi, Jinmen, Taiwan—nuchao xuesheng Zhang Shenghua de shengming shi" 江西、金門、臺灣-怒潮學生張盛華的生命史 [Jiangxi, Kinmen, and Taiwan: The life history of Chang Sheng Hua, a student of the Raging Tide Academy]. *Zhonghua xingzheng xuebao* 中華行政學報 [The journal of Chinese public administration] 21: 83–112.

Rahul Rao

Is the Homo in Homocapitalism the Caste in Caste Capitalism and the Racial in Racial Capitalism?

In March 2023 when the Government of India filed an affidavit in the Supreme Court opposing the legal recognition of same-sex marriage, an Instagram user called parambanana (2023) asked indignantly whether the government understood "how much the [queer] community and their members are bringing to the ECONOMY?" The post went on to draw attention to the contribution of queer designers, queer-owned businesses and entrepreneurs including chefs, wedding planners, "creative marketing Mavericks," musicians, artists, CEOs, film directors, models, producers, costume, hair and makeup stylists, and others to the "billion dollar economy of INDIA." The focus on these industries may be a function of the author's own self-location within them in his Instagram bio (turban model, fashion, business). The post concludes with the lament that "all this money is pouring in, when the LGBTQIA community is time and again suppressed, and have never ever been recognized in its full respect and potential by the Government!"

In response to the Ugandan Parliament's passage of a draconian Anti Homosexuality Bill in the same month—the second such legislation in less than a decade—the Open for Business

The South Atlantic Quarterly 123:1, January 2024
DOI 10.1215/00382876-10920678 © 2024 Duke University Press

Coalition (2023) wrote a letter to Ugandan president Yoweri Museveni to express its concern that the law would "make it harder for Uganda to foster a dynamic and diversified modern economy that is attractive to investors, tourists and skilled workers," undermining its attractiveness as a place to do business. Bringing together leading firms in the technology, industrial, airline, financial, healthcare, consumer products, entertainment, and consulting sectors, the letter is signed by global giants such as American Express, Google, Ikea, McKinsey and Unilever. It makes a series of claims in an attempt to persuade the President not to give his assent to the bill, including that "LGBTQ+ inclusive economies" are more competitive, receive higher foreign direct investment (and are less likely to be the target of punitive sanctions), experience stronger growth as a result of being able to attract entrepreneurial talent and high-value industries, are more inviting to tourists, and provide citizens with a better standard of living.

I am interested in parambanana's response to the Government of India's refusal to recognize same-sex marriage and the Open for Business Coalition's response to the Government of Uganda's passage of antiqueer legislation not because they are exceptional but because they reflect a common sense of our time that is operative on a variety of scales. To understand how we have got here, it may be useful to recall the most significant political and theoretical developments in the trajectories of what David Eng (2010) has called queer liberalism. Writing in the aftermath of the attacks of September 11, 2001, Jasbir Puar (2007) illuminated the structures and itineraries of an assemblage that she named homonationalism, whereby configurations of sexuality, race, gender, nation, class, and ethnicity were realigned in relation to forces of securitization, counterterrorism, and nationalism. Focusing on the US, Puar described how liberal politics incorporates certain queer subjects, once cast as figures of death via the AIDS epidemic and now tethered to life and productivity through the tropes of gay marriage and reproductive kinship. This inclusion is premised on the production of perversely sexualized and racialized populations, making place within US nationalism for the new figuration of the "gay patriot" by distinguishing it from the "queer terrorist." Importantly, this process of fractioning homosexuality operates at multiple scales, producing rifts within the US body politic but also functioning as a standard of civilization at the international level, where recognition of liberal LGBT rights now functions as a rubric against which the fitness for sovereignty of states is judged (Puar 2011).

Yet queer liberalism's geopolitical muscle flexing has aroused considerable resistance over the last two decades. Political homophobia has increasingly functioned as a sign of defiance against Western imperialism (Weiss and Bosia 2013). We can see this, for example, in Russia's championing of "traditional values" (Wilkinson 2014) or in the self-positioning of a number of states including—at various times—Zimbabwe, Namibia, Nigeria and Uganda—in the vanguard of authentic "Africanness" through their deployment of "antihomosexuality" (Hoad 2007). Faced with the retort that homonationalism's tropes of civilizational progress are signs of moral decay from the perspective of its antagonists, I have argued that queer liberalism has had to change tack, working less through the civilizationist logics of homonationalism than through the political economy logics of what I have called homocapitalism (Rao 2020).

When the Ugandan Parliament passed an earlier Anti Homosexuality Act in 2014, notorious as much for its draconian provisions as for the well-documented involvement of US-based Christian evangelical activists in its passage, one of the most significant critical global responses came from the World Bank. Three days after its passage in February 2014, the Bank announced the suspension of a $90 million loan that was to have funded maternal and infant healthcare and family planning in Uganda (BBC News 2014). India was also a key terrain for the Bank's newfound interest in LGBT rights. In the same month as the withholding of the Uganda loan, the Bank released preliminary results of a study estimating the cost of "homophobia" to the Indian economy at between 0.1 percent and 1.7 percent of its 2012 GDP (Badgett 2014). A subsequent study of thirty-nine countries made the converse argument that the "inclusion" of LGBT people as measured by the recognition of rights enumerated by the Global Index on Legal Recognition of Homosexual Orientation (GILRHO) and the Transgender Rights Index correlated positively with increases in per capita GDP and a higher ranking on the Human Development Index. The study claims that every additional right on the GILRHO is associated with $1400 more in per capita GDP (Badgett et al. 2014: 2). Beyond international financial institutions, firms in a number of sectors, including in the global South, have increasingly come to articulate and internalize a "business case" for LGBT rights by arguing that equitable benefits and protections for queer workers yield higher rates of employee retention and loyalty, while providing access to their tacit knowledge of queer consumer preferences (Aaberg 2022a; Conway 2022: 8–12). Liberal activists strive to make the business case hegemonic by demonstrating the universality of its benefits. As Parmesh Shahani (2023), self-described "inclusion advocate" and a principal cheerleader for homocapitalism in India today, enthuses, "What's amazing is that so many progressive workplaces are having these conversations, are creating systems and structures to unpack some of the challenges and really creating opportunities for all their employees, including I would say their straight employees, to flourish and literally bring themselves to work so that everyone can do well, be happy, make tons of money, make the company profits . . . it's capitalism baby . . . it's win, win, win!" Across a range of sites, institutions and scales, then, the threat (and actualization) of capital withdrawal as punishment for queerphobia and the promise of capital accumulation as incentive for queerphilia have supplemented, and arguably supplanted, the polarities of barbarism and civilization in the homonationalist assemblage.

There is a great deal at stake in recognizing that queer liberalism increasingly speaks in a materialist rather than a moral register, promising the concrete futurity of capital accumulation rather than the more dubious attractions of Western modernity and "civilization" as reward for the recognition of LGBT rights. The dovetailing of queer progressiveness with discourses of rampant capitalism portrays queer commitments to anticapitalism and degrowth as counterproductive, unnecessary and unimaginable. Moreover, the effort to foster respect for rights by highlighting the economic cost of their violation makes recognition of the personhood of queers contingent on the promise of their future productivity, were such personhood to be fully recognized. Such gestures of conditional recognition cleave potentially productive queers from those who are unable or unwilling to be productive within the terms set by the market—the unemployed and underemployed, the disabled, the aged, the Indigenous, the anticapitalist. Further, as Wendy Brown (2015: 109) has argued, the valuation of human life in terms of its contribution to capital effectively justifies divestment from—in other words, the sacrifice of—those who do not contribute to capital accumulation. Such moves are all too visible in austerity-ridden economies, where the provision of welfare to those racialized, gendered and sexualized as the undeserving poor has increasingly come under attack (Shilliam 2018).

In many ways homocapitalism's fractioning of queer populations is immanent within Puar's theorization of homonationalism. As she argues, "the factioning, fractioning, and fractalizing of identity is a prime activity of societies of control, whereby subjects (the ethnic, the homonormative) orient themselves as subjects through their disassociation or disidentification from others disenfranchised in similar ways in favor of consolidation with axes of privilege" (Puar 2007: 28). In a persuasive account of how multiculturalism operates to shore up what Rey Chow calls the "ascendancy of whiteness," she repeatedly underscores how access to capital enables minoritized subjects to vault the hurdles of racialized, gendered and sexualized exclusion (24–32). And she is attentive to the temporal and other disjunctures through which such complex maneuvers of inclusion and exclusion operate, noting how the market can function as a foil for the state, simulating belonging when the state refuses it and thereby offering "placebo rights to queer consumers who are hailed by capitalism but not by state legislation" (62; see also 26–27). Indeed this observation offers a prescient explanation for the discursive and affective responses to the Indian state's refusal to recognize same-sex marriage with which this article began. Yet this important acknowledgement of disjuncture between state and market is immediately smoothed over in the text by Puar's insistence that

> the familial and kinship-delineating heteronormativity of the nation and the "value-free" homonationalism of the market are convivial and complicitous rather than oppositional entities. For this reason, my genealogy of homonationalism embraces both the emphasis of queer liberalism on the queer subject before the law and the coterminous and, in some cases, preceding presence of queer consumer citizenship offered by the market (62).

Puar is scrupulous about locating this genealogy in a particular spatiotemporal context. Drawing on the work of Alexandra Chasin, who in turn situates the advent of queer consumer citizenship in a longer history of immigrant assimilation into the US nation through consumption, Puar's temporal focus here is on an immediate post-9/11 moment in which US consumers were urged to spend as a means of restoring the psychic and economic health of a beleaguered nation. One limitation here is that queer liberalism's focus on consumer citizenship threatens to infect its critique, occluding other capacities in which queers are implicated in the market and its shadow economies as producers and as agents of social reproduction—questions to which I shall turn in subsequent sections of this article.

Moreover, if we were to shift the spatiotemporal focus of analysis to the post-post-9/11 world, when the "war on terror" was overlaid by the US subprime mortgage crisis and the European sovereign debt crisis—the "global financial crisis"—it is not clear that the conviviality and complicitousness of nationalism and capitalism in the US, let alone globally, can be assumed. In other words, such conviviality as might be said to exist is historically contingent rather than structural. How else to account for the sheer irrationality—on neoliberal capitalism's own terms—of Brexit, the dogged loyalty of Trump voters in the deindustrialized US heartland in the face of his demonstrated failure to restore their standards of living, or the popularity of Narendra Modi among the very populations on whom he inflicts spectacular economic suffering via ill-conceived policies of demonetization and Covid lockdown? In the early days of these regimes, the disjuncture between the imperatives of capitalism and nationalism was resolved through promises of their temporally deferred subsumption, exemplified in the quaintly hopeful futurities of already obsolete slogans such as "Take Back Control," "Make America Great Again," and "Achhe din aane waale hain" ("Good days are coming"). Yet increasingly, authoritarian populism in democracies and autocracies alike is sustained through the construction of racialized, gendered, and sexualized scapegoats—unaccompanied male migrants, Black bodies in need of incarceration, hypersexualized Muslims, "woke" intellectual elites—that purport to account for the permanent estrangement of capitalism, nationalism, and liberal democracy. We are no longer promised that things will get better, only encouraged to channel our frustration into a schadenfreude at the prospect that the Other has it so much worse.

If queer liberalism can no longer rely on the fantasy of the presumed coherence of liberalism, democracy, nationalism, and capitalism, perhaps it must now take its chances with the most reliable of these. It may be useful to recall here the aphorism that is variously attributed to Fredric Jameson and Slavoj Žižek, "It is easier to imagine the end of the world than it is to imagine the end of capitalism," which Mark Fisher (2009: 7) famously adopts as emblematic of his notion of capitalist realism. Indeed where queer and especially trans people are concerned, it has been all too easy for their antagonists to invoke their very existence as portending the end of the world in apocalyptic fantasies about the death of the family, the perversion of children, the demographic collapse of nation and the coming of Armageddon. How better, then, to persuade those antagonists to accord queer people the paltry freedoms of liberal recognition than by promising their frictionless participation in the only game in town, a game in which the barbaric queerphobes themselves eagerly seek success. This is why queer liberalism holds out the prospect that homocapitalism might yet succeed where homonationalism has faltered. It is also why homocapitalism calls for theorization as a potentially autonomous and sometimes discordant component of the homonationalist assemblage, even if it has sometimes and in some places been convivial and complicitous with the rest of it.

One concomitant of the recognition of the autonomous force and affect of homocapitalism is that this begs the question of its relationship with other theorizations of capitalism's fractioning tendencies—principally racial capitalism and, I would add, caste capitalism. Indeed Anjali Arondekar (2022: 471) has pointedly called for a consideration of the "continuities and/or discontinuities between the different economies of value founding homocapitalism, racial capitalism, caste capitalism, and more." Accordingly, the following section of the article turns to a consideration of the fractioning operations of racial and caste capitalism before exploring the continuities and discontinuities that Arondekar invites us to consider.

To do this, I offer a brief overview of a Marxist line of thinking about the fragmentation of the working class as a way of laying the ground for a consideration of how we might locate homocapitalism in the field of concepts and ideological tendencies that this opens up. While the force of homocapitalism is palpable globally, my interest in theorizing its relationship with caste capitalism alongside racial capitalism generates a partial focus on India. This should not be taken as implying that caste as a category of hierarchy is limited in its applicability to South Asia and its diasporas, a proposition with which the "caste school of race relations" has long disagreed. Suraj Yengde (2022: 343) has more recently made a case for the utility of caste as a global category to describe a "layered mechanism of immovable social hierarchy and absolute control that aims to dehumanize certain forms of labour through both structural and economical positions, as well as through the cultural practices of endogamy and ritual." Nonetheless, the prominence of India in this discussion is a function of the historical density of subcontinental theorizations of caste and its annihilation.

It is also a function of the conjuncture in which my analysis is offered in (homo)capitalism's avowed "Asian century." This notion has typically gestured at China's role as the engine of the global economy, yet even as I write these words India has overtaken China as the most populous country on the planet (Ellis-Petersen 2023). Given the centrality of both states to the trajectories of global capitalism, it is not surprising that much of the recent scholarship tracking the mutations of homocapitalism has focused on India and China (Aaberg 2022a; Conway 2022; Tian 2020; Wei 2023; Ye 2022). I am inspired by the broad thrust of Petrus Liu's (2015; 2023) work to suggest that questions of what capitalism does in, to and through India and China and specifically the forms of social differentiation in these locations on which its relentless expansion is premised have rarely been more pressing concerns for queer theory. I cannot pretend to offer an adequate account of these processes in an article of this length, but refer to these features of the current conjuncture to account for the geographies that inform my inquiry.

Racial/Caste/Homo Capitalism: Analytics and Ideologies

In *Black Marxism*, Cedric J. Robinson ([1983] 2000: 2) defines racial capitalism as follows:

> In contradistinction to Marx's and Engel's expectations that bourgeois society would rationalize social relations and demystify social consciousness, the obverse occurred. The development, organization and expansion of capitalist society pursued essentially racial directions, so too did social ideology. As a material force, then, it could be expected that racialism would inevitably permeate the social structures emergent from capitalism. I have used the term "racial capitalism" to refer to this development and to the subsequent structures as a historical agency.

Robinson is emphatic that racism was born not in the first encounters between European and non-European peoples, but in medieval and feudal European discourses of nobility that prized the purity of aristocratic bloodlines and in the "internal" relations between European peoples themselves. In his reading, with the global extension of capitalism in the sixteenth century, Africans and Asians came to be racialized, exploited and dominated through the technologies and idioms that had been deployed vis-à-vis Europe's internal others (the Slavs, Tartars, Jews and Irish) in prior historical conjunctures (26). Robinson thus challenges the Marxist notion that capitalism was a revolutionary negation of feudalism and suggests instead that it "emerged within the feudal order and flowered in the cultural soil of a Western civilization already thoroughly infused with racialism" (Kelley 2017).

Even as we recognize the originality of Robinson's contribution, it is salutary to recall that Marx and Engels were themselves belatedly cognizant of capitalism's mobilization of racial and colonial antagonisms. As a number of scholars have demonstrated, the expansion of European colonialism by the 1860s gave them a new appreciation for how colonialism ruptured the hitherto presumed identity of interests between the metropolitan and colonized working classes (Benner 1995: 197–99; Anderson 2010). This was particularly evident in relation to the Irish question, where Marx (1869; 1870) could see that the extraction of surplus value from Ireland strengthened the English aristocratic landowning class in its battle with the working class in England while also fracturing the latter on racial lines. Racialized as "backward" by their capitalist overlords, poorly paid Irish workers were resented by their English counterparts as competitors who drove the wage down; conversely, Irish labor regarded English workers as instruments of English domination over Ireland. This leads Marx to the resounding conclusion that the organizing imperative of the moment was "to make the English workers realize that *for them* the *national emancipation of Ireland* is not a question of abstract justice or humanitarian sentiment but the *first condition of their own social emancipation*" (Marx 1870).

Marx (1870) analogizes English workers' racism vis-à-vis their Irish counterparts to that of "poor whites" vis-à-vis Black workers in the former slave states of the US. More than half a century later, W. E. B. Du Bois illuminated this latter set of relations in considering the question of why working-class unity had failed to materialize in the aftermath of the US Civil War when poor whites were deserting the Confederate Army in droves and Black workers were abandoning the plantations. His answer is that "the race philosophy came as a new and terrible thing to make labor unity or labor class-consciousness impossible. So long as the Southern white laborers could be induced to prefer poverty to equality with the Negro, just so long was a labor movement in the South made impossible" (Du Bois 1935: 680). Du Bois (700–701) suggests that such inducement was offered to white workers through a "public and psychological wage" disbursed through symbolic gestures to poor whites that accorded them a semblance of equality with rich whites, access to white spaces in segregated facilities, employment in the lower echelons of the state, etc. Crucially, while these measures "had small effect upon the economic situation, it had great effect upon their personal treatment and the deference shown to them." The psychological wage does not simply supplement the material one but actively drives it down, as white workers—ever fearful of being supplanted by Black labor—settle for less, while being assuaged by the psychic compensation of the wages of whiteness.

In remarkably resonant terms at exactly the same time, the pre-eminent Dalit leader B. R. Ambedkar was pessimistic about the prospects of a proletarian revolution in India without the prior annihilation of caste. Absent a sense of fraternity and justice—the assurance, in other words, that they would be treated equally regardless of caste or creed—he argued that the oppressed castes would not feel motivated to join such a revolution. Among the most frequently quoted lines from his work is his reminder that "the caste system is not merely division of labour. *It is also a division of labourers*" (Ambedkar [1936] 2016: 233). As he elaborates, "it is a hierarchy in which the divisions of labourers are graded one above the other" with such divisions based not on aptitude or choice but on the dogma of predestination (234). This notion of a graded inequality, in which all the rungs of a hierarchical system except those at the very bottom have a stake in retaining or improving their position on the social ladder—crucially, keeping the ladder intact—offers a powerful account of the material as much as the psychic purchase that such systems of inequality have on all except the most disadvantaged of their participants.

I shall return in the following section to the complex question of the relationship between racial and caste differentiation and their instrumentalization by capital through a discussion of the emergent theorization of what some scholars are calling "caste capitalism." For now, I want to underscore that the line of rumination that runs from Marx to Du Bois and Ambedkar on the fracturing of a desired working-class unity by race and caste was not the only ideological response imaginable to the questions opened up by the recognition that race and caste continue to have a material force in life under capitalism. Beginning with Booker T. Washington who—in Du Bois's ([1903] 2008: 37) jaundiced view—preached "a gospel of Work and Money" urging Black people to focus on vocational education and the accumulation of wealth rather than political power and civil rights as a means of conciliating racist white Southerners—a discourse advocating Black capitalism has long been articulated in tension with Black Marxism. As Kelefa Sanneh (2021) writes, this tension ran through even the Black Panthers whose more typical anticapitalist stance was sometimes interrupted by endorsements of Black capitalism, albeit understood more prosaically as Black control of neighborhoods. More ominously, Black capitalism found a champion in the Nixon administration, for whom its abandonment of welfarist rhetoric and promotion of the virtues of ownership and self-reliance proved ideologically resonant.

The Dalit public sphere has similarly been polarized on the question of the relationship between caste annihilation and capitalism between discourses of Ambedkarism (privileging the struggle against caste over class), Dalit capitalism and Dalit Marxism—with both of the latter also laying claim to the legacy of Ambedkar. Outside these Dalit publics, Indian Marxists hailing from oppressor caste backgrounds have typically privileged the struggle against class over caste, relegating caste questions to the putatively superstructural realm. Dalit capitalism's emancipatory hopes are premised on the assumption—shared, ironically, by an early Marx as much as capitalism's liberal champions—that market exchange will dissolve or attenuate the salience of precapitalist identities such as caste. In the era of India's liberalization, its foremost proponents—Chandra Bhan Prasad and Milind Kamble—have welcomed intensified foreign direct investment, arguing that its putative caste neutrality would render it more encouraging of Dalit entrepreneurship and partnership (Teltumbde 2018: 239).

Against these expectations and rather more in line with what Robinson's account of racial capitalism would lead us to expect, economic anthropologists have consistently demonstrated the continuing centrality of caste to the way business is transacted in India by mediating access to employment, contracts, credit, insurance, welfare, and political patronage. Drawing on extensive fieldwork in Tamil Nadu, Barbara Harriss-White (2003) illuminates the phenomenon of "caste corporatism," whereby caste associations assume vital regulatory functions in the economy including that of mediating relations between capital and labor within caste groups in ways that weaken class politics. Dalit Marxist Anand Teltumbde (2018: 243) excoriates the political opportunism of Dalit apologists for capital, arguing that the prosperity that they promise only ever accrues to a few besides the state functionaries who eagerly oblige them. In Teltumbde's view, such alliances allow the state to project a concern for Dalit emancipation even as it withdraws material support for their welfare. Meanwhile the affluence of a few prominent Dalit figures, whose rise is attributed to the ostensibly meritocratic mechanisms of the market, intensifies calls for the reduction or termination of "reservations" (affirmative action) while also defusing the risks of a Dalit rebellion against capitalism (Yengde 2019: 212).

In offering this brief survey of the landscape of Black/Dalit Marxism and Black/Dalit capitalism, I seek to make two points that might refine our understanding of homocapitalism. The first is provoked by the distinction between racial capitalism (/caste capitalism) as an *analytical* frame that recognizes the persistence and deployment of race (/caste) in the workings of capitalism, and Black (/Dalit) Marxism and Black (/Dalit) capitalism as contrasting *ideological* responses to this recognition.[1] The distinction is easy to lose sight of given that we are introduced to the analytical frame of racial capitalism in a text named *Black Marxism* (which is itself a subset of a more expansive ideological formation that Robinson names "the Black radical tradition" in the book's subtitle)—even though Black Marxism is only one of several responses imaginable to a recognition of the material force of racial capitalism. These complexities also mark the discussion of homocapitalism, which is deployed rather unhelpfully (including in my own prior work) to name both an analytic that seeks to illuminate how capitalism deploys sexuality to "faction, fraction and fractalize" queer populations, and a triumphalist ideology that regards participation in capitalism as a vehicle for queer liberation. I want to suggest that we need to distinguish between usages of homocapitalism as analytic and as ideology.

As ideology, homocapitalism shares affinities with Black capitalism and Dalit capitalism in that these are all ideological formations in which variously marginalized subjects are promised liberation through their conscription into capitalism. A central implication of this is that homocapitalism does not simply fraction populations along lines of race and caste but also aligns with and intensifies ideological tensions *within* racialized and oppressed caste groups over the putative merits of capitalism as a vehicle for social mobility. In his ethnography of homocapitalism in the globalized information technology sector in the south Indian metropolis of Bangalore/Bengaluru, Lars Aaberg (2022b) explains that a crucial dimension of this process entails the "upskilling" by NGOs of working-class queer people, many hailing from oppressed castes, in preparation for their employment in white-collar corporate environments dominated by middle- and upper-middle class, oppressor caste employees. Upskilling involves, among other things, the acquisition of "soft skills" such as the internalization of norms of office etiquette and comportment in an effort to smooth out the gender trouble that such bodies introduce into the workplace. Aaberg's work demonstrates that marginalized groups are not simply left out of the lifeworlds of homocapitalism but unevenly, differentially, and hierarchically included (much as they are in the caste system). I suggest that this process is lubricated by the "cruel optimism" (Berlant 2011) of discourses of liberatory capitalism that have long circulated, however implausibly and chimerically, within such groups. It is in this sense that homocapitalism can be understood not only as fractioning but also fractalizing, its splitting tendencies operative not only along racialized and caste lines but also pulling apart the groups constituted by those lines.

One occupational hazard of spending time with the ideology of homocapitalism, even if only to critique it, is the risk of contagion whereby its premises and horizons—its *weltanschauung*—threatens to infect its analysts in a kind of reverse transference. Thus, critiques of homocapitalism as ideology (including my own), in dwelling on the images of consumption and high value-production through which queer liberalism's seductions operate, can sometimes take the form of a moralizing discourse that fulminates against privilege and, in a voluntarism that mirrors its bootstrapism, urges putatively elite queers to "do better." As Alexander Stoffel (2021: 174) argues, such critique "risks valorizing the bourgeois imaginary of the market as a sphere of equal individuals, free from normative constraints on their self-expression and cultural dispositions." Homocapitalism as analytic seeks to explain historic shifts in state formation and capital accumulation that produce and are predicated on particular sexual formations.[2] To put this somewhat differently, rather than judging individuals for their choices as if they could have done otherwise, homocapitalism as analytic seeks to illuminate how and why the space for doing and desiring otherwise is constrained. Yet even as it does so, it must acknowledge that agency is not constrained equally. Moreover, central to the deployment of homocapitalism as an analytical frame is the continued analysis of homocapitalism as ideology—the mythologies and yarns that it spins, the seduction techniques through which it elicits consent—as a means of understanding how it constructs hegemony. We need to grasp how ideology reproduces structure without buying into ideology's mythical account of that structure. This is why I want to hold on to both senses of homocapitalism—as analytic and ideology—insisting on their conceptual distinctness but also their unceasing interaction.

Dis/continuities across Racial, Caste, and Homo Capitalisms

My heuristic juxtaposition of racial capitalism and caste capitalism as analytical frames in the previous section of this article risks rendering them as analogous and separable analytics, when in fact they have a more complex relationship that is neither synonymous nor analogous. As I have argued extensively elsewhere, analogical reasoning occludes the intersection and co-constitution of categories (Rao 2020: 12–16, 177). This is why the animating question of my inquiry here is not whether homocapitalism is *like* racial capitalism and caste capitalism—a question that in its very posing would propose an analogous relationship—but whether it is, in some sense, occupying the same ground as, overlapping with, or working through these formations. Certainly Robinson's account of racial capitalism has been the inspiration for recent theorizations of caste capitalism. As Svati Shah (2023: 3) explains, just as racial capitalism attaches a theory of racialization to the exploitation of labor and natural resources, caste capitalism can serve a similar purpose in Indian historiography. Yet rather than positing analogy, Shah suggests that the relationship between the two is one of "imbrication"—a condition of "overlap, being mutually constituted, blended and sharing histories" (14–15). Building on Ambedkar's (1916) understanding of caste as endogamy, in this Special Issue they describe caste capitalism as relying on heteronormative, endogamous social reproduction that is maintained through the violence of gender binarism and compulsory marriage.

The imbrication of racial and caste capitalism is productively explored in a recent collection of essays that seeks to rethink difference in India through the notion of racialization (Cháirez-Garza et al. 2022). The editors of this collection speak of discourses of race and caste as becoming "syncretized" (196) in nineteenth century colonial India. This is particularly evident in sites of governmentality such as the census, in which colonial authorities drew on local norms of classification—relying on caste elites for knowledge of these—interpreted through Victorian ideas of race and eugenics. Homing in more specifically on the question of capitalism, these scholars seek to extend the utility of racial capitalism beyond the Americas by deploying the notion of racialization to explore how Indian regimes of social differentiation along lines of caste, tribe, religion and culture—including those that predate European colonization—"are transformed, reproduced and proliferated in service to global capitalism in new racial terms" (198). In this, they are inspired by Robinson's location of the origins of "race," not in the transatlantic slave trade but in the racialization of social hierarchies internal to Europe that predated and enabled enclosure and capitalism—a move that enables the deployment of "racialization" in a manner that is not tethered exclusively to particular geographies and histories. Racialization can be understood as the naturalization (sometimes even biologization) of the differential value ascribed to different groups, thereby justifying a variety of oppressive practices including the extraction of labour, expropriation of resources and, in settler colonial contexts (Wolfe 2006), the elimination of populations deemed surplus to the requirements of capitalist accumulation through genocide, assimilation and expulsion. In the Indian context, it is crucial to recall that the ascription of differential value antedates colonialism and capitalism in discourses of caste, but is mobilized through racialization by these latter processes for their own extractive ends. As Cháirez-Garza et al. (2022: 202) conclude, *"race cannot be reduced to caste any more than caste can be reduced to race.* Rather, both operate through continuous logics of racialization that yield profit and value through political-economic valuations of bodies and/in space."

We can appreciate the distinctness but also the collision of the analytics of racial and caste capitalism in accounts of the institution of indentured labor. Although Indians from different regional and caste backgrounds crossed the oceans as indentured labor (Carter and Torabully 2002), Purba Hossain has demonstrated how in the immediate aftermath of the British abolition of slavery in 1833, the architects of indenture identified the "hill coolies" of British Bengal as ideal replacements for enslaved plantation workers in the Caribbean. Central to their attractiveness was the perception that they were strong, docile, and easily manageable, able to labor in tropical climates and, crucially, outside of caste society and therefore amenable to leaving the country unencumbered by caste restrictions. Described as "more akin to the monkey than the man" in some of the early colonial correspondence that instituted the lineaments of indenture, discourses of bestialization and racialization produce oppressed castes and outcastes as idealized indentured workers (Hossain 2022: 61). Looking at the question of return rather than recruitment through an examination of ship registers for more than 16,000 Indian indentured workers in British Guiana between 1872 and 1911, Neha Hui and Uma S. Kambhampati (2022) conclude that workers from oppressed castes were less likely to return "home" after their contractual period of indenture, perhaps adding to their allure for employers. They suggest that this was because the reduced salience of caste in plantation economies meant that despite the considerable privations of indenture, it offered an escape from the unfreedom of caste on the subcontinent. Even as an analytic of caste capitalism tells us something about the recruitment and retention of indentured labor, as Lisa Lowe (2015) reminds us, Indian and Chinese indenture unfolded contemporaneously with the continuation of slavery and settler colonialism and the emergence of European liberalism, thereby participating in global processes of race making and racial capitalism. Caste capitalism thus lubricates the "shift" from slavery to indenture, enabling the mutation and expansion of racial capitalism.

If in these examples, the racialization of caste operates to extract value from marginalized subjects, it can conversely also be deployed to enhance the value of dominant subjects in economies of all kinds including economies of desire. Drawing on ethnographic work on the use of the gay dating platform Grindr in India, Dhiren Borisa (2020: 93) notes the pervasiveness of self-ascriptions of caste on oppressor caste profiles and the association of caste identity with the virility of the body and especially the penis.[3] Such trends are also visible in online gay Indian pornography and resonate with the fetishistic depiction of racialized bodies especially in "interracial" gay porn aimed at white western audiences (McBride 2005: 88–131). At work here is the somatization of caste in ways that enable the accumulation of erotic capital (hookups), on a platform that makes possible a more conventional accumulation of capital. The most popular gay dating app worldwide, Grindr was valued at $2.1 billion in 2022 (Sweney 2022). Two years earlier, the US government had forced Grindr's Chinese owner, Kunlun Tech Co., to sell the company to US firms. Citing Chinese ownership of Grindr as a "national security risk," US regulators argued that its collection of personal data including information about location and HIV status could make government employees and military personnel who used the app vulnerable to blackmail. John Wei (2023: 5–6) places these concerns in the context of the US government's broader "tech war" against Chinese companies such as Huawei and Tiktok (the latter of which was banned by India in 2020), reminding us that the forced sale of Chinese owned technology to US firms was also seen as way for the US to acquire advanced algorithms that would allow it to maintain technological supremacy and market share. In attending to the narratives of self-making and unmaking, corporeal intimacies, kin formation and rupture, structures of ownership and profit, technological know-how and geopolitical posturing that Grindr assembles, we can see how the production of racialized difference in the affective modes of desire as much as paranoia is central to enabling accumulation of various kinds at multiple scales.

What is needed at this juncture is a more systematic account of how capital accumulation requires and produces gendered and sexually differentiated populations. Liu (2023) has recently provided one such account that begins from the familiar Marxist premise that capitalism requires noncapitalist and noneconomic relations for its expanded reproduction. Scholars such as David Harvey (2005) have tended to view the "constitutive outside" that capitalism needs in terms of space and time. In his now familiar argument, crises of overaccumulation are addressed through a spatiotemporal fix whereby capital surpluses are temporally displaced through investment in long term capital projects and/or social expenditures, or spatially displaced through the search for new markets and sites of production. For Liu, capitalism's "outside" is also socially differentiated, marked by gender and sexuality. As he argues, "accumulation of capital by dispossession does not take place across undifferentiated spaces, bodies, and genders" but "by grounding immobilized, racialized, and gendered subjects in territorially segregated and splintered spaces," with the ideology of the so-called Beijing Consensus providing the justificatory basis for these processes as they unfold in China (Liu 2023: 26). In his account the restructuring of US-Asian labor relations, the financialization of China's agrarian hinterlands, the privatization of its socialist institutions and the burgeoning of its globe-straddling infrastructural investments have reconfigured notions of race (in locations into which Chinese investment and labor flow) and created new classes of gender and sexuality in China including female migrant laborers, rural-to-urban sex workers, and transnationally mobile queers. Without framing their accounts in such explicitly Marxist terms, theorists of queer South asia have also unpacked the complex relationship between capitalist expansion and queer lifeworlds in a variety of ways—in the discourses of "compulsory individuality" fostered by 1990s discourses of economic liberalization (Bhaskaran 2004), in the novel subjectivities such as MsM (men who have sex with men), kothi, and panthi that proliferate in the interstices of HIV/AIDS funding and governmentality (khanna 2016), in the role of class- and caste-segregated urbanism and urban imaginaries of the rural in the discursive production of sexuality and gender-based activism in India (Shah 2015), etc.

Homocapitalism as ideology reflects the interests of only the most elite fractions of the queer subjectivities that these capitalist dynamics produce, but this does not make it any less significant in the production of value—not least because it functions as an aspirational horizon for those for whom its promised futurities are beyond immediate reach. Writing about an "LGBT Talent Job Fair" in Shanghai, Ian Liujia Tian (2020: 56) notes an "uneven distribution of desirable queerness" in employers' evident preference for urban and cosmopolitan subjects with the requisite education over rural and working-class queers who remain unwelcome in such spaces. While such fractionings of queerness are now banal, Tian illuminates how they serve global racial capitalism. Emphasizing that postsocialist queer Chinese lifeworlds have emerged in tandem with China's (re)incorporation into global racial capitalism, he suggests that desirable forms of queerness are those that embody the cultural knowhow (languages, techne) that service global racial capitalism. In her ethnographic work on "inclusion" in "LGBT-friendly" organizations in London, Olimpia Burchiellaro (2021) goes further, suggesting not only a correlation between desirable forms of queerness and the possession of valuable cultural capital but rather that the appropriate performance of queerness might *itself* be productive of value for the employer and should concomitantly be understood as labor undertaken by the employee.

While these perspectives grapple with the queering of production, a feminist commitment demands that we also attend to questions of social reproduction—questions that are directly implicated in Liu's evocation of capitalism's constitutive outside. In her attempt to set up a conversation between social reproduction theory and racial capitalism, Gargi Bhattacharyya (2018) begins with the familiar observation that the reproductive labor necessary to produce workers for capital accumulation has historically been disproportionately performed by women and has not been recognized as work. She argues that this hidden and unvalued work on which waged labor is premised is central to the techniques by which humanity comes to be divided into groups that are accorded differential value (Bhattacharyya 2018: 42). In a striking formulation that draws on the work of sociologist Maria Mies, she suggests that patriarchal accumulation might offer a "blueprint" (45) for racial capitalism. Following feminists who call for a reframing of the economy as structured around "productive-reproductive" relationships, she argues that the sheer variety of forms that this nexus takes might account for the hierarchies of racial capitalism:

The discussion of racial capitalism . . . centres on the manner in which people are constituted as different kinds of participants in capitalist formulations, both of production and consumption. In relation to questions of production, the interplay between reproductive and productive spheres
constructs different kinds of creatures—from fully serviced ready-for-work-
ers to hybrid beings who survive through a combination of "productive"
work and other forms of economic activity to those who exist at the edges or
in the crevices of capitalist life-worlds. In each case, the degree and character of the reproductive work that makes such lives possible becomes a
marker of racialised difference. The production-reproduction nexus, in its
variation, offers a naturalised rationale for the racialised differentiation of
workers and even for a racialised understanding of uneven development.
One key lesson, then, is that reproductive labor is the input that enables
workers to be highly differentiated and differently constituted as workers,
sometime workers and non-workers (50).

Among other things, Bhattacharyya's gendering of racial capitalism asks us
to consider that its hierarchies might stem as much, if not more, from the
realm of reproduction ("how these people live"—that all too familiar formulation of disgust reserved for racialized others) as from that of production
(how and what these people work). Think here of how centrally food and sex
function as sites for the reproduction of caste. If we shed the assumption
that reproduction requires heterosexuality, we can begin to map the fractioning of queerness on the basis of its potential (or lack thereof) to reproduce
full-fledged workers and to make sense of the narratives and images around
which ideologies of homocapitalism cohere.

At one end of a hierarchy of queer reproduction, the sexuality of queers
who are thought to be best positioned to reproduce workers (facilitated by
socially intelligible monogamous relationships, access to assisted reproductive technologies, surrogacy and outsourced domestic care work including in
their transnational racialized variants) ceases to be political at all. As Bhattacharyya might argue, their very capacity to produce workers becomes a
marker of their racial and caste status, an indicator of "full humanness" (52).
Where legal routes to reproduction are blocked off, the ideology of homocapitalism kicks into overdrive to demonstrate the productivity of queers *as
workers* (as opposed to more precarious sometime workers or non-workers)
in order to overcome moral qualms about queer reproduction. It is not coin-
cidental that parambanana (2023) lists a series of high-status professions
allegedly dominated by queers in his lamentation about the Indian state's

non-recognition of same-sex marriage; or that such professions (dancer, journalist, chef, hoteliers, businesswoman) provided the requisite respectability for the petitioners who persuaded the Indian Supreme Court to decriminalize queer sex in 2018 (*Navtej Singh Johar & Ors. Versus Union of India* 2018); or that some of the queer lawyers currently arguing for same-sex marriage before the Court themselves prefigure and perform through normative forms of coupledom, parenthood and religiosity the queer futures for which they seek legal recognition. Perhaps this is why, finally, the most degrading forms of racialization are reserved for queers who are thought to be incapable of social reproduction and whose attempts at kin formation are therefore suspect or criminal: hence the toxic association of hijras with kidnapping (Jain 2017: 48) and of kuchus in Uganda with the "recruitment" of children (Sadgrove et al. 2012).

In an important sense, the moral panics of a society provide a powerful indication of the forms of queerness that most threaten the modes of social reproduction that shore up racial and caste capitalism. Jules Joanne Gleeson and Elle O'Rourke (2021: 26) argue that transphobia is a response to trans peoples' defiance—embodied in the act of transition—of tacit expectations that the normative family that is so central to the reproduction of capitalism will be maintained. In disrupting the operation of the family and demanding the redistribution of resources for healthcare, housing, and welfare (and, in the Indian context, increased affirmative action), trans people threaten the foundations of capitalism and fraying social democratic and developmentalist states. The stakes here are deeply material but also psychic. Alyosxa Tudor (2020) has read transphobia in the UK as "white distraction" in light of the overrepresentation of white women among TERFs (trans exclusionary radical feminists) as well as the temporality of their heightened attacks on trans people in the summer of 2020—a time when racialized groups were grappling with their disproportionate morbidity and mortality under Covid and with the carceral violence that made the Black Lives Matter movement necessary. One way of understanding this is that whereas Black and Third World feminists had long problematized binary gender and singular notions of womanhood (Spillers 1987; Amadiume 1987; Oyěwùmí 1997), cisgender white women experienced militant trans activism as uniquely destabilizing. In this light, we might read UK transphobia as a response to the declining wages of white womanhood.

If moral panics tell us something about perceived threats to regimes of material and psychic accumulation, then a comparison of the forms that they take might illuminate the relationships between different regimes of accumulation. Or perhaps we might come at the question of comparison and connection between regimes of accumulation from a different angle: if, as Bhattacharyya suggests, patriarchal accumulation provides a blueprint for racial capitalism, might racial and caste capitalism provide blueprints for homocapitalism? This seems likely especially if, following Foucault ([1976] 1981), we candidly acknowledge the novelty of sexuality (relative to gender, race and caste) as an aspect of personhood. Writing about section 28—the legislative provision that the Thatcher government introduced in 1988 into the (UK) Local Government Act to prohibit the "promotion of homosexuality" by local authorities—Anna Marie Smith (1994: 22) argues that the homophobic moral panic that produced section 28 drew on prior racist moral panics whipped up by the likes of Enoch Powell. Both panics (as well as more recent ones such as that around Brexit) borrowed from a common stock of codes, tactics and metaphors—foreign invasion, unassimilable others, dangerous criminals, the threat of disease, subversive intellectuals, excessive permissiveness and, in the case of gay and trans panics, that hardy perennial: the corruption of the Child. In a remarkably resonant argument, Shamira Meghani (2020) demonstrates how the grammar of caste and specifically untouchability is mobilized to represent HIV stigmatization in Indian literary and cinematic texts. In both examples, the sexualized vilification of subjects who in different ways threaten social reproduction looks very much like racialization—a powerful indication of the shared arsenal of racial capitalism, caste capitalism and homocapitalism. While the folk devils at the heart of these moral panics shift in successive historical moments, there is a remarkable continuity to the methods by which they are demonized.

If capitalism must constantly expand to manage crises of overproduction and overaccumulation and if it always needs an "outside" into which to expand, then its survival requires a ceaseless proliferation of difference as a means of producing this outside from which to extract value. Racial capitalism, caste capitalism and homocapitalism name different modes in which such difference is produced, their historicity marking a spatial and temporal situatedness. They may not anticipate or subsume modes of differentiation that are yet to come, for which we will need new names. Yet they all function through a naturalization of difference that may still best be described as racialization.[4] Of course the extraction of value never proceeds smoothly, unencumbered by resistance. In this regard, the panic in moral panic indexes a systemic fear that its victims will become its gravediggers. Sometimes the folk devils at the heart of moral panics really are the system's nemesis; at other times, they are a foil, a distraction or scapegoat, hypervisibilized to thwart the realization of revolutionary antagonism. One method of managing the instabilities introduced by the production of difference is to, quite literally, split the difference through the incorporation into market/ nation/state of privileged fractions (the petty bourgeoisie, the creamy layer, the gay patriot) of those who have been differentiated. Yet unrelenting systemic instability means that such processes of incorporation are themselves dynamic with lines between those who are included and excluded never static (how else to understand the enormous ongoing investment in splitting off the "LGB" from the "T"?). Perhaps more pertinently they are not inexorable, with apparently settled questions around issues such as abortion and contraception, not to mention sexuality and gender identity, being reopened with detrimental existential consequences for many. As capitalism, nationalism and liberal democracy become ever more disentangled, questions of belonging and entitlement may increasingly be adjudicated in the realm of necessity rather than freedom. Yesterday's folk devils may have become today's gay patriots, but they may yet be spat out of a system that cannot metabolize them.

Notes

My thanks to Evren Savcı and Rana M. Jaleel for their editorial comments, and to the editors and production team at *South Atlantic Quarterly*. Thanks also to Akanksha Mehta, Jasbir Puar, Lars Aaberg, Sita Balani, and Svati Shah for conversations over several years that have shaped this piece

1   The central import of this sentence—namely that there is a meaningful distinction between analytical frames that seek to demonstrate the salience of race and caste in capitalism, and ideological formations that aspire to bring preferred utopias into being—can be read with either the racial or caste categories in mind. I have placed the caste categories in parentheses for ease of reading and in the expectation that readers will be more familiar with racial capitalism than with the emergent theorization of caste capitalism, to which I shall pay greater attention in the following section. As will become clear, these categories should not be understood as synonymous or even analogous, but as syncretized, imbricated, enmeshed.

2   In a very similar vein, sketching an agenda for queer Marxism, Liu (2015: 31) argues that "the point is neither to return to the primacy of economic determinants by reinstating an intellectual foundationalism for queer theory, nor to reiterate a moralistic critique of bourgeois consumption brought about by transnational capitalism. Rather, queer Marxism emphasizes the possibilities of *systemic analysis* in investigating those configurations of gender, sexuality and social power that liberal critics characterize as mere contingencies."

3   For an acute analysis of how caste structures "cartographies of romance" in contemporary India including on the terrain of dating apps see Kisana (2023).

4   Although see Shah in this special issue on the notion of "casteification."

References

Aaberg, Lars. 2022a. "Corporate India after Section 377: Haphazardness and Strategy in LGBTQ Diversity and Inclusion Advocacy." *Gender, Place & Culture*: 1–18. doi.org/10.10 80/0966369X.2022.2146660.

Aaberg, Lars. 2022b. "Productively Queer: An Ethnography of the "Business Case" for LGBTQI Diversity and Inclusion in India." PhD diss., SOAS University of London.

Amadiume, Ifi. 1987. *Male Daughters, Female Husbands: Gender and Sex in an African Society.* London: Zed Books.

Ambedkar, B. R. 1916. "Castes in India: Their Mechanism, Genesis and Development." *Indian Antiquary* 41: 81–95.

Ambedkar, B. R. (1936) 2016. *Annihilation of Caste*, edited and annotated by S. Anand. London: Verso.

Anderson, Kevin B. 2010. *Marx at the Margins: On Nationalism, Ethnicity, and Non-Western Societies.* Chicago: University of Chicago Press.

Arondekar, Anjali. 2022. "Go (Away) West!" *GLQ: A Journal of Lesbian and Gay Studies* 28, no. 3: 463–71.

Badgett, M. V. Lee. 2014. "The Economic Cost of Stigma and the Exclusion of LGBT People: A Case Study of India." World Bank, Washington, DC. https://openknowledge.world bank.org/entities/publication/bd5d40a3-0247-5c44-a9eb-5675d86aea73.

Badgett, M. V. Lee, Sheila Nezhad, Kees Waaldijk, and Yana van der Meulen Rodgers. 2014. "The Relationship between LGBT Inclusion and Economic Development: An Analysis of Emerging Economies." The Williams Institute, UCLA School of Law. https://williams institute.law.ucla.edu/wp-content/uploads/LGBT-Inclusion-Economic-Dev-Nov-2014.pdf.

Benner, Erica. 1995. *Really Existing Nationalisms: A Post-Communist View from Marx and Engels.* Oxford: Clarendon Press.

BBC News. 2014. "World Bank Postpones $90m Uganda Loan over Anti-Gay Law." February 28. https://www.bbc.co.uk/news/world-africa-26378230.

Berlant, Lauren. 2011. *Cruel Optimism.* Durham, NC: Duke University Press.

Bhaskaran, Suparna. 2004. *Made in India: Decolonizations, Queer Sexualities, Trans/national Projects.* New York: Palgrave.

Bhattacharyya, Gargi. 2018. *Rethinking Racial Capitalism: Questions of Reproduction and Survival.* London: Rowman & Littlefield.

Borisa, Dhiren. 2020. "Hopeful Rantings of a Dalit-Queer Person." *Jindal Law & Humanities Review* 1, no. 1: 91–95.

Brown, Wendy. 2015. *Undoing the Demos: Neoliberalism's Stealth Revolution.* New York: Zone Books.

Burchiellaro, Olimpia. 2021. "Queering Control and Inclusion in the Contemporary Organization: On 'LGBT-Friendly Control' and the Reproduction of (Queer) Value." *Organization Studies* 42, no. 5: 761–85.

Carter, Marina, and Khal Torabully. 2002. *Coolitude: An Anthology of the Indian Labour Diaspora.* London: Anthem Press.

Cháirez-Garza, Jesús F., Mabel Denzin Gergan, Malini Ranganathan, and Pavithra Vasudevan. 2022. "Introduction to the special issue: Rethinking difference in India through racialization." *Ethnic and Racial Studies* 45, no. 2: 193–215.

Conway, Daniel. 2022. "The Politics of Truth at LGBTQ+ Pride: Contesting Corporate Pride and Revealing Marginalized Lives at Hong Kong Migrants Pride." *International Feminist Journal of Politics*: 1–23. https://www.tandfonline.com/doi/full/10.1080/14616742.2022.2136732.

Du Bois, W. E. B. (1903) 2008. *The Souls of Black Folk*. Bensenville, IL: Lushena Books.

Du Bois, W. E. B. 1935. *Black Reconstruction in America: Toward a History of the Part Which Black Folk Played in the Attempt to Reconstruct Democracy in America, 1860–1880*. New York: Harcourt Brace and Company.

Ellis-Petersen, Hannah. 2023. "India Overtakes China to Become World's Most Populous Country." *The Guardian*, April 24. https://www.theguardian.com/world/2023/apr/24/india-overtakes-china-to-become-worlds-most-populous-country?CMP=share_btn_link.

Eng, David L. 2010. *The Feeling of Kinship: Queer Liberalism and the Racialization of Intimacy*. Durham, NC: Duke University Press.

Fisher, Mark. 2009. *Capitalist Realism: Is There No Alternative?* Winchester, UK: Zero Books.

Gleeson, Jules Joanne, and Elle O'Rourke. 2021. "Introduction." In *Transgender Marxism*, edited by Jules Joanne Gleeson and Elle O'Rourke, 1–32. London: Pluto Press.

Harriss-White, Barbara. 2003. *India Working: Essays on Society and Economy*. Cambridge, UK: Cambridge University Press.

Harvey, David. 2005. *The New Imperialism*. Oxford: Oxford University Press.

Hoad, Neville. 2007. *African Intimacies: Race, Homosexuality, and Globalization*. Minneapolis: University of Minnesota Press.

Hossain, Purba. 2022. "'A Matter of Doubt and Uncertainty': John Gladstone and the Post-Slavery Framework of Labour in the British Empire." *The Journal of Imperial and Commonwealth History* 50, no. 1: 52–80.

Hui, Neha, and Uma S. Kambhampati. 2022. "Between Unfreedoms: The Role of Caste in Decisions to Repatriate among Indentured Workers." *The Economic History Review* 75, no. 2: 421–46.

Jain, Dipika. 2017. "Shifting Subjects of State Legibility: Gender Minorities and the Law in India." *Berkeley Journal of Gender, Law & Justice* 32, no. 1: 39–72.

Kelley, Robin D. G. 2017. "What Did Cedric Robinson Mean by Racial Capitalism?" *Boston Review*, January 12. https://www.bostonreview.net/articles/robin-d-g-kelley-introduction-race-capitalism-justice/.

khanna, akshay. 2016. *Sexualness*. New Delhi: New Text.

Kisana, Ravikant. 2023. "Dating Like a Savarna." *The Swaddle*, April 29. https://theswaddle.com/dating-like-a-savarna/.

Liu, Petrus. 2015. *Queer Marxism in Two Chinas*. Durham, NC: Duke University Press.

Liu, Petrus. 2023. *The Specter of Materialism: Queer Theory and Marxism in the Age of the Beijing Consensus*. Durham, NC: Duke University Press.

Lowe, Lisa. 2015. *The Intimacies of Four Continents*. Durham, NC: Duke University Press.

Marx, Karl. 1869. "Letter to Ludwig Kugelmann." November 29. https://marxists.info/archive/marx/works/1869/letters/69_11_29.htm.

Marx, Karl. 1870. "Letter to Sigfrid Meyer and August Vogt." April 9. https://www.marxists.org/archive/marx/works/1870/letters/70_04_09.htm.

McBride, Dwight. 2005. *Why I Hate Abercrombie & Fitch: Essays on Race and Sexuality*. New York: New York University Press.

Meghani, Shamira. 2020. "HIV Stigma, Gay Identity, and Caste 'Untouchability': Metaphors of Abjection in *My Brother . . . Nikhil*, *The Boyfriend*, and 'Gandu Bagicha.'" *Journal of Medical Humanities* 41, no. 2: 137–51.

Navtej Singh Johar & Ors. Versus Union of India, AIR 2018 SC 4321. 2018.

Open for Business Coalition. 2023. "Investment Concern at the 2023 Anti-Homosexuality Bill." March 28. https://drive.google.com/file/d/1A4FmuFP__GwnZhqyYcYrs8Pjb-op2XYSx/view.

Oyěwùmí, Oyèrónké. 1997. *The Invention of Women: Making an African Sense of Western Gender Discourses*. Minneapolis: University of Minnesota Press.

parambanana.2023. "Everytime I think we went one step ahead, IRL we go ten step backwards!" Instagram, March 13. https://www.instagram.com/p/Cpu6mKIp1qf/.

Puar, Jasbir K. 2007. *Terrorist Assemblages: Homonationalism in Queer Times*. Durham, NC: Duke University Press.

Puar, Jasbir K. 2011. "Citation and Censorship: The Politics of Talking About the Sexual Politics of Israel." *Feminist Legal Studies* 19, no. 2: 133–42.

Rao, Rahul. 2020. *Out of Time: The Queer Politics of Postcoloniality*. New York: Oxford University Press.

Robinson, Cedric J. (1983) 2000. *Black Marxism: The Making of the Black Radical Tradition*. Chapel Hill: University of North Carolina Press.

Sadgrove, Joanna, Robert M. Vanderbeck, Johan Andersson, Gill Valentine, and Kevin Ward. 2012. "Morality Plays and Money Matters: Towards a Situated Understanding of the Politics of Homosexuality in Uganda." *Journal of Modern African Studies* 50, no. 1: 103–29.

Sanneh, Kelefa. 2021. "The Plan to Build a Capital for Black Capitalism." *New Yorker*, February 1. https://www.newyorker.com/magazine/2021/02/08/the-plan-to-build-a-capital-for-black-capitalism.

Shah, Svati. 2023. "Agriculture, rivers and gender: Thinking with 'caste capitalism', migrant labour and food production in the Capitalocene." *Agenda* 37, no. 1: 12–18. doi.org/10.1080/10130950.2023.2177555.

Shah, Svati P. 2015. "Queering Critiques of Neoliberalism in India: Urbanism and Inequality in the Era of Transnational 'LGBTQ' Rights." *Antipode* 47, no. 3: 635–51.

Shahani, Parmesh (with Shrabonti Bagchi). 2023. "Moving Towards Inclusivity." *BIC Talks*, March 16. https://bangaloreinternationalcentre.org/audio/228-moving-towards-inclusivity-with-parmesh-shahani-shrabonti-bagchi/.

Shilliam, Robbie. 2018. *Race and the Undeserving Poor*. Newcastle, UK: Agenda Publishing.

Smith, Anna Marie. 1994. *New Right Discourse on Race and Sexuality: Britain, 1968–1990*. Cambridge, UK: Cambridge University Press.

Spillers, Hortense J. 1987. "Mama's Baby, Papa's Maybe: An American Grammar Book." *Diacritics* 17, no. 2: 64–81.

Stoffel, Alexander. 2021. "'Homocapitalism': analytical precursors and future directions." *International Feminist Journal of Politics* 23, no. 1: 173–78.

Sweney, Mark. 2022. "Gay Dating App Grindr to Float in \$2.1bn deal." *The Guardian*, May 10. https://www.theguardian.com/business/2022/may/10/gay-dating-app-grindr-float-spac-deal.

Teltumbde, Anand. 2018. *Republic of Caste: Thinking Equality in the Time of Neoliberal Hindutva*. New Delhi: Navayana.

Tian, Ian Liujia. 2020. "Perverse Politics, Postsocialist Radicality: Queer Marxism in China." *QED: A Journal in GLBTQ Worldmaking* 7, no. 2: 48–68.

Tudor, Alyosxa. 2020. "Terfism Is White Distraction: On BLM, Decolonising the Curriculum, Anti-Gender Attacks and Feminist Transphobia." *Engenderings* (blog), June 19. https:// blogs.lse.ac.uk/gender/2020/06/19/terfism-is-white-distraction-on-blm-decolonising -the-curriculum-anti-gender-attacks-and-feminist-transphobia/.

Wei, John. 2023. "Rethinking Queer (Asian) Studies: Geopolitics, Covid-19, and Post-Covid Queer Theories and Mobilities." *Journal of Homosexuality*: 1–23. https://doi.org/10.1080 /00918369.2023.2174471.

Weiss, Meredith L., and Michael J. Bosia (editors). 2013. *Global Homophobia: States, Movements, and the Politics of Oppression.* Champaign: University of Illinois Press.

Wilkinson, Cai. 2014. "Putting 'Traditional Values' into Practice: The Rise and Contestation of Anti-Homopropaganda Laws in Russia." *Journal of Human Rights* 13, no. 3: 363–79.

Wolfe, Patrick. 2006. "Settler Colonialism and the elimination of the native." *Journal of Genocide Research* 8, no. 4: 387–409.

Ye, Shana. 2022. "*Word of Honor* and Brand Homonationalism with 'Chinese Characteristics': The *dangai* Industry, Queer Masculinity and the 'Opacity' of the State." *Feminist Media Studies*: 1–17. https://doi.org/10.1080/14680777.2022.2037007.

Yengde, Suraj. 2019. *Caste Matters.* Gurgaon: Penguin.

Yengde, Suraj. 2022. "Global Castes." *Ethnic and Racial Studies* 45, no. 2: 340–60.

Svati P. Shah

Caste Capitalism and Queer Theory: Beyond Identity Politics in India

This article takes up a central question of this special issue, asking what the transnational travels of queer of color critique look like and what kind of reconfigurations of racial capitalism are necessitated and enacted by such travel. I use this question as a point of departure to propose "caste capitalism" as a framework for thinking through how entanglements of sexuality politics, caste, and capital operate in contemporary India. I develop this frame through a queer hermeneutic of heritability and endogamy, drawing inspiration from Indian feminist, anti-caste, and Marxist critiques, and from critiques of racial capitalism as they have circulated in American critical race and queer studies. There is an urgency for this argument with respect to the Indian context, where the rise of autocratic Hindu nationalism is being waged in the terms of upper caste Brahminism and extractive capitalism. This project of Hindu nationalism, known as Hindutva, relies on the ruse of "identity" as being distinct from questions of political economy, offering limited forms of legibility on the basis of caste, gender, and sexuality, while attempting to cut off democratic processes that enable access to justice, or even advocacy for social welfare. Binding Hindutva to an autocratic turn, this

The South Atlantic Quarterly 123:1, January 2024
DOI 10.1215/00382876-10920750   © 2024 Duke University Press

mode of governance aggressively targets criticisms of the state and political dissent, pitting them against the logic of privatization and the consolidation of wealth, while steadily waging the erasure of the public sector. My argument builds on critiques of "casteification" (the ongoing production and processual iteration of caste categories) and its imbrications within and relations to class and the political economy of land and enclosure. Aligned with the projects of "queer of color" (Ferguson 2004) and "objectless" (Eng and Puar 2020) critiques, I seek to center South Asian historical and political referents in general and Indian historiography in particular. A key provocation for this piece is the need to countermand the ways in which questions of queer and transgender existence are conflated with liberal individualist notions of identity that are hived off from questions of material survival, economic subjectivity, and wealth redistribution. Throughout the piece, I think with historically contingent relationships between endogamy, heritability, stigma, and status, to illuminate how these are embedded within a problematic that requires a theory of "caste capitalism" and a queer hermeneutic of endogamy.

Caste as a term has an enduring history in South Asia, used to delineate a complex system of social hierarchies that stem from varied interpretations of cosmologies and texts grouped under the rubric of Hinduism; at the same time, the practice of caste-ism is not limited to Hindu religious or community contexts. In the sections below, I review much more detailed definitions of caste and concomitant debates. Suffice it to say at the outset that caste, like race, is always already implicated within critiques of class and economic status. As with racialization, caste status tracks closely with economic power, but does not predict it entirely. To tease out these discrepancies, I build upon Indian feminist critiques of caste-based endogamy in order to discuss seemingly minor shifts in what is acceptable regarding caste and marriage. These shifts show that, while caste-based endogamy activates strict adherence to rules for marriage and reproduction, these rules are also contingent, at times even elastic, evidencing broader shifts over time of social norms and rules of property. Using a queer hermeneutic for caste capitalism, we can understand how caste rules are both enforced through violent social norms, and *at the same time* selectively or intermittently ignored, e.g., in spaces of non-normative sexuality and gender expression, and how both enforcing and ignoring caste rules facilitate the normative functions of caste-based endogamy.

The problematic of how to account for "political economy," by which I am referencing macroeconomic processes that foreclose access to land rights, economic subjectivity, and wealth redistribution, in developing a more nuanced understanding sexuality, gender, and caste politics, is an integral concern of this piece. This means undoing the conflation of bio-normative individualism, freedom of (personal) expression, and queer and transgender politics, which turns on excluding questions of economic survival and iterative histories of caste-d and racialized sociality. In research that centers historical and social referents in the Global South, this conflation posits heteronormativity as immanent to life lived at the economic margins, while delimiting the possibility of queer existence to that of cisgender, bourgeois, urban, elite subjects. Such scholarship occludes the range of non-heteronormative negotiations that occur on a daily basis across a broad swathe of social and economic contexts. Within South Asian Studies, it contributes to shrinking the discursive space in which economic impoverishment and non-heteronormativity can be framed as concomitant social phenomena. In India, this framing is increasingly reduced to certain forms of transfemininity, such as hijra and kothi identities, which are currently in the process of being reframed and domesticated within a larger myth of a timeless "Hinduism" that has existed unchanged for millennia (Goel 2019). This discursive foreclosure of the intersections of sexuality and impoverishment is upcycled into a heroic narrative of the modern Hindu nationalist state's tolerant liberalism, while effectively excising the majority of India's population, whose survival is waged within informal economies, from non-heteronormative relations of caste and capital. This prolegomenon begins to intervene in this problematic by arguing for the possibilities of a queer hermeneutic that foregrounds the production and maintenance of caste hierarchies and boundaries within capitalist relations of extraction, enclosure, and commoditization.

Caste capitalism is a concept that is finding purchase in a growing number of critical contexts, which I also reference below. Here, I derive *caste capitalism* from Cedric Robinson's "racial capitalism" (Robinson 1983) as a means of undoing the idea of sexuality as a scientized aspect of the individual self, privatized and "private," the product of an idea of the body that is hived off from questions of land rights, economic autonomy, and historically contingent iterations of caste categories and relations. I begin by showing how caste capitalism turns on heteronormative, endogamous social reproduction as a system of heritability, with many caveats and "leaks" that cannot fully control sexuality and gender expression, even as it imposes the violence of biometric surveillance (Rao and Nair 2019) and compulsory marriage (Basu 2015; John 2021), without necessarily imposing compulsory heterosexuality. Caste capitalism cannot exist without Brahmanical patriarchy's iterations of controlled upper caste female sexuality as the limit of caste purity (Chakravarti 1998). The instability of this system is important to mark as a condition that vests economic subjectivity in male heads of households and the discourse of endogamy (Mitra 2021). Therefore it is a system that, like binary gender, must be policed, iterated, and re/iterated constantly. Within its auspices, there is queerness and gender transgression everywhere, in numerous forms that do not necessarily conform to the rubrics of identity, even as they necessitate creative approaches and limits in dealing with access to administrative legibility, heritability rights, and householding.

Building on this observation, I elaborate the rubric of caste capitalism as a way to read the discourse and histories of caste in India, using the work of Dalit radical scholar Anand Teltumbde as a signal example. The English word *caste* is derived from the Portuguese word *casta*. *Caste* has limited value on its own in describing normative discourses of touch, commensality, marriage and heritability rules that are often referenced by colloquial uses of the term in English. Structuralist ideas of the sacralization of purity and pollution as driving these rules are, by sociologist Janaki Abraham's reckoning, a "mask" and a "cloak" that overlay a materialist set of relations that maintain the status quo (Abraham 2014). These relations are negotiated within and among the thousands of localized forms of caste-based hierarchies throughout South Asia that are better described through terms like *jati*, which can be loosely translated as "type" or a social "category" verging on the notion of "community." For the purposes of my argument here, I focus on the iterative quality of these hierarchies through the language of casteification, a term that has resonances with the concept of racialization without reducing or subsuming the production of caste to that of race. This, too, requires a queer hermeneutic, in order to denaturalize the career of heteronormativity in caste-driven forms of social reproduction. In subsequent sections on endogamy and heritability, I extend the discussion of caste's production in relation to capital by invoking a reading caste capitalism's valuable potential for critiquing the idea of "the global" in queer studies and the transnationalization of queer theory. My argument concludes with a discussion of caste, stigma, and abjection through the lens of sex work, circling back to the queer hermeneutics of caste capitalism, and the ways in which this implicates questions surrounding processual hierarchies of the category of the human. In the following section, I begin by proposing the discursive terrain in which to situate caste capitalism in conjunction with a queer hermeneutic frame.

Queer Hermeneutics of Caste Capitalism

The formation *caste capitalism* provides an interpretive frame that is capacious enough to hold both historical and ongoing iterations of caste and capitalism. Thus conjoined, this language allows us to address the ways in which hiving off an understanding of sexuality from caste and political economy produces disciplinary spaces in which sexuality and gender identity are stripped of their historical and iterative qualities. Caste capitalism signals a multilayered understanding of gender and sexuality as processual categories that are configured and inflected by the dispersal of capitalism and the "casteification" and racialization that this dispersal demands. This is not to say that capitalism "originates" caste and race, though a certain reading of Robinson may draw such a conclusion with respect to the latter. It is to say that, in South Asia, for example, caste and caste-like social formations are very old, but they have had extremely divergent and localized expressions throughout history. In theorizing caste capitalism, the origins and development of caste expand to include charting its transformations under the conditions of colonial extraction and both commercial and industrial capitalism. This means we are as interested in the economic transformations that capitalism manifests, as in the ways in which "contemporary postcolonial capitalism, according to [Sanyal], is not revolutionary, it does not transform pre-capitalism in its own image; in contrast, it often preserves and sometimes creates forms of labour and production that that do not belong in the domain of capital" (Chatterjee 2007: x). If we are interested in centering the economic domain cited here, which is sometimes referred to as the "informal economy" or the space of (non-upper caste) "subalternity," then we are also interested in the late-nineteenth- and early-twentieth-century discursive consolidation of "Hinduism" as a coherent, singular religion with a stable textual tradition and cosmology (Doniger 2009). This is because this consolidation also required modified and renegotiated instantiations of caste-based hierarchies (Sakthidharan 2019) that implicated a host of lifeworlds, including the split between rural and urban life, "traditional versus "modern," and between formal and informal economic domains.

Caste capitalism, then, does not describe a new phenomenon, but proposes a new lens for reading the historical conjunctions, conditions, and ongoing iterations of caste and capitalism as inextricable from one another. My reading of the conjunction of caste and capitalism does not serve to present a more extreme form of oppression via aggregating the respective terms. Rather, caste capitalism, like the relation between racialization and racial capitalism, offers a reading of the ways in which "casteification"—the formation of caste—is inextricable from capitalist extraction and expansion. As a mode of inquiry, caste capitalism sheds light on the current crisis of autocratic, Hindu supremacist governance in India that has been built on the terms of upper caste ontologies and anti-Muslim ethnonationalism. This rhetoric is weaponized alongside a consolidation of Muslim "otherness" via challenges to citizenship, the suppression of political dissent, and the rapid consolidation of wealth. The rapid social consolidation of Hindu nationalism and its subsequent sanction of violence against minorities buttresses wholesale captures of land and mineral wealth, expanding commercial sectors while methodically dismantling the public sector to the point of erasure. Heightened juridical and extra-judicial assaults on intercaste and interfaith marriage have been co-constitutive with these trends, as well as, at this writing, troubling efforts to legalize same-sex marriage in India without challenging jurisprudential support for caste-based endogamy, which I discuss below.

Caste is better understood as a regional phenomenon that mobilizes religious discourse and sentiment, rather than being understood as "religious" per se. This means that caste capitalism does not only impact those subjects marked as "belonging" to Hinduism. At the same time, given the terror that is being waged against Muslims in India under the aegis of Hindu nationalism, it is crucial to emphasize the ways in which Brahmanism has been used to pave over and countermand India's long-standing syncretic traditions, and to mark India's vast Muslim minority as foreigners, invaders, and terrorists. This has been used to justify anti-Muslim violence and murder that draws no state sanction (Ellis-Petersen 2020) and is, if anything, increasingly celebrated (BBC 2023). Looking through the lens of caste capitalism, earlier instances of state sanctioned anti-Muslim violence that are sometimes referred to as "communal riots" (e.g., in Muzzafarnagar in 2013, outside of New Delhi [Singh 2016] or the infamous Gujarat "riots" in 2002 in which more than two thousand Muslims were killed and over one hundred thousand displaced [Jaffrelot 2012] in the northwestern state of Gujarat) can now be read as moments that consolidate "Hindu" identity across caste, while reifying caste as a naturalized form of ethnicity. In the sections that follow, I examine this effort through examples like proposed laws that attempt to criminalize intercaste and interfaith marriage. I also turn my attention to the campaign for "same sex marriage," reading both as discursive nodes that help us comprehend caste capitalism's varied forms in the ongoing iterations of sexuality- and gender-based norms within the contemporary Indian political context. These seemingly divergent attempts to intervene upon the institution of marriage serve to reify normative modes of heritability, Hindu supremacy, and access to land and capital through a recommitment to and reiteration of caste-based hierarchies that track with hierarchies of wealth and impoverishment.

Endogamy and Heritability

If scholarly and literary works on caste, and spaces of anti-caste activism, have consistently framed caste and class as coterminous, the same has not necessarily been true within Marxist academic critiques, the organizing spaces of trade unionism, and the parliamentary left in India. The history of Indian left perspectives on caste is extremely diverse, and ungeneralizable. It has included, but is not limited to, perspectives that relegated caste to "identity" and class to "structure," thereby analytically maintaining a central pillar of hierarchy, enclosure, and extraction by marking caste as a form of inequality that would recede with the end of private property. Again, this claim must be contextualized by the fact that there is no singular "Indian left." In the aftermath of the implementation of recommendations to expand affirmative action quotas for lower caste groups in university admissions and government employment in 1990 (Jaffrelot 2000), for example, Indian left intellectuals and organizations, on the whole, did expand their thinking on questions of caste. The vastness of "the Indian left" includes Maoist (Naxalite), Marxist-Leninist, and Trotskyist orientations, all of which, broadly speaking, have been critical in resisting the kind of enclosure that is also described by "caste capitalism." This resistance has been met with state repression, in the form of arrest and intimidation, often through use of anti-sedition and anti-terrorism laws. The Indian state has also targeted spaces of academic freedom and student organizing in central public universities (JNUTA 2017) in addition to mounting attacks on the independence of the press and judiciary. The urgency of countering these foreclosures institutionally is a call to theorize the workings of power that produce this context and ongoing resistance to it, and a key reason why caste capitalism is in the process of being elaborated in various scholarly literatures (e.g., Hota 2023).

My own development of this concept began[1] in a paper given at the Fifth International Conference on the Unfinished Legacy of Dr. B. R. Ambedkar at the New School for Social Research (Shah 2019), portions of which were later elaborated and published in a briefing for the South African feminist journal *Agenda: Empowering Women for Gender Equity* (Shah 2023). In this briefing, I defined caste capitalism as a relation produced within the Capitalocene, a term that emphasizes the ways in which the Age of Man (the Anthropocene) can be understood as the Age of Capital (Ruccio 2011; Haraway 2015; Moore 2015; Malm and Hornborg 2014):

"I use the term "caste capitalism", inspired by "racial capitalism", to describe the uneven distribution of the effects of "the Capitalocene" on landless lower caste agricultural workers. This situation concerns gender-based inequality inasmuch it implicates other forms of social hierarchy, including those of casteism and the re/production of caste-based social categories. (Shah 2023)

Elaborating upon this definition and drawing from long-standing research on the imbrications and intersections of class and caste, I propose that binary gender and endogamous heteronormative householding are of importance in facilitating casteification and enclosure, and are indispensable to reproducing social and material capital, including the ownership and heritability of movable and immovable property. Far from being a hermetically sealed system of regulated reproduction within a predefined social category, I understand endogamy here in quotidian terms, as a system that is constantly made, broken, and remade. Kornberg references the quotidian in defining casteification as "a term that indicates the mundane practices through which casted actors, groups, and structures are produced" (Kornberg 2019: 49). In this definition, Kornberg also cites a 1989 paper on everyday practices of caste differentiation among Goan Christian women in India (Ifeka 1989). Work on the shifting boundaries of caste-based categories and their relation with class mobility is too vast to summarize adequately here (e.g., Gidwani 2008, Abraham 2014, Chowdhry 1994, Rajaram 2021). As I discuss below, shifting the boundaries of caste-based categories is important for understanding the possibilities for queer life in diverse economic and social worlds, as well as understanding the ways in which the boundaries of social norms are policed, porous, and historically contingent. Understood through this lens, caste capitalism shows how forms of existence that mimic juridical autonomy through familial sanction are being accumulated in India among the few, by centering the history, production, and re/iteration of binary gender identity and heteronormativity in relation to land rights and economic autonomy. This reading of caste capitalism builds upon scholarship that figures caste as a system of violent extremes, especially for cisgender women, while asking not only what caste represses, but also what it produces. This necessitates unpacking how caste capitalism represents a set of contingencies that iterate abjection, privation, privilege, and power, and how these turn on the porosity of endogamy and heteronormativity.

The discursive relation between the preservation of caste-based categories and endogamous social reproduction is uncontroversial in scholarly understandings of how caste is re/produced. This relation has been at the heart of anti-caste and feminist critiques that expose how caste hierarchies are enforced through controlling women's sexuality. Dr. B. R. Ambedkar, perhaps India's most famous Dalit intellectual, author of India's constitution and a founder of Indian anti-caste and anti-caste discrimination movements, argued that endogamy was at the heart of maintaining caste, and advocated for intercaste marriage as a way to end caste-based categories, and therefore, hierarchies. In a 2014 article on the permeability and contingency of endogamy in the production of caste and the ways caste-based categories change over time, sociologist Janaki Abraham references historical critiques of endogamy in arguments advocating the abolition of caste:

> Critics of caste such as E[.] V[.] Ramasami Naikar (Geetha and Rajadurai 1998; Dirks 1996) and B[.] R[.] Ambedkar ([1936] 2004) saw endogamy at the heart of caste and stressed that inter-caste marriage was one way of ridding India of caste. This image of caste with endogamy as its central principle is not only shared by those who seek to maintain caste and those who have sought to destroy it. In both popular and scholarly understandings, endogamy (and hypergamy) are presented as defining features of caste. (Abraham 2014: 56)

Abraham argues that the much-critiqued Dumontian ideal of caste as an ahistorical, stable hierarchy that "characterizes" Indian society in turn activates an immutable reading of endogamy. She also argues that endogamy maintains caste through the control of women's sexuality, citing Uma Chakravarti's work on Brahmanical patriarchy (Chakravarti 1993) and on gender, caste, and labor (Chakravarti 1995). Drawing from Chakravarti's work, Abraham argues for a cross-caste concept of "caste patriarchy."

Uma Chakravarti describes the workings of Brahmanical patriarchy in her work on Pandita Ramabai, a young Brahmin woman who was widowed and went on to become one of the most important social reformers of mid-nineteenth-century colonial India (Chakravarti 1998). Ramabai's role in advocating for the emancipation of women and for wider access to education went against Brahamanical codes of propriety for widowed Brahmin women, who were expected to retire permanently from any mode of public life after the death of their husbands, including injunctions against remarriage. Chakravarti shows that it was not only Brahmins who sought to sequester widows from public view, but people of lower castes as well, who saw adopting Brahmanical social mores as aspirational. Lower caste people adopting such mores was met with fierce opposition from Brahmins in the nineteenth century who actively tried to prevent the adoption of Brahamanical injunctions against widow remarriage among non-Brahmins.

> As noted earlier, the Prabhus whom the Peshwa regarded as unfit for the higher status they were seeking, were also prohibited from enforcing a ban on the remarriage of widows because this would establish their case for high status equivalent to that of the Brahmanas. In Brahmanical patriarchy the relationship between caste and gender is crucial: ultimately the degree to which the sexuality of women is controlled is the degree to which a caste group is regarded as maintaining the purity of blood and can thereby establish its claims to be regarded as high. (Chakravarti 1998: 17)

This situation has changed in the contemporary right-wing Hindu dispensation, where the idea of Hinduism is actively being consolidated in upper caste and Brahmanical terms across castes and tribes, catalyzing, in turn, an oppositional idea of Muslims as terrorists and colonial invaders (e.g., see Bhushan 2021 for anti-Muslim citizenship laws and protests against these proposed laws.) However, this does not change the fact that "caste patriarchy" maintains caste-based categories as ideal types even as the boundaries of endogamy shift, sometimes idiosyncratically, sometimes categorically. These shifts include transgressive heterosexual "love marriages" (the colloquial term for a marriage negotiated by the couple themselves and not the families) that are unsanctioned, as well as queer and transgender transgressions that I discuss below. Abraham describes shifting parameters of endogamy for some upper and dominant caste groups in the southern state of Kerala, and that these have precedents elsewhere. She cites Beteille, for example, who "points out in relation to Tamil brahmins, the horizons of endogamy have expanded from sub-subcaste to sub-caste and to caste ([Beteille] 1996: 164)" (Abraham 2014: 58). Beteille here refers to shifting "horizons of endogamy" among *jatis* (sub-castes, or local caste and caste-like formations) and among broad categories of caste. Abraham also describes the shifting boundaries of non-endogamous marriages that are tolerated and accepted by families, as well as pointing out that hypergamy—women marrying men of a higher caste—is a form of non-endogamy that is built into the shifting definitions of caste-based categories (58). Abraham cites Chowdhry in describing changes in the bounds of acceptable hypergamy with changes in property and the desire for upward mobility, which delimited the possibility of hypergamy in the postcolonial period, whereas it had been accepted during British colonial rule (Chowdhry 1994). The elasticity of endogamy and hypergamy, Abraham and other feminist scholars note, is unevenly distributed. They cite the fact that lower caste women were historically tied to feudal relations of power that included being required to be sexually available to landlords (Rege 2003), while being bound to uncompromising relations of caste capitalism and endogamous marriage rules.

The relations of gender-caste-land-capital[2] here open up the possibility for a queer hermeneutic of caste capitalism in two ways. First, a queer hermeneutic illuminates how heteronormativity is produced and maintained through caste capitalism's work to interpolate issues like heritability rights and dowry within agreed-upon rules about acceptable marriage partners. Janaki Abraham, for example, discusses honor killings committed by male siblings against sisters who could retain property rights that would otherwise be theirs if not for the marriages that their sisters enter into. Some of these marriages could technically be thought of as violating caste endogamy, because they are defined as cross-cousin marriages in which women can make a claim to ancestral property (Abraham 2014). The second possibility for a queer hermeneutic of caste capitalism requires grappling with a new juridical discourse of queer and transgender subjectivity that at points has explicitly aligned itself with the project of upholding caste in the wake of the decriminalization of homosexuality in India in 2018 (Mandal 2018).

The juridical discourse of queer and transgender subjectivity I reference here pertains to advocacy for new possibilities for queer and transgender legibility in India. These have included advocacy around affirmative action in employment and education for transgender people, and subsequent debates regarding which specific categories of transgender identity would have access to these quotas, and whether a specific category of caste-based affirmative action, known as "reservations," would apply. These debates have pitted variously positioned transgender and gender non-conforming groups against one another, while raising the question of whether, in effect, some transgender categories will now function as "intermediate caste" categories that are neither upper caste nor Dalit (CLPR 2018) for the purposes of social welfare programs. The second domain of critique surrounds intra-movement debates regarding efforts to win legalized gay marriage in India. For example, aspects of the 2023 campaign for gay marriage in India were criticized for their refusal to engage with the thirty-day provision of the Special Marriage Act, a law that requires intercaste and interfaith couples to post a public notice in a local magistrate's office for thirty days prior to marriage, in case there should be any objections. The law effectively protects the rights of family and kin networks over those of couples, favoring couples who have familial support. For cisgender queer and transgender people, even if "gay marriage" were passed, only those with family sanction could access it. (Same sex marriage in India, at this writing, is being argued as a provision that should be included in the Special Marriage Act, but without challenging the thirty-day notice.) A 2023 report produced by the National Network of LBI (Lesbian, Bisexual, Intersex) Women and Trans Persons ("The Network") argued that there is a continuum between honor killings that police intercaste and interfaith marriages and the violence that queer and transgender people face within their natal families. The levels of violence faced by queer couples who are also intercaste invariably reference class as well:

> The ideology of the endogamous heterosexual marriage arranged by the family fuels natal family violence in both situations. A deeper analysis of the intersection of caste, community and sexuality is required to understand the particular intensity of the violence directed at queer/ trans couples who come from different religions and castes. Sexual othering always deploys class, caste and community and in certain contexts queer couples are acceptable if it can be sufficiently distanced from one's own class, caste and community. . . . The intersectionalities of sexualities and faith and caste particularly in the case of intercaste and interfaith queer relationships argues for a stronger and safer Special Marriages Act for couples which revisits the requirements of the notice period and domicile. (PUCL and National Network of LBI Women and Trans Persons 2023: 143–45)

Because caste, class, and capital are so entwined, we can think of caste as the shifting outline of how capital is accessed. As queer and transgender politics and debates develop through the post-2018 era of decriminalized homosexuality, they will inevitably test and elaborate the ways in which caste capitalism produces new accommodations and limitations within normative endogamy.

The Myth of Timelessness

The myth of caste as a timeless phenomenon is a defining feature in galvanizing the forces of Hindu nationalism, driven by the ideology of Hindutva that began to be articulated at the turn of the twentieth century (Chaturvedi 2022). Hindutva's version of Hinduism as a millennia-long tradition interrupted by Mughal rule is deeply dependent upon caste as we understand it today as a central feature of the Hindu tradition. Ironically, Hindutva is appropriating mid-twentieth-century anthropological arguments of caste as the defining feature of India, derived from Orientalist notions of the immanence of Eastern social hierarchy.[3] This version of caste, like any social category, requires a great deal of labor and social reinforcement in order to be continuously reproduced. The twenty-first-century production of caste in this Brahmanical image offers an acceptable rational for contemporary Islamophobic violence and the disenfranchisement of Muslims. If caste capitalism explains why caste and class track with one another so closely, stigma helps to explain how casteism is practiced and maintained by people of all castes in the present.

Since the seventeenth century, caste has been of foundational interest to the development of political theory and the social sciences, comprising a central object of Orientalist and Indological philology. While there have been varying anthropological views on caste, most mid-twentieth-century anthropologists and sociologists, and their Indological ancestors, agreed that caste was a signifier of tribalism and connoted premodern structures of selfhood. The existence of caste was taken as proof of a persistent lack of individuation and individual reason in non-Western, coeval subjects (Uberoi, Deshpande, and Sundar, 2007). The drone-like functionalism that characterized caste had variants among them, from Hocartian theories of the primacy of warrior castes and kings over Brahmin priests (Hocart 1950), to Dumont's idea of caste as a state of mind and a unique form of social stratification and inequality (Dumont 1970). All generally agreed that caste was a sign of an earlier stage of human social development, and that "the caste system," like the non-Western world that was its progenitor, had remained basically unchanged for centuries.

That caste has changed dramatically over the centuries is a fairly uncontroversial statement in historical terms. In Ancient India, caste was a mode of social organization that seems to have been akin to a guild system. The Arthashastra, a text on statecraft dated between the second century BCE and the third century CE, includes a short passage on taxation concerning sex workers in a manner that looks as though sex workers were a guild-based caste, or a caste-based guild (Shah 2014). The idea of caste-based occupations and their relationship with wider social organization were inevitably shaped by the various forms of local governance that were practiced throughout South Asia over time (Dirks 1996). These forms of governance were regionally specific throughout South Asian history, up to and including the early twentieth century. Part of the post-independence project of Indian nationalism in the late 1940s and 1950s was to try to regularize an extremely diverse and localized set of practices, categories, and modes of legal recognition based on caste, class, and language that varied widely across post-partition India, where there remained territory within the boundaries of "India" that had yet to accede to the new national dispensation. By the time of Indian independence and the partition of India and Pakistan in 1947, the definition of caste as an unchanging form of stratification was fairly familiar. Anand Teltumbde cites it as follows:

> Caste, as such, is a form of social stratification involving a mode of hierarchically arranged, closed endogamous strata, membership to which is ascribed by descent and between which contact is restricted and mobility impossible. The [North] Indian word for caste is *jati*. When we refer to "caste", we really speak of *jati*, although many tend to confuse it with *varna*, which refers to the basic "classes", four in number, established in Hindu scripture. (Teltumbde 2010: 12)

However, as Teltumbde goes on to explain, historical change, contemporaneous regional variation, and the innumerable forms that caste has assumed over time, all undermine the stability of caste as a singular, historically, and socially inflexible "system" that is uniformly applied throughout India. The variability of caste-based access to land and other forms of capital increasingly elicits a violent normative response that engenders yet newer iterations of caste-based hierarchies. One example is the violent 1990 protests by upper caste students in response to the government implementing the recommendations of the Mandal Commission Report, which would expand reservations in college and university admissions, and in a range of government jobs, for lower caste groups (Jaffrelot 2000).

> The commonplace understanding of the caste system as having held Indian society in fossilized form for over two millennia is therefore not quite correct. While it is accurate so far as the broad varna framework is concerned, the castes within this framework have been fluid. Many new castes were formed and many have disappeared; many split up and many merged with others over time in response to local political and economic demands. (Teltumbde 2010: 15)

For our purposes here, the most important aspect of this perspective on caste is how it undermines the idea that caste is like a single tree with myriad branches, unchanged for millennia. Teltumbde argues to the contrary that the violence and brutality of caste has actually intensified since 1947. In *The Persistence of Caste*, Teltumbde offers a social history of the horrific 2006 murders of four members of a Dalit family in the village of Khair-lanji, in the Western Indian state of Maharashtra. The term *Dalit* means "downtrodden" or "oppressed" and is used by people who belong to India's so-called "untouchable" or "lowest" castes as a signifier of a politicized posi-tion against caste-based oppression. This is an originating space of anti-caste movements. In Khairlanji, the Dalit Bhotmange family was beaten, tortured, mutilated, and murdered by local people who were of an "interme-diate" caste (OBC, or Other Backward Caste, in official parlance). They were of a slightly higher caste but still classified as "lower caste," and apparently harbored resentment that this family of Dalits were accumulating wealth and status commensurate with their own. Teltumbde argues that, while casteism has historically been characterized by what he terms "crimes of contempt," *atrocities* like those that took place in Khairlanji are, in historical terms, relatively new. He cites changing land distribution policies in the post-independence era, as well as the rise of the Hindu Right "vote bank pol-itics,"[4] as major factors in the rise of this kind of caste-based violence, rather than seeing intercaste violence as somehow inevitable (Teltumbde 2010).

> There is also a difference between the nature of atrocities earlier and now. Previously they were committed as an integrated part of the interaction between savarnas and avarnas, and hence tended to be casual, more humil-iating than injurious. Today, they are far more violent, more physically destructive and more brutal than before. Earlier caste violence was mostly committed by individuals in a fit of rage. Now it is carried out collectively, in a loosely planned manner, as a spectacle of demonstrative justice. (Tel-tumbde 2010: 3)

It is difficult to overstate the threat that this kind of critique poses to the for-mation and aims of the current state. At this writing, Teltumbde was released from prison on bail several months ago, after having been arrested and imprisoned in a sweep of activists and advocates working within Dalit radical and tribal politics, in a case known as Elgar Parishad (Prasanna 2021). The potency of this critique is in showing the ways in which caste *adapts* within and in relation to the political economy of its era. Teltumbde's oeuvre is foundational for thinking with caste capitalism because of its clear view of caste and capitalism as explicitly linked in the politics of land and wealth redistribution. This is commensurate with the field of the study of caste as a whole, which can also be characterized as always already conjoin-ing caste and class, if not capital. This critique has taken a variety of forms, and is characterized by a number of key defining tensions, including the charge that spaces of left intellectualism are bourgeois, upper caste, and male, with arguments that are sometimes reinforced by the stage-ist notion that once class-based oppression falls, all other forms of social hierarchy will follow suit.[5] Another key tension animating the field is that between "representation" and "production" of forms of unfree and exploited labor. In 2003, historian Anupama Rao, in synthesizing the literature on gender and caste in her foundational edited collection on these themes, characterized this tension as being between critiques of "representation" and "dispossession." (Rao 2003: 15)

I will return to these tensions in the context of queer Marxist critique in the concluding section of this article. In the section below, I elaborate the problematic of caste-based stigma that animates this tension, providing a crucial affective mechanism that maps boundaries of different *jatis*. Stigma, and its lack, are foundational to the ways that caste-based distinctions are maintained in contemporary life. This is happening amid ongoing efforts to ban interfaith marriages (Sinha 2021) and to rescript marriages between Muslim men and Hindu women as "Love Jihad" (Rao 2011) and, in the process, to cast Muslim men as dangerous to Hindu women. These efforts to legislate caste-based endogamy are situated upon a continuum that necessarily includes the reification of heteronormative marriage, despite calls for legalizing gay marriage in the wake of the decriminalization of homosexuality in 2018.

Queer Hermeneutics, Stigma, and Processual Hierarchies

Along with referencing the spaces of queer non-cisnormative gender expression, and "leaky" heteronormative endogamy, it becomes necessary to mention sex work as another area in which caste norms are routinely, temporarily, transgressed. In my book *Street Corner Secrets: Sex, Work and Migration in the City of Mumbai* (Shah 2014), I focused on the solicitation of clients for paid and traded sexual services. In discussing spaces of solicitation that were semi-secret, I narrated conflicts that took place between lower caste and tribal women at a street corner that served as a public day-wage labor market in Mumbai. The fact that women solicited sexual services from this space was an open secret, but a secret, nonetheless. Women of different caste groups regularly berated one another for being indiscrete with contractors, or simply accused one another of allowing male contractors to have sex in exchange for paid work, a phenomenon that I termed "sex for work" (Ibid. 2014: 78). These accusations were usually deployed by relatively more upper caste women against more lower caste women, or by Dalits against tribal women ("adivasis"). In this vein, Dalit women regularly accused adivasi women of being sex workers and taking paid work that they felt was rightfully theirs. This dynamic resonated with dynamics in brothels and in the Indian sex workers' rights movement, which evinced their own hierarchies. These hierarchies are manifested in these spaces, but hardly originate there, reflecting hierarchies that are widely dispersed, and maintained through discourses of stigma inasmuch as they are through contact rules, violence, and gendered economic subjectivity, for example. Sex workers of all genders are far more stigmatized for selling sexual services than are their clients for buying them. While much of the prevailing discussion on sex work has focused on the juridical debates (on whether and how sex work should be de/criminalized), these debates cannot stand in for a critique of stigma, respectability, harm, survival, and caste. Such a critique of stigma must also account for the fact that because selling and trading sexual services is done as mode of economic survival among the very poor, it is primarily (but not exclusively) people from non–upper caste backgrounds who earn all or part of their living from selling sexual services.

In India, the debate on sex work and caste is fraught, because the claim that many women who sell sex are Dalit and tribal invokes the history of the sexual assault of lower caste women by the rural landowners whose land lower caste peasants have historically worked as bonded laborers and sharecroppers. As in the era of chattel slavery in the United States, when enslaved women were routinely raped and assaulted by white slave owners, the history of sexual assault and brutalization experienced by Dalit women is not remote, and is invoked readily in feminist debates on sex work. The kernel of this debate is a question about the role of history. If Dalit women in India were historically the objects of sexual assault by upper caste landowners, then what does the significant presence of Dalit and other lower caste women among the ranks of sex workers mean today? How would this historical context shape our response to sexual commerce? This problematic is salient in showing how analytic frames collapse around questions of sexuality. If sex work is one answer to the problem of poverty, then the question moves from what it means for Dalit women to do sex work, given the historical context of upper caste landowners sexually assaulting Dalit women, to include what it means to relegate the entire population of lower caste and tribal people in India to the status of subsistence, to eking out survival in the economic spaces of informality, where there are fewer and fewer resources to go around?

Indian scholarly debates on caste and sexuality have addressed some of these questions through discussions of the uses of honor (*izzat*), and the confluence of "degradation" (as external, objective) and humiliation (as internal, subjective) (Guru 2011: 28). This literature deals less with "stigma" than with "humiliation" and "honor," in part because the history of dealing with stigma has tended toward critiques of access to mental health services (Kleinman and Hall-Clifford 2009). In the US, for example, "stigma" has become a sociological tool used for measuring access to university admissions, or certain kinds of employment. This literature has focused less on stigma as *producing* or re-iterating race, racialization, or "types" of persons, and more on the effects of stigma on the individual psyche. Considering critiques of humiliation, such as Gopal Guru's, as well as V. Geetha's critique of abjection in the same volume, are important in seeing stigma as a materialist concern that, in this case, collides with the trope of caste. Of the production of caste-based abjection, V. Geetha notes, "These fictions of the caste imagination do not merely damn the Dalit, like racial myths damn the black-skinned. Rather they construct the Dalit as an expendable negative other, who is also wholly necessary" (V. Geetha 2011: 98). This "expendable negative other" is Julia Kristeva's (1982) definition of abjection, where the abjected other is not separate from the non-abjected self but is required for the continued production of that self. This "other" in V. Geetha's formulation is also surplus labor, the Gramscian subalterns of left historiography. In the figure of the Dalit sex worker, the stigma of sex work, the abjection of caste and the surplus of labor that is commensurate with uneven accumulation converge. And yet, Dalit sex workers survive, not because they are particularly "free" or "heroic" but because elaborating these constraints does not point toward the impossibility of survival; it analyzes how everyday life is waged, and in which caste is re/produced in relation to the elasticity of regulations of sexuality and gender expression. Gopal Guru, in his introduction to his edited volume on humiliation, explains this in relation to the social mechanisms by which humiliation is generated, and in the process, elaborates the context for V. Geetha's gesture toward abjection:

> Transgression of the boundaries between the private and the public was considered as the context for humiliation (Habermas 1991: 39). Secondly, the capacity to control the corporeal body (both male and female) in the public domain defines individual dignity and 'decency of the bourgeois society (ibid.). (Guru 2011: 1)

These arguments ultimately reference the hierarchical problematics of the category of humanity, in a mode that is resonant with racialization, but not equivalent to it. Because these arguments elaborate casteificiation, they necessarily focus on the spatialization of material dispossession through social stratification.

Conclusion

In this article, I have discussed the productive possibilities for a reading of caste, sexuality, gender identity, and land rights in India using caste capitalism. This is one approach to theorizing caste capitalism, which is in the process of being articulated in light of the changing political economy of land rights (Hota 2023), sexuality politics (Rao 2020; Rao 2024), and caste politics per se (Arondekar 2022; Yengde 2019). The argument I have developed here is inspired by the productive capacities of racial capitalism, while insisting on a queer hermeneutic that is routed through historical and historiographical referents that can account for the production of caste through anti-capitalist and feminist critique in South Asia. Racial capitalism has already had many lives and interpretations, as does any generative theory. Many of those interpretations, especially of late, use it to demonstrate the brutality of both capitalism and racism, and the fundamental of role enslaved labor and the transatlantic slave trade in the processes of industrialization and the birth of capitalism. By the same token, a few recent uses of "caste capitalism" perform similar work, using each term to enhance the marginalizing force of the other, particularly with reference to the brutality of each system as experienced by those at bottom of each hierarchy. Here, I have referenced the violence of the re/iterations of caste as physical violence against marriage and commensality, as well as marking the violence of caste as that of economic exclusion, played out in differential access to health care, nutrition, and stable formal sector employment. These "iterations of violence" matter because they consolidate lower casteness and untouchability as grounds for social and economic exclusion.

I have proposed that racial capitalism and caste capitalism both offer a valuable interpretive lens to unravel processes of racialization and casteification that cannot be separated from questions of sexuality, gender identity, and political economy. This is not to say that there is a particular, localized, "culturally specific" brand of queer critique that should be thought of as "South Asian." It is to emphasize historical referents within unique discursive contexts that support a given queer hermeneutic, and to question why the flow of academic critique seems to go North to South, but not in the reverse, within queer studies, with a number of notable exceptions (e.g., Macharia 2019). Given the relatively robust history of leftist organizing and spaces in the Global South, particularly in comparison to the ways in which Marxist critique and socialism were marginalized and suppressed in the US (Daulatzai 2012), it behooves us to think with the centrality that critiques of political economy have had in Southern academia, including in queer and gender studies. Differences in regimes of administrative legibility between India and the West also raise interesting issues for thinking with abjected and abnormal embodiment, especially in the context of queer recognition and India's new regime of compulsory, universal biometric identification (Rao and Nair 2019) that is tied with patrilineal householding and legibility.

The stakes of materialist critique using a queer hermeneutic frame are fairly high at this point in time, particularly as queer and transgender scholarship on and from the Global South expands in scope and reach. In India, this is a moment in which bourgeois, urban, upper caste, cisgender queer subjects are being reified as national subjects along with narrowly defined members of a "traditional" "third gender." This is happening in the context of the rise of Hindu nationalist majoritarianism that is consolidating Hindu vote banks through the rhetoric of anti-Muslim eugenicism, while proposing a slate of laws seeking to strip Indian Muslims of citizenship rights (Bhushan 2021). The homonationalist overtones of the uses of queer legibility are unmistakable, as Hindu nationalism shores up its legitimacy, invoking a narrative of national economic progress and Hinduism as a religion of tolerance. At the same time, questions of survival in informal economies, rural development, and the protection of minority rights are further marginalized, while the uses of anti-terrorism and anti-sedition laws expand toward a wholesale crackdown on activism, advocacy, and journalism. The importance of discourses of queer progress within these rhetorical shifts cannot be overstated, especially in the wake of the 2018 Supreme Court decision to decriminalize sodomy. The appropriation of queer individual rights by majoritarian rhetoric is ironic given that, since the early 1990s, queer social movements in India LGBTQI+ and autonomous feminist social movements have been sites of resistance against these forces, and against the notion that "real" queerness in India is urban, English speaking, elite, and upper caste. Addressing this problematic here has entailed taking up the question of the "transnational travels of queer of color critique" and offering a perspective on the possibilities of caste capitalism, both for a queer hermeneutic of caste and class and as a new lens on a very long-standing set of debates and histories of how caste and capitalism come to be, how they are weaponized, and how they continue to operate as sites of struggle.

Notes

The author would like to offer sincere thanks to Rana Jaleel and Evren Savcı for the invitation to contribute to this special issue and for critical feedback on this piece, to Inderpal Grewal and Chitra Ganesh for invaluable suggestions on earlier drafts, and to Prisha Dayal for editorial support. All shortcomings remain my own.

1   This term was also developed in a transnational context within a Law and Society Association sponsored International Research Collaboration (IRC) organized by myself and Rahul Rao. The IRC was framed within the rubric of Sexuality, Political Economy and the Law, and organized four panels over 2021 and 2022 during the annual Law and Society Association meetings. See https://www.lawandsociety.org/lsairc08/.

2   On this relation of gender-caste-land, also see Ramaswamy (2022).

3   These claims were often based on readings of Indian ancient texts, the search of which was conducted in a similar vein as looking for a textual tradition like that which exists for the "revealed" religions of the Levant. Orientalist notions of caste were attached to a reading of the Manusmriti ("Manu's book" or "the Book of Manu"). The Manusmriti was one of first ancient Hindu texts translated into English by renowned Sanskrit scholar William Jones, in 1794, as part of British efforts to look for a local, "traditional" basis for colonial governance (Dinkar 2017).

4   "Vote bank politics" are efforts to garner votes based on "banks" of people that are seen to be of the same social category. The rise of the Hindu Right in India has been facilitated by differential treatment of various social groups, such that larger numbers of lower caste and tribal groups are supporting Hindu Right candidates as part of a consolidation of majoritarian "Hindu" identity.

5   An article on these tensions reports the following retort in a conversation between the upper caste leftist author of the piece and his friend, an Ambedkarite (anti-caste activist working in the tradition of Dr. B. R. Ambedkar): "You communists, just how many Dalits are there in your leadership? Your leaders lead a life of luxury even as you people send innocent tribal youth to die at the hands of the paramilitary. . . . Dalits do not need people like you; we can fight for our rights without support from the upper castes."

References

Abraham, Janaki. 2014. "Contingent Caste Endogamy and Patriarchy: Lessons for Our Understanding of Caste." *Economic & Political Weekly* 49, no. 2: 56–65.

Ambedkar, B. R. 2018 [1936]. *The Annihilation of Caste*. New Delhi: Rupa Publications.

Arondekar, Anjali. 2022. "Go (Away) West!" *GLQ: A Journal of Lesbian and Gay Studies* 28, no. 3: 463–71.

BBC. 2023. "Naroda Gam Massacre: India Court Acquits All Accused in 2002 Gujarat Riots Case." *BBC*, April 21. https://www.bbc.com/news/world-asia-india-65334381.

Bajpai, Vikas. 2017. "The Continuing Debate on the 'Annihilation of Caste': Understanding Tensions Between Ambedkarites and Communists." *Social Change* 47, no. 2: 1–18. https://doi.10.1177/0049085717696383.

Basu, Srimati. 2015. *The Trouble with Marriage: Feminists Confront Law and Violence in India*. Oakland: University of California Press.

Béteille, André. 1990. "Race, Caste and Gender." *Man* 25, no. 3: 489–504.

Béteille, André. 1996. "Caste in Contemporary India." In *Caste Today*, edited by C J Fuller, 150-179. Delhi: Oxford University Press.

Bhushan, Bharat. 2021. "Citizens, Infiltrators, and Others: The Nature of Protests against the Citizenship Amendment Act." *South Atlantic Quarterly* 120, no. 1: 201–8.

Chakravarti, Uma. 1993. "Conceptualising Brahmanical Patriarchy in Early India: Gender, Caste, Class and State." *Economic & Political Weekly* 27, no. 14: 579–85.

Chakravarti, Uma. 1995. "Gender, Caste and Labour: Ideological and Material Structure of Widowhood." *Economic & Political Weekly* 30, no. 36: 579–85.

Chakravarti, Uma. 1998. *Rewriting history: The Life and Times of Pandita Ramabai.* New Delhi: Kali for Women.

Chatterjee, Partha. 2007. "Foreword." In *Rethinking Capitalist Development: Primitive Accumulation, Governmentality, and Postcolonial Capitalism*, by Kalyan Sanyal, ix–xiii. New Delhi: Routledge Press.

Chaturvedi, Vinayak. 2022. *Hindutva and Violence: V. D. Savarkar and the Politics of History.* New Delhi: Permanent Black.

Chowdhry, Prem. 1994. *The Veiled Women: Shifting Gender Equations in Rural Haryana 1880–1990.* New Delhi: Oxford University Press.

CLPR (Centre for Law and Policy Research). 2018. "Policy Brief: Making Rights Real Implementing Reservations for Transgender & Intersex Persons in Education and Public Employment." Bangalore, India. https://clpr.org.in/wp-content/uploads/2018/12/Policy-Brief-2018-Implementing-Reservations-for-Transgender-and-Intersex-Persons.pdf.

Daultatzai, Sohail. 2012. *Black Star, Crescent Moon: The Muslim International and Black Freedom Beyond America.* Minneapolis: University of Minnesota Press.

Dinkar, Niharika. 2017. "The 'New Conquering Empire of Light and Reason': The Civilizing Mission of William Jones." In *Light in a Socio-Cultural Perspective*, edited by Ruth Lubashevshy and Ronit Milano, 33–48. Newcastle upon Tyne: Cambridge Scholars Publishing.

Dirks, Nicholas B. 1996. "Recasting Tamil Society: The Politics of Caste and Race in Contemporary Southern India." In *Caste Today*, edited by C. J. Fuller, 263–95. New Delhi: Oxford University.

Doniger, Wendy. 2009. *The Hindus: An Alternative History.* New York: Penguin Press.

Dumont, Louis. 1970. *Homo Hierarchicus: The Caste System and Its Implications.* Chicago: University of Chicago Press.

Ellis-Petersen, Hannah. 2020. "Inside Delhi: beaten, lynched and burnt alive." *The Guardian*, March 1. https://www.theguardian.com/world/2020/mar/01/india-delhi-after-hindu-mob-riot-religious-hatred-nationalists.

Eng, David, and Jasbir Puar. 2020. "Introduction: Left of Queer." *Social Text* 38, no. 4: 1–23.

Ferguson, Roderick. 2004. *Aberrations in Black: Towards a Queer of Color Critique.* Minneapolis: University of Minnesota Press.

Gidwani, V. 2008. *Capital Interrupted: Agrarian Development and the Politics of Work in India.* Minneapolis: University of Minnesota Press.

Goel, Ina. 2019. "India's Third Gender Rises Again." *Sapiens*, September 26. https://www.sapiens.org/biology/hijra-india-third-gender/.

Guru, Gopal. 2011. "Introduction: Theorizing Humiliation." In *Humiliation: Claims and Contexts*, edited by Gopal Guru, 1–22. New Delhi: Oxford University Press.

Habermas, Jürgen. 1991. *The Structural Transformation of the Public Sphere.* Cambridge: MIT Press.

Haraway, Donna. 2015. "Anthropocene, Capitalocene, Plantationocene, Chthulucene: Making Kin." *Environmental Humanities* 6, no. 1: 159–65.

Hocart, A. M. 1950. *Caste: A Comparative Study.* London: Methuen and Co. Ltd.

Hota, Pinky. 2023. *The Violence of Recognition: Adivasi Indigeneity and Anti-Dalitness in India.* Philadelphia: University of Pennsylvania Press.

Ifeka, Caroline. 1989. "Hierarchical Woman: The 'Dowry' System and Its Implications among Christians in Goa, India." *Contributions to Indian Sociology* 23, no. 2: 261–84.

Jaffrelot, Christopher. 2000. "Sanskritization vs. Ethnicization in India: Changing Identities and Caste Politics before Mandal." *Asian Survey* 40, no. 5: 756–66.

Jaffrelot, Christopher. 2012. "Gujarat 2002: What Justice for the Victims? The Supreme Court, the SIT, the Police and the State Judiciary." *Economic and Political Weekly* 47, no. 8: 77–89.

JNUTA. 2017. *What the Nation Really Needs to Know: The JNU Nationalism Lectures.* New Delhi: HarperCollins.

John, Mary. 2021. *Child Marriage in an International Frame: A Feminist Review from India.* New Delhi: Routledge India.

Kleinman, Arthur, and Rachel Hall-Clifford. 2009. "Stigma: A Social, Cultural and Moral Process." *Journal of Epidemiology & Community Health* 63, no. 6: 418–19.

Kornberg, Dana. 2019. "From Balmikis to Bengalis: The 'Casteification' of Muslims in Delhi's Informal Garbage Economy." *Economic and Political Weekly* 54, no. 47: 48–54.

Kristeva, Julia. 1982. *Powers of Horror: An Essay on Abjection.* New York: Columbia University Press.

Macharia, Keguro. 2019. *Frottage: Frictions of Intimacy across the Black Diaspora.* New York: NYU Press.

Malm, Andreas, and Alf Hornborg. 2014. "The Geology of Mankind? A Critique of the Anthropocene Narrative." *The Anthropocene Review* 1, no. 1: 62–69. https://doi.org/10.1177/2053019613516291.

Mandal, Saptarshi. 2018. "Section 377: Whose Concerns Does the Judgment Address?" *Economic and Political Weekly* 53, no. 37. https://www.epw.in/sites/default/files/engage_pdf/2018/09/12/152629.pdf.

Mitra, D. 2021. "'Surplus Woman': Female Sexuality and the Concept of Endogamy." *The Journal of Asian Studies* 80, no. 1: 3–26.

Moore, Jason. 2015. *Capitalism in the Web of Life.* New York: Verso Press.

Prasanna, Pooja. 2021. "Bhima Koregaon-Elgar Parishad: A Timeline of Events." *The News Minute*, July 5. https://www.thenewsminute.com/article/bhima-koregaon-elgar-parishad-timeline-events-151798.

PUCL (People's Union of Civil Liberties) and National Network of LBI (Lesbian, Bisexual and Intersex) Women and Trans Persons. 2023. *Apnon Ka Bahut Lagta Hai (Our Own Hurt Us the Most): Centering Familial Violence in the Lives of Queer and Trans Persons in the Marriage Equality Debates.* New Delhi: People's Union of Civil Liberties.https://pucl.org/wp-content/uploads/2023/05/Combined_all_2_compressed.pdf.

Rajaram, Poorva. 2021. *"Normal Prospects of Life": Pensions and Insurance in Colonial India, 1813–1947.* PhD diss., Centre for Historical Studies, Jawaharlal Nehru University.

Ramaswamy, Gita. 2022. *Land, Guns, Caste, Woman: The Memoir of a Lapsed Revolutionary.* New Delhi: Navayana Press.

Rao, Anupama. 2003. "Introduction." In *Gender and Caste*, edited by Anupama Rao, 1–49. New Delhi: Kali for Women.

Rao, Mohan. 2011. "Love Jihad and Demographic Fears." *Indian Journal of Gender Studies* 18, no. 3: 425–30. https://doi.org/10.1177/097152151101800307.

Rao, Rahul. 2020. *Out of Time: The Queer Politics of Postcoloniality*. Oxford, UK: Oxford University Press.

Rao, Rahul. 2024. "Is the Homo in Homocapitalism the Caste in Caste Capitalism and the Racial in Racial Capitalism?" *South Atlantic Quarterly* 123, no. 1.

Rao, Ursula, and Vijayanka Nair. 2019. "Aadhaar: Governing with Biometrics." *South Asia: Journal of South Asian Studies* 42, no. 3: 469–481, https://doi.org/10.1080/00856401.2019.1595343.

Rege, Sharmila. 2003. "A Dalit Feminist Standpoint." In *Gender and Caste*, edited by Anupama Rao, 90-101. New Delhi: Kali.

Robinson, Cedric J. 1983. *Black Marxism: The Making of the Black Radical Tradition*. London: Zed Books.

Ruccio, D. 2011. "Anthropocene—or how the world was remade by capitalism" *Occasional Links & Commentary on Economics, Culture and Society* (blog), March 4. https://anticap.wordpress.com/2011/03/04/anthropocene%E2%80%94or-how-the-world-was-remade-by-capitalism/.

Sakthidharan, A. V. 2019. *Antigod's Own Country: A Short History of the Brahmanical Colonisation of Kerala*. New Delhi: Navayana Press.

Shah, Svati. 2014. *Street Corner Secrets: Sex, Work and Migration in the City of Mumbai*. Durham, NC: Duke University Press.

Shah, Svati. 2019. "Caste Capitalism, Sexuality Politics and Stigma in India: Producing Inequality Through Public Space." Fifth International Conference on the Unfinished Legacy of Dr. B. R. Ambedkar Dalits in Global Context: Rethinking Gender and Religion, New School for Social Research.

Shah, Svati. 2023. "Briefing: Spices, Rivers and Gender: Reviewing the Literature on Climate Change and Exports for a Critique of Caste Capitalism." *Agenda: Empowering Women for Gender Equity* 37, no. 1: 1–7. https://doi.org/10.1080/10130950.2023.2177555.

Singh, Jagpal. 2016. "Communal Violence in Muzaffarnagar: Agrarian Transformation and Politics." *Economic and Political Weekly* 51, no. 31: 94–101.

Sinha, Chinki. 2021. "India's Interfaith Couples on Edge after New Law." *BBC*, March 15. https://www.bbc.com/news/world-asia-india-56330206.

Teltumbde, Anand. 2010. *The Persistence of Caste: The Khairlanji Murders and India's Hidden Apartheid*. London: Zed Books.

Uberoi, Patricia, Satish Deshpande, and Nandini Sundar, eds. 2007. *Anthropology in the East: Founders of Indian Sociology and Anthropology*. Calcutta: Seagull Press.

V. Geetha. 2011. "Bereft of Being: The Humiliations of Untouchability." In *Humiliation: Claims and Contexts*, edited by Gopal Guru, 95–107. New Delhi: Oxford University Press.

V. Geetha, and S. V. Rajadurai. 1998. *Towards a Non-Brahman Millennium*. Calcutta: Samya.

Yengde, Suraj. 2019. *Caste Matters*. Gurgaon: Penguin Press.

Hentyle Yapp

The Ubiquity of Asia:
Cai Guo-Qiang's Fireworks and Spectral Marxism

China supplies 129,000 tons of fireworks to the United States, accounting for 95 percent of the market. In 2019, its value was over $270 billion. One nation in Asia provides the vast majority of the objects used to celebrate mass events, notably the celebration of US independence. This single nation amasses hundreds of billions of dollars through a small, everyday item. Further, a single man primarily manages this global industry. Through his shipping companies, Shanghai Huayang and Firstrans International, Ding Yan Zhong controls 70 percent of the trade. Based out of Southeastern China, Ding exported on average, as of 2019, an estimated seventy-two shipping containers into the US every day. This is not an anomalous story about fireworks; it is rather an emblematic parable for contemporary capital. Considering that the very material used for spectacles, particularly for the celebration of nation-states, is supplied by Chinese capital and logistics, what might this tell us about racial capital today?

Mr. Ding's involvement in the fireworks industry is illustrative of China's and, more broadly, Asia's relationship to capital. Beyond the fireworks industry, China and Asia are central to the global

The South Atlantic Quarterly 123:1, January 2024
DOI 10.1215/00382876-10920696 © 2024 Duke University Press

supply chain. Further, Asia saturates popular culture, as Korean pop, beauty, and dramas and Japanese anime are now not viewed as exotic imports but rather as part of culture at large (Lee 2016; Fung 2013). Put differently, Asia has become a driving force across popular culture and beyond. It feels like Asia is everywhere. Asia is ubiquitous. In the American cycle of capital accumulation, under Giovanni Arrighi's schema, the dominance and overrepresentation of the United States was marked through notions like Disneyfication (Baudrillard 1994) and "the ascendancy of whiteness" (Chow 2002). Through these rubrics, minoritarian and non-Western groups and spaces have routinely come to be measured against the racialized modernity of Western nation-states and according to their *representational proximity* to whiteness. And now under our contemporary Asian cycle of accumulation, this geographic area's affective ubiquity appears much like that of the US by preoccupying global public sentiment.

However, Asia as a region forces us to question if the previous measures that relied on a representational proximity to whiteness and modernity, both anchored by the earlier centers of capital accumulation within Western Europe and the US, can continue to explain racial capital today. Asia's affective intensity and spread emerge across sites like China, South Korea, India, and Japan, among others. Asia's ubiquity indexes how its cultural objects become imports, but its influence also shapes how global industries and cultural tastes operate. Asia's own standards for culture are not simply replacing whiteness but are rather complicating the very terms that have helped us make sense of the world. Asia is not merely redefining the norm, displacing white supremacy for some imagined yellow supremacy. The area does not replace the old symbolic standard to simply become the new one, nor does it merely enter into a supranational frame of other modern nations; instead, we witness its permeation that shifts old ways of functioning. Naoki Sakai astutely names this juncture as "the end of Pax Americana, for the end of the geopolitical order that has been accepted in the last several decades," whereby "in a decade or two, East Asia may well be the center of gravity in the global economy" (2022: 1). For example, many Western media companies continue to primarily cast white entertainers, with a few Asian Americans and other people of color involved. But these companies actively shape their narratives and appeal for the Chinese market, even though production primarily happens in the West (Anderson 2019). The Chinese renminbi, as such, saturates representational demands. In this way, unlike the symbolic and representational force of the US through Disneyfication and the predominance of white norms, Asia's ubiquity does not fully arise through equivalent representational logics. Instead, it affectively shapes how things operate. Thus, how do we discuss the operations of capital today in light of this notion of *affective ubiquity* that is related to yet unique from capital accumulation under the American cycle? At what scale do we engage capital, and what methods exist to track and comprehend capital in this shift toward Asia?

Further, the historic racialization of this area requires that we move beyond a discourse that primarily frames the other as an underrepresented racialized victim toward one that grapples with the other as racialized generators of capital. Asia is not only a site of extreme capital extraction as many (primarily gendered) laborers fuel the production of goods, but also a site of capital accumulation and rampant consumption. Since Asia drives accumulation through both consumption and production, how then do we discuss racialized subjects when they become not solely the compradors or extracted laborers of capital but also its generators and consumers? Asian American studies has identified this change by examining how some within this minoritarian community are coming closer to identifying with majoritarian, capitalist values. Scholars emphasize how the model minority myth continues to predominate with the need to reconcile the past with the future of the field (Chuh 2017; Kang 2014). Asian studies has identified a similar dynamic through what Rey Chow astutely names the figure of the Maoist: those invested in deploying discourses of "lack, subalternity, and victimization . . . often with the intention of spotlighting the speaker's own sense of alterity," which results in "rob[bing] the terms of oppression of their political import" (1993: 13) and ignoring "the power, wealth, and privilege that ironically accumulate from their 'opposition' viewpoint" (17). Beyond Asian and Asian American studies, others have identified a larger trend called elite capture, whereby a marginalized group's interests come to be limited and predominated by the wealthy and elite from such a minoritized group (Táíwò 2022). Another term of art for this dynamic is what Marxists have come to identify as the professional managerial class (Liu 2021). Following these insights, I examine additional avenues to reconsider our notions of the subject as they have related to representation, victimization, and exclusion. Asia as ubiquitous is emblematic of it becoming central to the globe rather than simply the West's particular, Oriental other. By asking us to move away from representationalism and exclusion as primary measures for the racialized subject, I do not ask us to simply celebrate inclusion. Instead, I situate Asian racialization in the past to its present ubiquity. By doing so, this essay explores how we might redefine the subject to shift away from victimization narratives that have become standard for minoritarian discourse. Considering the shift from representational difference toward Asia's affective ubiquity, I explore what type of subject we might need in light of our current cycle of accumulation.

This essay then examines what methods are available to catalyze such a project to rethink our notions of the subject and the racial.

As such, this essay first considers the subject. Marxism offers different notions that situate the figure in relation to the structural to produce a more relational and class-engaged definition of the term. This focus on the structural places us in the "realm of implication: a realm where people are entangled in injustices that fall outside the purview of the law and where the categories into which we like to sort the innocent and the guilty become troubled" (Rothberg 2019: 8). I specifically focus on the figure of the comrade, rather than the proletariat, as the means to make sense of Asian racialization as it shifts from the West's whiteness to Asia's ubiquity, alongside a rethinking of the subject as implicated and relational.

Second, this essay explores the methods available for contending with a shift in our ideas of the subject. Marxism often emphasizes relations through production relying on historical materialism and economic circulation as key methods. Take, for example, fireworks. In the start of this essay, fireworks helped illustrate a shift in accumulation through a methodological approach of historicization and the tracking of commodities. However, fireworks themselves provide another level of analysis to track Asia's ubiquity and to consider the subject in ways that are about spread and affect. Beyond historical materialism, I explore what the aesthetic offers. Some strands of queer of color critique have been developing the aesthetic, with its attention to form and the production of sense, to reconsider our ideas of the subject and the world (Musser 2018; Amin, Musser, and Pérez 2017). The aesthetic is a method that works across multiple scales and offers additional insights that complement political economy. Although the social sciences have provided effective approaches to these questions, alongside critiques of human rights and other social and legal formations, the aesthetic holds a curious place within queer of color critique, racial capitalist discourse, and political economy. This essay is less interested in arguing for the aesthetic's equivalence to or import for the political. Such approaches could be demonstrated by arguing for the aesthetic as a mode of resistance, on one hand, or by using the aesthetic to illustrate the circulation of goods, on the other. Instead, this essay focuses on aesthetic form to further the project of queer of color critique that has been pushing toward modes of aesthetic analysis that do not default into the established logics of politics or political economy. Instead, the aesthetic produces an analytic that helps us shift out of these routinized approaches to the questions raised by racial capitalism.

I thus utilize fireworks to suture the political economic with the aesthetic. This minor object is both a material commodity that circulates and a metaphorical aesthetic that helps us rethink the subject amid changes in capital. Fireworks provide both an analysis of commodity circulation and an aesthetic form to reimagine the subject in relational and structural ways. I specifically examine the practices of Chinese artist Cai Guo-Qiang to ground our approaches to the subject and world. Many artists have been working with fireworks as a medium beyond nationalist pageantry. From Judy Chicago to Ana Mendieta, and Cai to Desmond Lewis, artists deflate the grand sublime of fireworks with minor experimentation. I focus on Cai to situate Asian racialization. More specifically, I engage racial and aesthetic forms akin to Colleen Lye by focusing on "the theoretical generativity of speaking not of identity but of form, of trying to investigate race and nation through the relationship between aesthetic and social modalities of form" (2007: 6–7). Through form and aesthetics, I hope that such a "deeper historicization via closer attention to form . . . will lead us beyond the political and cultural dualisms of Orientalism" (9). By engaging form to shift our focus beyond Orientalism, I connect racial form to histories of socialism that are crucial in grappling with Asia's ubiquity. As Shu-mei Shih has articulated, "The Cold War divided the world around a particular kind of dichotomy of East and West—socialism and capitalism—not the East and the West of Orientalism and Occidentalism" (Shih 2012: 28). Put differently, the form of fireworks provides apertures to contend with changes in racial capital within the ubiquity of Asia, which can also be understood as grappling with postsocialism.

My emphasis on aesthetics and form is not meant to dismiss the need to account for the material history of objects but rather to bring to the fore the aesthetic as a key method. This essay thus engages queer of color critique less through legible subjects and objects. In particular, I shift away from examining bodies that are often taxed with the representational burden of showing the material realities of race. Instead, I build on calls for subjectless (Eng, Halberstam, and Muñoz 2005) and objectless (Eng and Puar 2020) critiques, which emphasize the need to engage queerness beyond the presumptive terms and subjects that originated the field. The aesthetics and form of fireworks provide a way to rethink the "'proper objects' of study for the field" beyond "the nation-state, sexuality, the sexed body, race and sex" (Eng and Puar: 14). For this reason, I consider the aesthetic as the queer method to ground such forms of critique, particularly in light of legible demands that often come out of Marxist and racial capitalist approaches.

I explore a methodological question inherent to situating racial capitalism with aesthetic inquiry: can the latter produce much for the former beyond simply illustrating the circulation of goods and consumption?

Lastly, through an exploration of the comrade as subject and the aesthetic as method, this essay reconsiders what we do with Marxism and what kind of relation we must develop with Marxist discourse as queer of color critique and racial capitalism further develop their analytics. In particular, the aesthetic as method and a reworking of the subject, alongside the racial, retool Marxism and its established approaches. How do we locate the ways both queer of color critique and racial capitalism amplify the relational orientation of Marxism, particularly its frameworks that highlight the connections across groups that exist as objects of history and commodities of exchange? I define this particular relationship to Marxism as spectral, building off of Jacques Derrida. In brief, a spectral relationship to Marxism is one that exceeds immediate legibility and forces us to bring to the fore the relational import of Marxist approaches. Spectrality entails shifting beyond Marx's model minority, the proletariat, as the primary means for revolution; beyond the state or a global party to define a movement; and beyond a meta narrative of class and capital that obscures the histories of racialized extraction, dispossession, conquest, and enslavement that have produced modernity. Further, a spectral relation to Marxism considers the category of postsocialism as not simply the end of Marxism nor its desired resurgence. Rather, the spectral enables the return of socialism to revitalize and reframe what we do with Marxism.

Further, a spectral relation to Marxism allows us to work across scales of analysis, from the comrade subject to others across time and space; and from the representational model of white modernity to the affective spread of Asia. I thus center Derrida's focus on phenomenology to explore how exactly we might work across temporal and spatial scales. By doing so, however, we must attend to the levels of abstraction we operate within. As Stuart Hall reminds us, "Some of the greatest problems in Marxist analysis have resulted from misunderstanding the level at which abstractions are working" (2016: 90). Hall's attention to scale and the level of abstraction is a critical reminder for both queer of color critique and racial capitalist discourse. Both approaches certainly emphasize social difference as it relates to Marxism; however, this is not simply done to remedy "the so-called silence in Marx's discourse" because "[Marx] thinks these other determinations are insignificant" but rather because these silences "are the result of the relevant level of abstraction" (Hall: 92). Both queer of color critique and racial capitalist discourse direct us to a level of abstraction that requires that we attend to the specificities of capitalism's subjects—in particular, how we define, conceptualize, and methodologically track such subjects amid the Asian century.

Beyond Individuals, Toward Comrades

In order to traverse the scale from the subject to cycles of accumulation, we must understand the place of race in shaping both ends. Arrighi offers a helpful starting point; he notes how capitalism has changed through systemic cycles of accumulation. He traces how these shifts occurred across Europe and the US toward Asia. Building off of world-systems theory, Arrighi originally noted four "long centuries" from the Italian city-states of the sixteenth century, the Dutch of the seventeenth century, and the British of the nineteenth century to the United States after 1945 (Arrighi 1994). Throughout each cycle, two shifts occur from material expansion into accumulation through finance capital. This model led Arrighi to account for the waning of the US century into the rise of the Asian century, with China as a key site (Arrighi 2007). It would be a mistake, however, to simply consider China as representationally embodying and entering a universal model of modernity or becoming part of a racial capitalist order that had previously been held by Western colonizers (Ong 2006; Rofel 2007). This representational logic undergirds notions of (white) modernity that have dominated how we have understood race during earlier cycles. China, instead, is a "market economy" that mediates capitalist classes and projects within a historical and existing East Asian state system that can be differentiated from the European world system (Arrighi 2007: 24 and 331–32). Put another way, this differentiation is critical since it allows us to understand how the Chinese state has more autonomy to operate beyond the complete interests of the capitalist class; the state itself has the choice to operate for national interests that are not always bound to class interests, unlike say the US. China and Asia are not simply fitting into a representational standard of a racialized modernity; instead, they are affectively shifting the terms in how the world operates.

I briefly outline Arrighi's contributions to illustrate how and why it is critical to understand the Asian century as it relates to our ideas of race and the subject. In particular, our previous models of difference, based on a representational proximity to a dominant norm, occurred amid accumulation located in Western Europe and the US. Whiteness thus became the predominant measure for situating difference. However, this shift toward the Asian century requires that we rethink how we define difference and how we have heavily relied on representationalism for critique. In particular, the established discourse of Orientalism emphasizes being outside of a representational standard of whiteness and victimized as perpetual outsider, rationalizing warfare and capitalist extraction. As Lye has noted, "Asian American cultural studies can be said to have not yet moved beyond Orientalism . . . that we have not found a way to exceed its critique" (2007: 6). Although previous frames continue to provide explanatory power, they cannot fully explicate Asia's ubiquity. Earlier theorizations of race, as Lye reminds us, depend on a narrative that emerged from the nineteenth century during British and American cycles of accumulation (2). These narratives often rely on notions of subject exclusion. These models use representational notions of the subject to compare how a group symbolically fails in degree from a norm, like whiteness. In turn, the logic undergirding liberalism argues for inclusion and increased representation as the remedies for historic exclusion.

Take, for example, the funding from a mix of Chinese, Asian American, and white donors that supports Asian American "activism" against affirmative action (Day 2019; Hsu 2018). Although some in the Asian American community use past victimization to argue against what they perceive as race-based state discrimination within the realm of education, it comes at the expense of a larger coalitional politics. Those having recently immigrated from China with a differentiated and distant relationship to histories of US-based racialization desire and presume access to institutions, particularly for those from the expanding upper-class elites or those desiring such positions. In turn, they fund those from within the Asian American community who rely on forms of nineteenth-century anti-Asian discrimination enduring today. However, the mix of Chinese and American capital forces us to pause and rethink a model of race premised upon victimization; this is an instance of elite capture, whereby the reliance on past anti-Asian forms of victimization is used to obscure the underlying bourgeois interests of the wealthy elite in ending affirmative action. Historical victimization and discourses of Orientalism can only explain so much; how might we attend for class mobilizations of race that benefit the racialized petite bourgeoisie? Do our current approaches to the subject provide enough explanatory power to fully grapple with class, alongside the international (primarily gendered) division of labor?

Orientalism, as an analytic, is not a problem in and of itself. Rather, it requires that we locate the notion historically. The frame illustrates how the other is represented and understood as distinct from the legible norms of whiteness and Western modernity. Drawing from this model, Takashi Fujitani astutely identifies how Japan approximates whiteness through modernization; he historicizes racial logics during the early twentieth century and locates how Japan represents itself as symbolically an almost white modern nation (2011). This is what we might call race being understood as illustrating a representational proximity to white modernity. Fujitani historicizes forms of racialization to avoid race becoming a transhistorical signifier. This move is critical, as Lye has identified. She articulates this need through her critiques of Omi and Winant's racial formation theory, arguably the most influential theorization of race during the late twentieth century. Lye illuminates how racial formation theory "emerged as a brand of postmarxism whose theoretical intervention was the irreducibility of race to class analysis, it overcompensated for past neglect by turning race into a kind of transcendental signifier, emphasizing the foundational status of racism to U.S. society at the expense of describing its historical variability" (Lye 2007: 2).

Our established models primarily operate through such a representational frame, where the larger emancipatory project comes to be premised upon the eventual disappearance of race from modern thought. Denise Ferreira da Silva identifies the limits of such approaches due to what she calls the "sociohistorical logic of exclusion," which "assumes that racial difference and the exclusionary symbolic (cultural or ideological) strategies it entails are extraneous to the modern ethical landscape, it can write the racial only as an unbecoming aid to (economic) class subjection" (2007: xxvii). As a result of these models of race, the larger project of emancipation is presumed to arise "when the (juridical and economic) inclusion of the racial others and their voices (historical and cultural representations) finally realizes universality in postmodern social configurations" (xxiv). In this way, Ferreira da Silva locates how the logic of exclusion and victimization ultimately reaffirms non-Europeans as the other and considers race as extraneous to "post-Enlightenment, modern, social (moral) configurations" (xxxvi). Race, under the sociohistorical logic of exclusion, has primarily been understood through this logic of representation, within a racial paradigm of symbolics that measures racialized others in their proximity to whiteness and racialized nations in their proximity to modernity. This model has been helpful for understanding race within British and American cycles of accumulation. During the rise and establishment of the American century, the predominance of US global capital *and* the representational symbolics of cultural norms established by white standards both became the measuring sticks for minoritarian and non-Western others. In other words, the logic of representation was an important way to explicate race as national and global forms from the mid-nineteenth century into most of the twentieth, a time period that aligns with Arrighi's sites for accumulation.

These changes in capital accumulation highlight the need to update how Asia and notions of the subject have been understood. Asiatic racial form operates both representationally and affectively/phenomenologically, as evinced by Asia's ubiquity. We must rethink our models of racial form to produce a more complex understanding of the subject as it relates to changes in capital accumulation, alongside class, gender, sexuality, and nation-states. David Eng and Shinhee Han engage such a model through property: "Notably, with the rise of Asia globally and the shift of economic and political power to the East, we must factor into the history of the Asian American subject a more expansive account of the subject of racial history connected to different empires (the United States, China, India) and their organizations of race and caste into social hierarchy and subordination. Indeed, we must begin to account how the enfranchised subjects of these countries have their own particular histories of race and property" (2019: 168). Their focus on race and property within the rise of Asia is a critical reminder of the need to situate race not only geographically but also historically. Such theorizations are indebted to Cheryl Harris, whose work on whiteness as property emerges from a focus on the founding of the US. Her analysis is situated within nineteenth and early twentieth-century theorizations of race, with a keen attention to Indigenous dispossession and Black enslavement. She notably highlights the need to attend to "issues of relative power and social relations [that are] inherent in any definition of property" (1993: 1729). As such, property is indicative of larger historical modes of social power, structures, and relations. In other words, property helps us theorize subjects as always relational as they constellate with social structures and others. A different account of the subject beyond solely representation is needed in order to produce this more expansive way to suture race to class, considering how within the Asian century and late liberalism there are consistent mobilizations of race to benefit privileged classes.

The need to historicize race becomes even more critical considering how Asia's ubiquity problematizes narratives of victimization, exclusion, and representation. Kandice Chuh identifies this as "the potency of model minority discourse and its sustaining political economic structures in both inducing identification with the exceptionalism that is Asian difference and affirming the unquestionable value of majoritarian U.S. culture and politics" (2017: 231). There are those racialized subjects that desire normativity and majoritarian life—the life of global capital. There are those who seek to access a particular "genre of the human," to use Sylvia Wynter's words, which is that of "the Western and westernized (or conversely) global middle classes" (2003: 313). Race, in other words, when historicized within this contemporary juncture, can provide access to capital and does not fully operate representationally. Yet, many continue to rely on representational ideas of victimization as the primary formulation for subjects.

As such, we need to update how the subject is conceptualized so as to contend with individualist notions that have come to shape critique. I place pressure on minoritarian-oriented studies for the way a narrative of exclusion and a measure of a symbolic or representational proximity to whiteness cannot fully account for these historic shifts. What Ferreira da Silva, Wynter, Chuh, and others suggest is that race must be understood as ontoepistemological to modernity, which is to say that race informs the very terms and functions of our world. Broadly, what these theorists suggest is the need to shift away from appealing to bids to be humanized and to become part of a universal (modern) whole through better or increased representation. Instead, they collectively ask us to examine the structures that maintain the logics of modernity—to understand the racial as both a key structuring force of discourse and a mode of relation across different groups. Ferreira da Silva, in particular, emphasizes ways to conceptualize race that refute exclusion not through a simplistic inclusion. Instead, she emphasizes how racial logics are the products of "modern strategies of power" (2007: xxxvii). The goal should not entail the disappearance of racial difference; instead, we must understand it as central to modern thought. By doing so, we track the structural over the individual liberal subject.

In order to emphasize the structural, the subject must be understood as always in relation to others across space and time. The figure of the comrade serves as an alternative to rethink the subject in this way. The comrade is a figure that is politically oriented and connected to socialist histories. Unlike the proletariat, Marx's preferred subject, the comrade opens up Marxism beyond dogma toward a broad ethical orientation, whereby the comrade comes to be always in relation, suturing self to others in time and space. In this way, the comrade can be understood as affective in the sense that this subject's bounds are not individuated; rather, the comrade extends beyond a singular self. Comrade in mandarin Chinese (*tongzhi*) is also slang that refers to queer subjects. This notion of the comrade allows us to understand the subject not as defined through the liberal individual. Instead, the comrade allows us to conceptualize the subject as always in relation to others—these relations are both in solidarity and in antipathy. In this way, the comrade allows us to phenomenologically track self to others across and with difference. Asia's ubiquity demands that we grapple with race as it relates to class so as to avoid further class mobilizations of race meant to highlight victimization without accounting for class difference.

Cai Guo-Qiang's art practice directs us to this sense of the comrade; the artist uses aesthetics to produce a sutured and implicated subject whose phenomenological perception extends beyond the self. Cai is an art world star, who originally trained in stage design but whose work now spans performance art, installation, video, and fireworks. The artist, born in 1957, is from Guangzhou and worked in Japan from the mid-1980s to the mid-1990s and has been working out of New York since 1995. He won the Golden Lion prize at the Venice Biennale in 1999 and has continued to produce at a rapid pace. He has worked with gunpowder and fireworks as media since early in his career and continues to deploy them. Later in this essay, I focus on some of his more well-known fireworks, but I begin with his initial and ongoing preoccupation with fireworks that engage those beyond the human: extraterrestrial life. The artist often speaks about fireworks as a way to extend beyond the earth and to communicate with aliens. If we read this as simply directing us to the unknown universe, we miss the opportunity to think about the formal innovation in his works. Cai does not simply rethink the human and shift us to a nonhuman subject; instead, he turns toward the sky to direct us to what lies beyond us. The body and its representability are obliterated in his focus on space, particularly in *Sky Ladder* (2015; fig. 1). In this piece, he produces a literal ladder to the sky, removing our focus from the world to what is above. He diverts our attention away from the drama of the everyday and ourselves toward what exists beyond. Rather than being lost in the sublime effect of fireworks, he encourages us to ponder what lingers apart from our immediate world. Since 1989, Cai has described his gunpowder works as attempts to communicate with aliens. His *Human Abode: Project for Extraterrestrials No. 1* (1989) at the Tama River initiated this focus. In 2012 at Los Angeles's Geffen Museum, many of Cai's works used images of aliens and UFOs. Rather than debating the veracity of alien life, I take this focus on aliens as a way to further define what constitutes us differently from an imagined being—forcing us to clarify our sense of humanity. Cai deploys the metaphysical (what is beyond the human) to contend with how we have historically defined the human. This push to imagine beyond the self or the anthropocentric encourages searching for relations that exceed our locations in national forms, what I describe later as a spectral grasp that develops what Derrida calls the "New International" that works beyond established nation-based discourses.

Beyond aliens, Cai has used fireworks to consider comrades. Beginning in 2005, Cai began to document and curate homemade flying saucers,

Figure 1. Cai Guo-Qiang (b. 1957, Quanzhou, China; lives in New York), *Sky Ladder*, 2015, Realized off Huiyu Island, Quanzhou, June 15, 4:45 am (dawn), 100 seconds. Gunpowder, fuse and helium balloon, 500 x 5.5 m. Photo by Wen-You Cai, courtesy Cai Studio.

airplanes, and submarines made by rural workers across China. When Cai was the curator of the China Pavilion at the Venice Biennale in 2005, he exhibited Du Wenda's artwork *Flying Saucer*. Du is a comrade, a farmer from Anhui, and he was invited to construct and attempt to launch his structure imagined as a flying saucer, which involved fireworks. In 2010, Cai furthered this curatorial project and presented works by fifty artists in *Peasant Da Vincis* at Shanghai's Rockbound Art Museum. Cai highlights the peasant as an artist, expanding an understanding of peasants beyond routinized notions as solely laborers or even workers outside of the privileged class, known as the proletariat. The peasant becomes a comrade, which allows us to shift away from locating a Marxist subject based upon a political party affiliation (à la the alienated and enlightened proletariat) toward a less defined relation. The figure of the comrade redefines how we orient ourselves to others across space and time; the comrade is not per se the proletariat. Cai's aesthetics thus offer a method that directs us to the ethics surrounding how we engage others: rather than demanding a Marxist orientation based in proletariat identification, Cai's comrade aesthetics shifts away from didactic means. His form and aesthetics gesture toward comrades rather than dictate a proper Marxist way.

Cai's works additionally play with a viewer's phenomenological orientation in order to amplify this notion of the comrade. Popular art discourses often frame Cai as using gunpowder across a flat canvas or plane (the sky and ground, respectively). However, his works extend beyond a singular dimension, directing our phenomenological foci beyond the sky and ground. This aesthetic effect guides one's focus without being overly didactic or completely overwhelming. His fireworks do not simply direct our focus outward to be lost in the formless sublime; rather, he constellates the self to structure and other comrades. The aesthetic and form of fireworks provide a method for grappling with the sublime and scattered effects of late capital, toggling across phenomenological registers from individual to comrades, background to foreground, and self to structure. This phenomenological effect and formal approach require that the subject always be understood in relation to others across time and space. In turn, Cai's fireworks expand our understanding of the subject from one with singular feelings to one broadly situated across time, space, structure, and others. Cai's comrade aesthetics thus produce a model of a subject that revises our understanding beyond representation and individual advancement. As such, Cai's work resonates and lands where Fredric Jameson leaves us in his essay on postmodernism: cognitive mapping (1989). Although most have explored cognitive mapping in relation to affect (Flatley 2008), I rely on phenomenology because it provides the means for a more directed political engagement beyond affective dispersal. Cai's works do not simply encourage us to be lost in the affective sublime; rather, he tethers the subject via phenomenology to structure and to others beyond the self. These aesthetics enact an ethics of relation.

Asia's ubiquity indicates that race operates at this interplay surrounding affect and phenomenology. Asian racial form reveals how our ideas of the subject have become less about its degree of representational difference from whiteness. Instead, race's porosity highlights its availability for multiple means; its malleability can be used for various political ends—race as affect means that it is a site of governance. This is to say that race as affect is not per se a net positive. On the one hand, race's affectiveness and ubiquity indicate that it does not immediately enable victimization and subjugation. Instead, as indicated by Asian racial form, it can be used toward majoritarian, capitalist ends. On the other hand, race as affect enables one to relate race to others well beyond one's subject position. I consider race as affect not to dismiss historical exclusion. However, these modes often come to be deployed toward a liberal focus on individual feeling and self-advancement— used in the interest of elite capture. Instead, we must turn to the structures that maintain forms of victimization across multiple groups. These structures not only produce a relation across forms of difference, but also highlight the material privileges and varied property interests that groups differentially possess. Put more explicitly, Asian racialization is not only critical to highlight a relational and solidarity politic across groups, but also difficult to contend with due to changes in how capital accumulation functions. As such, we must grapple with not only structure and relations, but also difference in dispossession. Such an account relies on studying and locating the subject in its historicity—an approach that phenomenology centralizes.

Through Cai's use of form to illustrate how a subject senses space and time, he directs us to areas that expand beyond representation: phenomenology and affect. However, phenomenology amends affect by revealing the historical and structural relations that produce a subject. Phenomenology works against the untethered, hyper-individualist subject that liberal frames enact and the universalized subject that some affective approaches produce. I thus emphasize how phenomenology operates in Cai's works to revise representational approaches toward a relational one. A reconceptualization of the subject through the comrade involves approaching the subject in affective and phenomenological ways—to shift away from a fully representational account. Affect, however, runs the risk of what José Muñoz describes as a "crypto-universalism," rendering any subject equivalent to all others (Muñoz 2006:

675). Phenomenology provides the means to theorize the subject as always sutured to history and difference and not simply dissipated into pure affect. Both representation-based and affect-based approaches have distanced themselves from phenomenology as its analytics have often been understood as being centered around an ableist reliance on visuality, presumptions of a holistic sense of perception, the universalization of a subject and experience, and an overreliance on intention (May 2014; Peden 2014). Accounts from intellectual history have revealed that the shift toward affect, with the increased reliance on Spinoza and Deleuze, historically emerged as a move away from phenomenology (Peden 2014). However, phenomenology provides some key theoretical tools to contend with an affective turn that has often universalized and deracialized discourse.

Maurice Merleau-Ponty and Frantz Fanon developed their phenomenological approaches against universalizing impulses, specifically existentialism. They each questioned Jean-Paul Sartre's reliance on universalist frames. For Merleau-Ponty, Sartre's focus on the dialectic could not provide sufficient answers to how political change occurs (1973: 204). For Fanon, Sartre could not account for the fact of Blackness. However, for both, Sartre informed their reliance on phenomenology as the mode to shed self-interest. Judith Butler articulates how Sartre's theorizations of violence inspire Fanon to develop a phenomenology that directs one beyond the self toward others (2006). This development of phenomenology as the means to move beyond the self is critical for how we understand the aesthetic as a method.

Merleau-Ponty's ideas are not based on a universal ethic. The practice of phenomenology, by tracking the self within totality, leads to both critique and action. His commitment to a humanist Marx relies on what he identifies as a located I, a subject that tracks the self with social structure. Merleau-Ponty's corporeal schema thus emphasizes how this situated I negotiates space, time, and others. This schema becomes the basis for intersubjective connection. Although intersubjectivity is often dismissed as a romantic mode of connection (Nancy 2000: 62), it is the phenomenological mechanism necessary to produce relationality. Merleau-Ponty's intersubjectivity is not a simplistic connection between bodies. Fanon reformulates Merleau-Ponty's frameworks through a deeper consideration of history, particularly in relation to the fact of Blackness. Fanon produces the historical racial schema to amend Merleau-Ponty's corporeal schema: "In the white world, the man of color encounters difficulties in elaborating his body schema. . . . It is not imposed on me; it is rather a definitive structuring of myself and the world-definitive because it creates a genuine dialectic between my body and the world" (2008: 90–91).

Fanon locates the historical-racial schema "below" the corporeal schema, whereby the racial undergirds and revises the universalist notion of the corporeal (92). These models of phenomenology allow us to situate notions of race to affect, history, and others in relation. Retooling the subject via phenomenology is critical considering how we cannot fully understand Asia's ubiquity and its contemporary racialization through representation.

Historical Materialism and Aesthetics

Asia's affective ubiquity requires that we shift our conceptualization of the subject. However, how do we methodologically enact such a shift to contend with the comrade alongside changes in capital? To consider method, I return us to the object I began with. Fireworks offer a model to grapple with Asia's ubiquity through not only production, but also its aesthetics and form. Although tracking the circulation of objects is a helpful move, it primarily involves a symbolic and representational approach. Aesthetics and form provide additional and critical modes to highlight the limits of representationalism. The aesthetic as a method operates beyond the routinized and, at times, predictable narratives when situating objects, even aesthetics ones, in relation to Marxism proper: commodities, fetish, ideology, and circulation.

The material history of fireworks reveals a connection between the affect of the sublime and the production of nation-states through warfare, gunpowder, and commemorative displays of the birth of nations. As Kevin Salatino (1997) and Simon Werrett (2010) have argued, the sublime's connotations of awe and the grandiose are achieved through a nation-state's use of fireworks. During the Enlightenment in Great Britain, Edmund Burke, who influenced Kant's theorizations of the sublime, imagined this affect as a form of mortality that involved terror, with fireworks representing a mathematical sublime that was formless (Kant [1764] 2003). Fireworks thus came to be imagined as a medium apart from painting and etchings, whose static forms could be used to represent reality. In particular, fireworks were framed through the medium of performance. The French playwright and librettist Jean-Louis de Cahuzac described the Enlightenment conceptualization of fireworks as spectacle: "In all the Arts it is necessary to paint. In the one that we call *spectacle*, it is necessary to paint with actions" (cited in Salatino 1997: 47). The sublime became the organizing affect for this practice due to its ephemerality and formlessness.

The sublime of fireworks also became a metaphor for war. The French word for fireworks, *feu d'artifice*, translates into artificial fire, whereby the semblance of war produces the sublime since one is removed from combat. Salatino delineates this association across medium and war: "What is significant here, however, at least in the context of the eighteenth-century notion of the sublime, is the recognition that the *terribilità* of war can be an experience that elicits pleasure when it resembles, but is not in actuality war; that the loud noises and brilliant lights, the cacophonic explosions and bursting rockets are intrinsically satisfying to the spectator, granting a frisson of delight mingled with fear" (1997: 49). Fireworks typically operate as a stand-in for the experience of war. Put differently, performance and spectacle are key frames as they situate fireworks as a rehearsal for war. Performance and the idea of rehearsal buttress what some scholars describe as a modern relation to control and order. Lihong Liu carefully connects the use of fireworks as ornament to represent this modern mode of control (2017). Depictions of fireworks emerged throughout the production of clocks and other pictorial representations in not only China but also the broader early modern world. Fireworks, in other words, came to serve as a transnational mode of ordering in which one could rehearse time and existence. Further, fireworks and gunpowder circulated across global trade routes tied to both commerce and warfare, representing the relationship across the medium, the sublime, and capitalist networks. Most accounts trace the emergence of this technology and its circulation within China's Silk Road during the thirteenth century and beyond. One might thus understand fireworks as aiding the production of a world system.

This history reveals how the affective goal for nationalist deployments of fireworks has been to overwhelm a viewer to a point of losing one's sense of time and space. Fireworks, in other words, fuel a crisis in representation. By getting lost in the formless sublime, a nation's subject becomes overwhelmed and isolated from others, space, and time. Put differently, the sublime of fireworks produces a form of individualism detached from history, others, and totality. The formlessness of the sublime scatters one's focus so to be overwhelmed to a point of losing oneself. As Jameson has established, the postmodern, as a cultural dominant, conditions subjects to forget history with the sublime as a central aesthetic of late capital. This forgetting is amplified due to late capital's sense of the sublime being tied to questions around representability, order, and totality (1989: 34). It is the impossibility of representing totality that leads to the affect of what he identifies as a "camp" and "hysterical" sublime. Amid constant warfare and sensorial intensity, a camp sublime emerges as *the* vehicle to forget history. For Marxists, the task of tracking totality thus becomes the critical project for which the aesthetic can provide insight.

The question of method becomes central as the established methods of historical materialism and political economy provide key but limited apertures into understanding late capital. Further, within the context of the Asian century, the limits of representationalism, as related to the sublime affects of late capital, are brought further to the fore. Historical materialism and the tracking of objects and commodities allow us to trace totality and to provide a grounded analysis of how capital works and how to work against its pull. However, I have focused and will continue to focus on the aesthetic because it extends such critical and established analyses. When situating queer of color critique in relation to racial capitalist discourse, a tension arises around method that could be broadly understood as differences across the humanities and social sciences. Although one can certainly focus on established methods surrounding the social sciences and political economy, queer of color critique has additionally emphasized the aesthetic with its emphasis on form and sense-making. This difference across methods can be indexed through fireworks themselves. They are, on one hand, a commodity within circulation, distribution, and accumulation. On the other, fireworks possess an aesthetic and form that track other ways of imagining a subject beyond an individualist self through the interplay across representation, phenomenology, and affect.

Cai's aesthetics offers insights to this tension surrounding method. His fireworks deal with the problem of history by not reproducing the sublime of capital; they formally direct our attention toward other comrades in relation. When viewing his work, one's phenomenological field is subdued and not lost, allowing one to trace one's location in space and in relation to others. Cai's (fire)works thus force individuals to get out of themselves as an enactment of relation, not as a universalizing connection or a sublime escapism. Although we are pushed to get out of ourselves, it is done with a socialist inflection, relation to histories of subjugation, and phenomenological guidance rather than simply a dispersed aspiration or prescribed and transparent politic. Individual subjects are compelled to place themselves in a constellation with comrades across history and geography. For example, in *Black Ceremony* (2011; fig. 2), Cai ignites a stream of black fireworks at Qatar's Mathaf: Arab Museum of Modern Art. Both the visual and sonic elements muffle the sublime into "stuplimity." Visually, the work does not deploy the usual nationalist multicolored and exploding form of fireworks and instead ignites small black spots, reminiscent of a flock of birds. Cai tempers the grandiose display of saturated colors against a night sky by igniting black flecks across a crisp blue sky. In addition, the sonic effects of *Black Ceremony* take us out of the body. The reverberations from this piece produce a more minimal impact when compared to public displays of fireworks during the celebration of nation-states, like the Fourth of July with the playing of "The Star-Spangled Banner" amplifying the affective mood of fireworks. The cascading soft booms of the ignitions in *Black Ceremony* congeal together into a sonic reverberation that almost whimpers when compared to the fireworks of the Beijing Olympics (which Cai served as creative director). This softer sonic touch does not operate as sublime distraction. Cai creates a shock of the muted boom rather than of the bombastic new.

We can understand this shift from the sublime by the ways Cai deploys fireworks akin to Sianne Ngai's category of stuplimity, which is "astonishment" that is "paradoxically united with boredom" (2012: 271). Ngai's aesthetic of "stuplimity reveals the limits of our ability to comprehend a vast extended form as a totality, as does Kant's mathematical sublime, yet not through an encounter with the infinite but with finite bits and scraps of material in repetition" (271). Cai's (fire)works deflate the affect of the sublime. Similar to the large-scale works Ngai focuses on, Cai's fireworks are not sublime "since here the initial experience of being aesthetically overwhelmed involves not terror or pain (eventually superseded by tranquility), but something much closer to an ordinary fatigue" (270). Cai does not scatter our attention. Instead, through form, his aesthetics plays with a viewer's focus. The stuplimity produced through phenomenological attention enables a viewer to not become overwhelmed by the immensity of late capital, utilizing attention as the means to extend the self outward to those past and present and across space and time.

Additionally, on December 2, 2017, as part of the seventy-fifth commemoration of the first self-sustained nuclear chain reaction, the University of Chicago invited Cai to ignite *Color Mushroom Cloud* (fig. 3). The minute-long piece involved the ignition of streams of gunpowder that burst into flecks of color. The cold Chicago wind then blows the flecks away as a subtle gray mushroom cloud slowly takes over the dissipating flecks. Debates circulated surrounding Cai's complicity with nuclear power. The aesthetic here is both a problem and possibility. At first, Cai's firework could be dismissed as simply a celebration and endorsement of nuclear power. Although the scientific breakthrough advanced medical imaging and other insights, the initial development of it benefited the Manhattan Project. The project's war machines catalyzed nuclear effects that linger in the populations, animals, and nature exposed, along with the generations that have followed.

Figure 2. Cai Guo-Qiang (b. 1957, Quanzhou, China; lives in New York) *Black Ceremony*, 2011, Realized outside Mathaf: Arab Museum of Modern Art, Doha, December 5, 2011, 3:00 pm, approximately 3 minutes. 8,300 smoke shells fitted with computer chips. Commissioned by Mathaf: Arab Museum of Modern Art [Ephemeral]. Photo by Hiro Ihara, courtesy Cai Studio.

However, Cai scales back the sublime effect of his fireworks beyond simply a nationalist celebration. Instead, he deploys stuplimity to direct our attention beyond pageantry. The muted transition from colorful flecks to grey mushroom subdues the effects of this work in ways that ask us to contemplate and direct our attention toward the larger conditions that structure how we understand nuclear power itself. The drive to "modernize," with nuclear technology as central, creates a specific world order. Cold War anxieties and the presumed demise of socialism amplify this world order. Cai uses the aesthetic neither to didactically celebrate nor to reject this order; instead, he directs our attention to focus beyond the immediate allure of critique or celebration. The aesthetic effect of stuplimity plays with phenomenological attention and affective ubiquity to scale back how we deploy critique.

Figure 3. Cai Guo-Qiang (b. 1957, Quanzhou, China; lives in New York) *Color Mushroom Cloud*, 2017, Realized above the former CP-1 site, University of Chicago in commemoration of the 75th anniversary of the first controlled self-sustained nuclear chain reaction, Chicago, December 2, 3:25 pm. Color comets and PixelBurst™ Aerial shells, 75 meters tall. Commissioned by UChicago Arts and the Smart Museum of Art. Photo by Wen-You Cai, courtesy Cai Studio.

Spectral Marxism and the New International

Both a reconceptualization of the subject as comrade and the aesthetic as method shift our relations to established Marxist analysis. These approaches, specifically the aesthetic and the racial, are unwieldy with regard to orthodox Marxism. They are promiscuous, or in the words of Derrida, they are spectral. To produce such an orientation to Marxism is critical, particularly at this historical juncture as it relates to Asia's ubiquity and China's postsocialist condition. In this vein, a focus on Asia, the racial, and the aesthetic form of fireworks provides the opportunity to define this shift in Marxist discourse. To deflate our relationship to Marxism means to retain its ethics and projects without returning to some of the predictable debates that surround orthodox Marxism.

Cai's approach to art indexes a spectral relation to Marxism. In 2018, the artist Cai and the philosopher Boris Groys explored questions surrounding the relationship between Marxism and socialism. The two discuss Cai's use of fireworks and gunpowder, swimming around the postsocialist conditions that shape China and Russia. Groys locates the issues of history and memory that are central to grappling with postsocialism: "It's precisely the structure of memory: at certain levels people remember, are ready to cry, but at some other level, they forget. It's very strange, layers of memory." Most critically, Cai identifies the aesthetic for contending with these layers of history, where Cai evokes a fairly Kantian idea: "To me, part of art's power resides in its non-practicality. These days, we are so utilitarian that we can't see the power of things that are useless" (Cai and Groys 2018). Rather than through the avenues of the representable and legible, the uselessness and non-utility of the aesthetic offer important ways to engage a global Marxist project.

In particular, Cai's aesthetics of fireworks expands the individualist subject toward one that engages others across history and space. As such, his comrade aesthetics highlights the import and problems of Asia's ubiquity, where Asia locates an uneasy divide across producers and consumers of capital. The aesthetic highlights this difficulty in China's postsocialist condition for Marxist futures.

Beyond the notion of uselessness, Cai's aesthetics index and capture a spectral effect. The aesthetics of gunpowder are ephemeral and dematerialize, as many have noted the way they burn images into the mind's eye. Although it might be tempting to focus on how Cai's fireworks disappear, they also remain as smoke or charred canvas. Further, a complicating factor from fireworks is how its momentary performance or sparkle can be archived, as captured through etchings, photography, and other visual and object-based means. For theorists of performance, then, this condition seems quite related—an ontological condition surrounding disappearance and remains. The medium of fireworks offers space to reconsider performance and how we grapple with the materiality of the subject's body. Without delving into the debates around the ontology of performance as dissipating and/or remaining, there has been a preoccupation with how we theorize the body's enactments and reenactments (Phelan 1993; Nyong'o 2009; Schneider 2011). Fireworks provide an avenue to rethink this central debate, specifically at the level of the subject. Rather than relying on a politics of representation and presence, fireworks utilize a spectral effect to reconsider these questions. Krista Thompson's work on shine within the context of the African diaspora helps retool a focus on the subject's body and its representation toward a framework that works "within yet beyond" visibility and representability (2015: 236). She contends "that the artists who draw on surfacism and its connection to black bodies implicitly call up the connection between surface aesthetics, capitalism, and the historical denial of subjectivity to enslaved persons of African descent" (233). The shine of fireworks provides space to move beyond discourses of representation and visibility toward the racial as it relates to the global. Cai's fireworks rejuvenate discourses on disappearance and remains, shifting away from the singular body toward a comrade collective. Fireworks, in other words, produce a spectral effect that remains, disappears, and returns.

This spectral effect informs how racial capitalist discourse and queer of color critique engage Marxism. A spectral relation involves a less orthodox relation to Marxism and deploys methods, like the aesthetic, that might initially appear illegible and useless. Derrida's *Specters of Marx: The State of Debt, the Work of Mourning, and the New International* lays the groundwork for defining this relationship to Marxism, as the work historicizes postsocialism within a global frame. For Derrida, the spectral involves a "question of repetition: a specter is always a *revenant*. One cannot control its comings and goings because it *begins by coming back*. Think as well of Macbeth, and remember the specter of Caesar. After having expired, he returns" (2006: 11). Written in 1993 for a conference grappling with the perceived withering of Marxism following the fall of the Berlin Wall and the liberalization of Chinese markets, *Specters of Marx* offers a framework that deals with the relational politics of socialism beyond political dogma. Derrida contends with the presumed rise of democracy, working against Francis Fukuyama's declaration of the end of history. Derrida critiques such declarations by examining the texture of the spectral, especially as it illustrates a lingering and less committed relation to Marxism proper. The spectral historicizes the postsocial expansively, relationally, and reparatively. Derrida encourages us to think about the postsocial in terms of not only nation-states, but also aesthetic form.

I traverse these divergent relations to the postsocial to highlight what Derrida names in the last part of his title as a "New International." This relational notion works "beyond the sovereignty of States" (105) and deploys international justice to "be inspired by at least one of the spirits of Marx or of Marxism . . . and ally themselves, in a new, concrete, and real way, even if this alliance no longer takes the form of a party or of a workers' international" (107). The spectral quality of a relational international that is ethically guided and inflected by Marxism emerges from phenomenology, whereby "the phenomenal form of the world itself is spectral" and "the phenomenological *ego* (Me, You, and so forth) is a specter" (169). For Derrida, phenomenology becomes the means by which to understand the spectral and a relational postsocial international—one that deploys the spectral to engage with and beyond

Marxism and to grapple with the fascist and authoritarian legacies of communism. Derrida's "phenomenology of the spectral" (237) indicates a relation to past socialisms that remains open and relational yet guided by a Marxist ethic, without relying on the state or larger global party. With the demise or presumed death of socialism, he contemplates what we do with this loss. The spectral thus becomes an ethical orientation that does not hold on to an identification as dogmatically socialist, Marxist, or communist. Phenomenology becomes not only the method that sutures past with present and future (a way to historicize), but also a guiding, nondidactic ethic informed by a socialist past. Ultimately, how we orient ourselves phenomenologically as spectral to the past and to comrades produces both a sense of self along with a sense of the world; the phenomenology of the spectral enables relations to others as comrades that form this "New International."

Derrida's phenomenology of the spectral departs from the state or party form, producing a transnational relationality that reworks the postsocial beyond these entities. Chinese experiments with market capitalism and socialism indicate a postsocialism that cannot be understood as simply beyond or the end. And spectrality allows us to contend with the inflections of leftist utopias and socialist longings and returns. Further, this articulation of postsocialism through spectrality directs us toward an understanding of the production of the modern world. Derrida contends that the "phenomenal form of the world itself is spectral" in order to highlight the conditions that frame our understandings of globality (169). Through the phenomenology of spectral Marxism, we become less concerned with identifying the correct political party (as Marxist or not) and more with the structure of modern thought—what Ferreira da Silva, Chuh, and others describe as ontoepistemological. Merleau-Ponty similarly wrestles with these questions. Although he identified with and was active with leftist causes, he refused to fully identify with a political party because modernity predicates a rationalism that occludes spectral and open engagements with the political—akin to what Cai describes as useless. Merleau-Ponty directs us to the insufficiencies of Marxism and calls for a "noncommunist left." This left exists beyond nation-state forms: "The first article of this new left should be that the rivalry between the United States and the U.S.S.R. is not between 'free enterprise' and Marxism" (Merleau-Ponty 1973: 225). To imagine a noncommunist left, one must navigate a "double position, positing social problems in terms of struggle and refusing the dictatorship of the proletariat" (226).

In light of Asia's affective ubiquity, the new international and noncommunist left arise through a spectral Marxism that emphasizes relation over nation, alongside ethics over dogma. As Asian/American neoliberal subjects further identify with majoritarian capitalist values, we must develop a spectral Marxism to refrain from reproducing a dogmatic political project that simply dismisses those things deemed "useless" or in excess to Marxism proper. Instead, we need the aesthetic to open up the non-utility and difficulties surrounding this moment of affective ubiquity amid Asia's rise. The point of the spectral then is to reorient how we approach the world and each other—our ethical orientations. The insights from Merleau-Ponty and Fanon resonate with Derrida's phenomenology of the spectral, as we contend with the "phenomenality of phenomenon"—the structuring forces of modernity that shape how we perceive one another, space, and time (2006: 187). Through Fanon, the structuring forces of modernity arise from an attention to race and Blackness. And through Merleau-Ponty, modernity's structuring forces cannot simply be identified through dogmatic positions from the left. Cai's aesthetics offer a glimmer of these phenomenological and spectrally Marxist approaches, gently orienting our ethical commitments toward comrades and a renewed sense of the transits occurring across the international.

Note

The author would like to thank engaged audiences at MIT, University of Michigan, UCLA, Boston University, and UC Davis for thoughtful feedback on this essay. The author would also like to thank the co-editors of and other authors in this special issue, Carolyn Jones, Iván Ramos, Diane Dah-Young Ahn, and Sean Metzger for helpful suggestions.

References

Amin, Kadji, Amber Musser, and Roy Pérez. 2017. "Queer Form." *ASAP/Journal* 2, no. 2: 227–239.

Anderson, Mae. 2019. "U.S. Companies Walk a Fine Line When Doing Business with China." *LA Times,* October 8. https://www.latimes.com/business/story/2019-10-08/nba-furor-shows-u-s-companies-walk-a-fine-line-with-china.

Arrighi, Giovanni. 1994, *Long Twentieth Century.* London: Verso.

Arrighi, Giovanni. 2007. *Adam Smith in Beijing.* London: Verso.

Baudrillard, Jean. 1994. *Simulacra and Simulation.* Ann Arbor: University of Michigan Press.

Butler, Judith. 2006. "Violence, Non-Violence." *Graduate Faculty Philosophy Journal* 27, no. 1: 3–24.

Cai, Guo-Qiang, and Boris Groys. 2018. "A Conversation from a Studio Visit." *e-Flux,* February. https://conversations.e-flux.com/t/boris-groys-and-cai-guo-qiang-a-conversation-from-a-studio-visit/7625

Chow, Rey. 1993. *Writing Diaspora.* Bloomington: Indiana University Press.

Chow, Rey. 2002. *The Protestant Ethnic and the Spirit of Capitalism*. New York: Columbia University Press.

Chuh, Kandice. 2017. "Asians are the New . . . What?" In *Flashpoints for Asian American Studies*, edited by Cathy Schlund-Vials, 220–38. New York: Fordham University Press.

Day, Iyko. 2019. "Accumulation by Education." *Public Seminar*, June 14. https://publicseminar .org/essays/accumulation-by-education/

Derrida, Jacques. 2006. *Specters of Marx*. London: Routledge.

Eng, David, Jack Halberstam, and José Muñoz. 2005 "What's Queer about Queer Studies Now?" *Social Text* 23, nos. 3–4: 1–17.

Eng, David, and Jasbir Puar. 2020. "Left of Queer" *Social Text* 38, no. 4: 1–23.

Eng, David, and Shinhee Han. 2019. *Racial Melancholia, Racial Dissociation*. Durham, NC: Duke University Press.

Fanon, Frantz. 2008. *Black Skin, White Masks*. New York: Grove Press.

Ferreira da Silva, Denise. 2007. *Toward a Global Idea of Race*. Minneapolis: University of Minnesota Press.

Flatley, Jonathan. 2008. *Affective Mapping*. Cambridge, MA: Harvard University Press.

Fujitani, Takashi. 2011. *Race for Empire*. Berkeley: University of California Press.

Fung, Anthony (Editor). 2013. *Asian Popular Culture*. London: Routledge.

Hall, Stuart. 2016. "Rethinking Base and Superstructure." In *Cultural Studies 1983*, edited by Stuart Hall, Jennifer Daryl Slack, and Lawrence Grossberg, 74–96. Durham, NC: Duke University Press.

Harris, Cheryl. 1993. "Whiteness as Property" *Harvard Law Review* 106, no. 8: 1707–91.

Hsu, Hua. 2018. "The Rise and Fall of Affirmative Action" *The New Yorker*, October 15. https:// www.newyorker.com/magazine/2018/10/15/the-rise-and-fall-of-affirmative-action

Jameson, Fredric. 1989. *Postmodernism, or, The Cultural Logic of Late Capitalism*. Durham, NC: Duke University Press.

Kang, Laura. 2014. "Late (Global) Capital." In *The Routledge Companion to Asian American and Pacific Islander Literature*, edited by Rachel Lee, 301–14. New York: Routledge.

Kant, Immanuel. (1764) 2003. *Observations on the Feeling of the Beautiful and Sublime*. Translated by John Goldthwait. Berkeley: University of California Press.

Lee, Sharon Heijin. 2016. "Beauty Between Empires." *Frontiers: Journal of Women Studies* 37, no. 1: 1–31.

Liu, Catherine. 2021. *Virtue Hoarders*. Minneapolis: University of Minnesota Press.

Liu, Lihong. 2017. "Pyrotechnic Profusion," *Journal18* no. 3: 1–31.

Lye, Colleen. 2007. "Introduction: In Dialogue with Asian American Studies," *Representations* 99, no. 1: 1–12.

May, Todd. 2014. *The End of Phenomenology*. Edinburgh: University of Edinburgh Press.

Merleau-Ponty, Maurice. 1973. *Adventures of the Dialectic*. Evanston, IL: Northwestern Press.

Muñoz, José. 2006. "Feeling Brown, Feeling Down," *Signs* 31, no. 3: 675–88.

Musser, Amber. 2018. *Sensual Excess*. New York: New York University Press.

Nancy, Jean-Luc. 2000. *Being Singular Plural*. Stanford, CA: Stanford University Press.

Ngai, Sianne. 2012. *Our Aesthetic Categories*. Cambridge, MA: Harvard University Press.

Nyong'o, Tavia. 2009. *Amalgamation Waltz*. Minneapolis: University of Minnesota Press.

Ong, Aihwa. 2006. *Neoliberalism as Exception*. Durham, NC: Duke University Press.

Peden, Knox. 2014. *Spinoza Contra Phenomenology*. Stanford, CA: Stanford University Press.

Phelan, Peggy. 1993. *Unmarked*. New York: Routledge.

Rofel, Lisa. 2007. *Desiring China*. Durham, NC: Duke University Press.

Rothberg, Michael. 2019. *The Implicated Subject*. Stanford, CA: Stanford University Press.

Sakai, Naoki. 2022. *The End of Pax Americana*. Durham, NC: Duke University Press.

Salatino, Kevin. 1997. *Incendiary Art*. Los Angeles: Getty Research Institute.

Schneider, Rebecca. 2011. *Performing Remains*. New York: Routledge.

Shih, Shu-mei. 2012. "Is Postsocial in Postsocialism the Post on Posthumanism?" *Social Text* 30, no. 1: 27–50.

Táíwò, Olúfẹ́mi. 2022. *Elite Capture*. Boston: Haymarket Books.

Thompson, Krista. 2015. *Shine*. Durham, NC: Duke University Press.

Werrett, Simon. 2010. *Fireworks*. Chicago: University of Chicago Press.

Wynter, Sylvia. 2003. "Unsettling the Coloniality of Being/Power/Truth/Freedom: Towards the Human, After Man, Its Overrepresentation—An Argument." *CR: The New Centennial Review* 3, no. 3: 257–337.

Şahin Açıkgöz, Howard Chiang, Debanuj DasGupta, Joao Gabriel, Christoph Hanssmann, Rana M. Jaleel, Durba Mitra, and Evren Savcı

Roundtable: Queer/Trans of Color Transits and the Imaginaries of Racial Capitalism

RANA AND EVREN: *Racial capitalism in US scholarship is necessarily and rightfully narrated through the transatlantic slave trade. While this is a globally relevant history for understanding the past and the present of transnational racial orders, what other histories and present modes of capitalist accumulation are relevant to telling a global history of racial capitalism?*

DURBA: As Cedric Robinson ([1983] 2000) shows, there is no other history in the global rise of racial capitalism made possible through the European colonial project that was not touched by entwined histories of slavery and dispossession in the transatlantic world. Systems of domination intimately tied seemingly disparate geographies of colonialism and slavery, to think with Lisa Lowe's potent conceptualization of intimacy across continents (Lowe 2015). In my own work, I ask what global histories might we be able to tell when we place the colonial enforcement of sexual difference and the control of sexuality at the heart of the project of racial capitalism? To understand the concepts, disciplines, and institutions foundational to racial capitalism, I argue we must center the modern "problem" of feminized sexuality, for it is through racialized ideas of sexual deviancy that society

The South Atlantic Quarterly 123:1, January 2024
DOI 10.1215/00382876-10920687   © 2024 Duke University Press

itself became an object and site of knowledge. With research rooted in the colonial domination of the Indian subcontinent, I demonstrate how the study of social life across the modern world—in institutions of law, policing, science, and emerging disciplines of modern social science—was built through the control and erasure of feminized sexuality (Mitra 2020). In thinking the queerness of feminized sexuality, my work builds on wide-ranging traditions in Black feminist thinking about the gendering work of enslavement and enforced reproduction (e.g., Davis 1983; Morgan 2021), postcolonial feminist critiques of the coloniality of sex (e.g., Arondekar 2009), Indigenous feminist theories of the enforcement of settler heterosexuality (Rifkin 2010; TallBear 2013), and queer of color theories that center racial domination in the project of heterosexual white supremacy (Ferguson 2003).

All of the wonderful scholars in our roundtable conversation offering parallel reflections on the obfuscation and elision of race and racism in the study of our histories across area studies geographies, from the Ottoman empire to South Asia, China, and the broader Sinophone world, to Latin America. These forced erasures of racial subjection have created limited understandings of the global nature of enslavement, indigenous dispossession, and interlinked histories of colonial capital. As Indrani Chatterjee (2002) has argued powerfully in South Asia, the history of slavery is always a history of intimacy and the violent hierarchy of the household. We know that, while India seems far from the transatlantic world, its resources as the capital of the empire were essential to the expansion of multiple systems of slavery, ongoing settlement and colonization, and new hierarchies of bonded labor. It was in colonial India that the British experimented and refined multiple systems of resource extraction and perpetual famine, enforced forms of exploited labor based in the permanent settlement of peasantry (the paradigmatic subaltern) alongside the forced migration of workers, and built enduring legal and scientific structures of social domination that traveled across the empire, enduring far beyond the formal end of colonialism. These multiple histories of social reproduction in racial capitalism—the uncounted productive and reproductive labor of the enslaved, the peasant, the colonized, the indentured, the Third World worker—offer a different view of capitalism when theorized together (Bhattacharya 2017).

HOWARD: In comparison to the transatlantic world, the concepts of race and indigeneity are no less socially salient and analytically important in the Asia Pacific. However, they suffer from being doubly marginalized in existing theoretical dialogues. On the one hand, scholars of Asia often ignore these analytical categories, even though there is a growing body of literature that considers indigenous communities across Asia, such as in the history of Japan, Siberia, the Philippines, and the Indian Ocean. On the other hand, critics of racial capitalism in the West tend to treat the transatlantic slave trade as the overriding framework for understanding the historical formation of race and capitalism. This elevates the conceptualization of racial orders in the Americas to an epistemologically privileged position. One enduring legacy has been the lack of approaching "other" races in the West (e.g., Asian Americans) on an equal footing. Another consequence has been the absence of critical attention to how race (and indigeneity) assumes social meanings and hierarchies that are no less potent in transpacific Asia than they do across the Atlantic.

In one of my current projects, I look at the politics of transness, especially how it intersects with the constructions of indigeneity, in Taiwan. Taiwan is often ignored by mainstream scholarly comprehension for its unstable geopolitical status: is it part of China (thus Chinese), an orphan of the earlier Japanese empire (thus postcolonial Japanese), or the face of right-wing America in the Cold War era (thus hegemonic American)? Further, much of the discourses surrounding queer Taiwan tend to ignore a defining feature of the island's history: it is also home to a diverse group of indigenous communities. According to one line of archaeological research, the tribes in Taiwan are possibly the ancestors of various Austronesian communities scattered across the Pacific.

Most of the Chinese people who migrated to Taiwan belong to the "Han" ethnic group. These Han majorities came to redefine the political landscape of Taiwan in the late 1940s, when Chiang Kai-shek's Nationalist regime retreated to the island and "took over" from the Japanese. There are ongoing tensions within the Han majority, including debates over the political meanings of nativity, Chineseness, and Taiwaneseness (for instance, being a "native" Taiwanese is not necessarily the same as being an "indigenous" Taiwanese). This certainly warrants a more careful inclusion into analysis of racial discourses in Taiwan. However, a realm of social tension more germane to my point lies in Han-Austronesia relations. Historically, the settler colonialism of Han Chinese in Taiwan has pushed Austronesia people into poverty. Therefore, I would argue that the history of indigenous subjects in Taiwan constitutes an important part of the global history of racial capitalism. A vocabulary for talking about Han capitalist accumulation is necessary for probing into the ways in which queerness and transness become intertwined with the racial and class hierarchies.

Şahin: As a researcher whose project seeks to rethink and reimagine trans and queer historiography in the Middle East, in particular, and the Global South, in general, I grapple with the workings of racial capitalism through a kindred but distinct history, namely, the East African slave trade and the Ottoman empire's multivalent involvement in it. It is quite frustrating but hardly surprising that the wide-reaching ramifications of this history are largely missing from the global accounts of racial capitalism produced in the Global North under some strands of trans/queer of color scholarship. Certain characteristics and specificities of this history might help explain why it is omitted from the dominant strands of US scholarship on racial capitalism. For instance, the gendered domestic space has historically been conceptualized outside of the domain of capital in hegemonic accounts. The fact that one common manifestation of the East African slave trade in the Ottoman empire was domestic slavery no doubt has played a pivotal role in this history's (and thus gender's) assumed irrelevance to racial capitalism. Furthermore, the East African slave trade was but one part of the Ottoman system of slavery, which, as Ehud R. Toledano (1998) convincingly argues, is best understood as "a continuum of various degrees of bondage rather than a dichotomy between slave and free" due to its complexity and inconsistency. In other words, its so-called incommensurability renders it a poor comparative framework to comprehend the global itinerary of racial capitalism. Neither of these potential rationales (among various others), however, justify or explain why this history is pretermitted from trans/queer of color scholarship, which not only rightly emphasizes the centrality of gender/sexuality to the workings of racial capitalism but also problematizes the presupposed incommensurabilities between discrete structures/geographies/temporalities. I argue indeed that such erasure is the corollary of the unwillingness of trans/queer of color scholarship from the Global North to reckon with the secular as ideology. On the one hand, this unwillingness reproduces the reductive and chronic culturalism that pervades the analyses concerning the particularities of the Global South shaped by the varicolored manifestations of religion. On the other hand, it fails to unpack the imbrication of race and religion in the East African slave trade, which is tantamount to effacing the polyvalent ways in which religious difference configured corporeal valuation, racial-ethnic formation, and gendered normalization. Through a theoretical prism saturated with the secular as ideology, it is difficult, if not impossible, to cognize that one cannot, in many geographies and time periods, narrate a history of racial capitalism without a concomitant history of religion.

CHRIS:

> "There are new and unpredictable modes of dispossession to be understood alongside the centuries-old carnage that moistens the earth beneath our feet."
> —Bhattacharyya 2018, p. x

In the fifth of their ten theses on racial capitalism, Gargi Bhattacharyya (2018) grapples with the imperative to trace its distinct, varied, and often contradictory emergences. The critical project of engaging capitalism's instantiations in, with, and through regimes of enslavement is far from complete. Of course, the "centuries-old carnage" to which they refer incorporates a history that is both longer and more expansive than this. If we are to fully grasp these "new and unpredictable modes of dispossession" we must engage the protracted dynamics of racialization and accumulation that both include and exceed this instantiation.

Let's take Sarmiento Park, the setting for the collective lives of *travesti* sex workers in Córdoba, Argentina, in Camila Sosa Villada's autofiction *Las Malas* (2019).As a workplace, Sarmiento Park is one site from which to engage racial capitalism to connect the violences of both past and present. Not only through the fact of criminalized sex trade among those pushed to the margins of formal employment, but also through the racist history of Argentine nationalism instantiated by the park's namesake, Domingo Faustino Sarmiento.

Sarmiento—Argentina's president from 1868 until 1874—formalized the nation's program of *blanqueamiento*, or "whitening," by promulgating the position he expressed in his 1845 book *Facundo: Civilization and Barbarism.* In it, he claimed that Argentina's postcolonial failure to thrive after its 1816 declaration of independence from Spain could be attributed to racialized "savagery." For Sarmiento, modernization had to do with the alleged failures of those living in the Pampas to sufficiently exploit the land on which they dwelled. He proposed "taming the wilds" of the country by importing the qualities of urban centers to advance order and prosperity. His infamous "Conquest of the Desert" instantiated whitening regimes through genocide and militarized terror, leaving behind "empty" land for privatization.

Moving both forward and back from Sarmiento (the historical figure) and Sarmiento (the park), we might trace the inequitable and unfree relations of labor that we aptly name "racial." Sosa Villada's nocturnal scene of Sarmiento Park—the wild green lung—reveals the textures of persistent racialization, gendering, and sexualization of classed dispossession in Argentina. For it is not only the echoes of colonization and enslavement that marginalize

Afro-descended, indigenous, and non-white Mestiza transfeminine laborers, but also the racist and racializing nationalisms of anticolonial rule. In this milieu, what sense might we then make of an assemblage of racial capitalism comprising Argentine workers' movements, IMF debts, repressive dictatorships, Peronism, and *travesti* rage (*furia travesti*)? In other words, what is racial capitalism from under the shadow of Dante's statue at Sarmiento Park?

DEBANUJ: My research focuses upon how the global governance of migration is felt at the scale of the queer and trans body. Presently my work interrogates the relocations and seasonal migrations of queer and trans communities from and within Latin America, as well as movement of transgender workers along the Indo-Nepal-Bangladesh borders. I conceptualize racialized capitalism through longer histories of Indian Ocean trade, and the ways in which present-day capital and labor circulates across urban centers across Asia, Latin America, and the US. I offer two broad meditations about racialized capitalism through an inter-Asian trans-regional perspective.

I want us to think about racial capitalism through histories of the Indian Ocean world; through scholars such as Aiwa Ong and Ananya Roy's work about worlding cities (Ong and Ray 2011), and Ayona Datta's ideas about Trans-local geographies (Brickell and Datta, 2016). Ong's ideas about flexible capital helps me to think about how owning class communities from East Asia (and, now increasingly from India as well) have been transferring capital following a longer history of feudal wealth, industrialization and present-day global movement of capital. Let us look at the US and Mexico border in Tijuana, where one encounters dense levels of East Asian investments crafted through the landscape of the city. Samsung sponsored huge neon arch welcomes you to Tijuana's Zona Rosa. Thus, one needs to incorporate movement of capital and production through Indian and Pacific Ocean worlds. Secondly, I am thinking about how elite upper caste, racial formations, wherein race and whiteness is being unmoored from corporeality and circulating through achievement, caste, and class status, engendering the formation of owning class migrant communities in the US and UK.

For instance, Rishi Sunak is now the first person of Indian descent to become the prime minster of the UK—the country that once colonized India. Sunak would also be the eleventh PM to have a degree from Oxford and second richest person to be the UK PM after the Earl of Rosebery. Rishi Sunak is Oxford educated, hails from a meritocratic family, and married into one of the richest families of India. As a figure Sunak, gestures toward the rise of upper caste, upper class, English educated Indian elites who are visibly aligned with white owning class and conservative politics. Sunak espouses an anti-immigrant, nationalist, pro-austerity politics that is akin to white own-ing class's conservative rhetoric. It is helpful to think about Sunak's figure through a trans-local scale, where capital circulates through the global cities network, while getting hooked to local sites and nationalist politics.

In returning to the question of racial capitalism through such an inter-Asia framework, one needs to think about long histories of Indian ocean trade between Indian merchants and East Africa. Scholars such as Pedro Machado examine the central role of Gujarat's Vaaniya merchants between western India and East Africa. Machado demonstrates not only that the Por-tuguese imperial infrastructures were dependent on Gujarati merchants but also that Gujarati actions determined European outcomes. Machado shows us how Vaaniya networks disguised slave trading as a "Hindu" activity amid Portuguese injunctions against the continuation of Islamic slave trades (Machado 2015: 220).

EVREN AND RANA: *How do queer hermeneutics reckon with global and transna-tional histories of social differentiation that ground in other or additional intellec-tual traditions of what we might expansively call "race"?*

DURBA: I would love to see queer and trans of color theorists more often in direct conversation with wide-ranging theorists in the postcolony who offer essential insights into the study of global domination and supremacy through and in excess of the social scientific concept of "race." In the mod-ern world, because of the global nature of colonial structures of knowledge that organize how we study modern society, all structures of domination are inflected through concepts of race. Yet our analytic language in the study of race and racism is largely inadequate to describe other global structures of subjection. In the study of South Asia, there are many productive ways to imagine a queer materialist analysis of gendered structures of caste, Hindu majoritarianism and anti-Muslim violence, the dehumanization of laboring people, emergency in borderlands, claims to indigeneity, and so much more.

In my view, the insights of feminist, queer, and trans of color critique, particularly by scholars and activists outside of the Global North, help in rethinking the very disciplines we have historically used to study the question of social domination. The social scientific categories of race, kinship, caste, endogamy, and descent offer little analytical insight into the mechanics and experiences of subordination, humiliation, and social violence. Thinking with Şahin Açıkgöz's important suggestion that race must be thought through the question of religion and scholarly critiques of the inadequacies of secularism, it is clear that the lexicon of concepts available to us is inadequate to understand social and political life in most of the world.

Rather than coining new social scientific concepts that might better describe social systems, what if we were to instead orient ourselves to the experiential and the sensorial, to the workings of domination for example as a project of smell or touch? Açıkgöz's reflection on religion as a place of domination, religious sociality, and embodiment offers ways we might to reorient our conceptual vocabulary. I can for example imagine exciting new directions in transnational queer studies that center the sensorium. Here I think with the extraordinary work of the late theorist of caste Aniket Jaaware (2018), who critiques the reliance on colonial social scientific categories in the study of caste and Hinduism to instead foreground the question of touch, of touching and not touching. He asks: What does it mean to touch? Who always has the power to touch without consent and inflict violence, and how is being *not* touched a profound mode of subjection? The concept of touch stands in stark contrast to the study of endogamy as a project of caste supremacy in the modern social sciences (Mitra 2021). Or as Black feminist theorist Hortense Spillers describes in a lecture, the manhandling of enslavement, the cruel intimacies of touch, in elaborating her earlier distinction between body and flesh. As she describes it, "Touching, here, is not a token of social cohesion or brotherhood or fellowship or fellow feeling, but rather the very breadth and depth of alienation, among other things, alienation from the laws, and perhaps even ways to distinguish human life from bare life" (2018: n.p.).

Alternatively, we might think of domination spatially, in the forced proximity in carceral structures and enforced social distance. What if, instead of foregrounding descriptive sociological categories like race, caste, class, we orient the study of queerness and non-normativity through the phenomenological subjection of confinement?

HOWARD: My work on the history of Chinese eunuchs serves as a good point of entry into this question. In imperial China, eunuchs were male castrated servants for the emperor and his royal family, occupying a range of positions from within the harem to becoming military commissioners and heads of naval expeditions. In certain epochs of Chinese history, most notably, the Eastern Han (25–220), the Tang (618–907), and the Ming (1368–1644), eunuchs rose to unprecedented political prominence. Over time, historians have debated—and often criticized—the political intrusion of eunuchs in state affairs. The eunuch system came to a halt in the early twentieth century, when the last Qing emperor Puyi dismissed the last cohort of eunuchs from his Qing court.

While this seemingly organic narrative of the demise of Chinese castration may appear to be unrelated to our topic, I would argue that a queer hermeneutic, imbued with a critical attention to race and ethnicity, is central to our deconstruction of the narrative. On the one hand, we see time and again—in fact, up to the present—the expression of a strong critique of eunuchs in terms of their bodily biology and socio-political presence. Throughout Chinese history, scholar officials and Confucian literati construed the activities of eunuchs as the antithesis of civic moral values. Han cultural elites would subsequently hold eunuchs, among other feminized agents, responsible for the failings of a Chinese political regime. In fact, the early record of castration in China suggests that eunuchs were enslaved captives, so they had always been deemed as "inferior" to non-castrated men from the very beginning. A queer hermeneutic, then, questions both the kind of sexual normalcy buttressing Chinese heteronormative patriarchy and the political positioning of eunuchs with respect to Han Confucian virtues.

On the other hand, critiques of Chinese castration began to accumulate with mounting evidence by the late nineteenth century, especially coming from European spectators. Some of the most detailed accounts of the Chinese castration operation itself available today came from these late-Qing Western accounts. By turning the castrated body "inside-out," the dissecting tone of these condemning statements associated a distinctively pathological identity with not just the body of Chinese eunuchs, but the Chinese civilization at large. Here, what appeared to be at stake is the entire Chinese "race," a construct that native voices sought to reconcile with, on the one side, white Europeans and, on the other, an increasingly powerful Japanese race. Because the castrated body became a material basis for the dissemination of new (scientific) knowledge about sex and sex change in the Republican period (1912–1949), a trans hermeneutic forces us to reconsider narratives of eunuchs that fail to acknowledge its queerness from ground zero.

CHRIS: Thinking with sex/gender in transnational inquiry about marginalization and subjugation might veer toward attunement and away from intellectual imperialism. These approaches might be called queer hermeneutics, "hemispheric cuir/queer dialogue" (Pierce et al. 2021), "disobedient epistemologies" (Sacchi et al. 2021), or transnational transfeminism (Hanssmann 2023), among others. Regardless of how we conceptualize them, such approaches might guide inquiries within which queer or trans (as well as *cuir, transgénero*, trans*, *travesti*, and many others) figure not only—indeed, not primarily—as objects of analysis, but rather as what sociologists call "sensitizing concepts."

As Kathy Charmaz (2003, 259) explains, "Sensitizing concepts offer ways of seeing, organizing, and understanding experience. . . . Although sensitizing concepts may deepen perception, they provide starting points for building analysis, not ending points for evading it."

Moving laterally from queer/trans objects, Kadji Amin (2018), Toby Beauchamp (2013), and Thelma Wang (2022) examine transnational regimes of knowledge production through the sensitizing concept of trans. In other words, "trans" becomes an analytic starting point to trace material and conceptual permeabilities of different orders—including and exceeding paradigms of racialization. In their work, "trans" is not an "ending point for evading" analysis. Neither stable nor confirmatory, it is instead a sometimes faltering means through which to consider diffuse and uneven circulations of power. To this end, Amin, Beauchamp, and Wang trace the workings of power across histories, borders, bodies, laboratories, racial projects, Olympic policies, DIY paradigms of gender affirmation, eugenics, and pharmaceutical manufacture and regulation through the organs (glands) and substances (hormones) of endocrinology.

Even in its methodological anti-determinism, however, sensitizing concepts may reify through their very lines of inquiry. This is central to Geeta Patel's (2006: 27) concerns with "scholars who have crossed borders in the chase to "discover" sex/gender difference" among Aravani or hijra as "reified embodiments of difference." For Patel, the intellectual pursuit of certain arrangements of difference can quietly efface the centrality of capital, state formation, colonialism, property, law, medicine, religion, and much more. Cole Rizki's (2020) work offers a refreshing antidote, taking as its sensitizing concepts both "sex/gender" and "state violence." He examines travesti subjectivity—as both lived experience and metonym for the violence of liberalism—to consider the persistence of Argentine state violence spanning both fascist and ostensibly democratic regimes. Here, queer/trans inquiry refuses reification, and instead traces the unevenly shared calamity of racialized, classed, indigenized, sexualized, and gendered state violence.

DEBANUJ: I have been thinking about how personhood is bestowed in the context of India through ideas of sanguinity, purity and profanity, caste status (broadly through categories such as Jati and Kula-which are ascribed at birth). Blood, sanguinity, caste status, as well as religious background provides frameworks for legitimacy of one's body, and thereby delimiting one's sexual and reproductive capacities. In my scholarship I highlight how caste, class, Hindu nationalism (in the case of India) operate as regulatory regimes upon diverse bodies and how caste purity bestows livability upon certain bodies, while rendering Dalit and non-Hindu communities as those marked for slow death. Such processes are yet to be fully taken up by queer hermeneutics, as well as by scholars of queer biopolitics.

Secondly, trans*studies as it has emerged in the US academy posits the formation of the trans*subject as a secular project. Majority of the literature considers religion and trans*politics as oppositional to each other (Strassfeld and Henderson-Espinoza 2019). However, in the context of South Asia, the emergence of trans* subject of rights remain entangled with religiosities. Throughout South Asia, each of the countries now have varying forms of legal recognition for diverse gender identities. The legal deliberations are framed through religious discourses about the timelessness of diverse gender identities in religions of South Asia. In Pakistan KhwajaSira is connected with ideas about piety, whereas in India, Hindu mythologies about Hijras, Aravanis, and Kinnars is written into the Supreme Court judgement. Hindu Brahmanical myths, practices, caste hierarchies provide the framework for the arrival of the transgender subjects of rights. Thus, thinking through caste, religiosities, and nationalism is vital to a rethinking of "trans," as a project of secular modernity.

ŞAHIN: I find this question very significant, and I believe that one way to respond to it is by inquiring into what kind of hermeneutics queer theory/critique has persistently deployed in its perusal of variegated texts, bodies, histories, geographies, and matters to make sense of racial difference. It would not be wrong to postulate that queer's predilect hermeneutics has historically been secular hermeneutics of suspicion, which, I argue, has very often resulted in what Boaventura de Sousa Santos (2014) termed epistemicide. Since such hermeneutics has been chiefly oriented toward resistance, demystification, and unearthing, it has tended to read particular global manifestations of difference through a complicit/subversive dyad. This, in turn, has occluded a generative reading of how secular modernity has systematically mystified both the kaleidoscopic self- formations of nonsecular communities/subjects and the coterminous materialization, in certain spaces/periods, of various constitutive analytical categories such as race and religion. As Muriam Haleh Davis (2022) reminds us in her work on Islam and racial capitalism in Algeria, the secular modern attachment to the division between race and religion has kept us from seeing the workings of the racial regime of religion. My own work on the black eunuchs of the Ottoman Empire also underscores the impossibility of fully grasping the gendered normalization of human proper in that context without rethinking how religious difference found articulation within racial difference. The answer to why there has been a pervasive dismissal of its obverse, namely queer hermeneutics of faith, in queer scholarship is not more complicated than a simple "queer hermeneutics has a faith and religion problem." Roger Rothman (2020) notes that even when Sedgwick acknowledges her debt to Paul Ricoeur in her critique of suspicion, she does not elaborate on what Ricoeur proposed as its antithesis (faith), opting instead for "hermeneutics of recovery of meaning" to avoid using the term "faith." Ironically though, in his own justification for why faith is a more appropriate term than recovery due to its refusal "to suppose a prelapsarian wholeness as the wellspring of meaning," Rothman feels the need to clarify that his understanding of faith is secular as opposed to religious. Although I completely agree with Rothman's argument that hermeneutics of faith is about imagining and recognizing that alternative frames exist, his clarification strikes me as odd given that the secular, as many scholars have shown (Strassfeld and Henderson-Espinoza 2019; Sanchez 2019), is not secular but itself a religious formation. To recapitulate why this matters for queer's relationally with race, I should note that early queer hermeneutics, on account of its reductive (and colonial) privileging of sexuality, had, inter alia, a race problem, which has been brilliantly taken to task by queer of color scholarship. Nonetheless, the "religion problem" still persists, obfuscating a much needed appreciation of the divergent formations of race and racialization across the globe. In that sense, in its complex reckoning with race, queer hermeneutics would no doubt benefit from having more "faith."

RANA AND EVREN: *How would queer of color critique as an analytic be useful to question the very making of abject and abnormal bodies, the structures of knowledge and regimes of truth that produce them, and the political economies that necessitate them?*

HOWARD: There is a thriving literature that addresses this question in Western queer studies. A queer of color critique is not limited to the deciphering of how such binaries as white/black and heterosexuality/homosexuality had been co-produced in the scientific literature from the start—from George Cuvier's depiction of Saartje Baartman to the eugenics vision of early-twentieth-century European sexologists. Asian American critics have also expanded this approach by exploring the interconnection between sexual and racial difference in concrete political-economic terms: the way queerness figures into the construction of Asianness in the history of railroad labor, immigration exclusion, bachelor societies, wartime internment, and beyond. More recently, historian Laurie Marhoefer has bridged these two seemingly separate approaches by bringing to light sexologist Magnus Hirschfeld's relationship with his Sinophone lover Li Shiu Tong. In so doing, Marhoefer demonstrates the way racism and ideas about race enabled both prejudiced and subversive conceptualizations of queerness.

I would like to bring the conversation back to the Sinophone Pacific again. There are numerous examples to which one can point, but the work of Francisca Lai deserves special mention in light of the groundbreaking nature of her work on Indonesian migrant lesbian workers in Hong Kong. Although not always couched in the language of race or ethnicity, the difference between native Cantonese Hong Kongers and migrant workers from the Philippines and Indonesia became particularly acute within local queer communities. One particular area where this can be seen is the rise of migrant lesbian activism at the grassroots level since 2006. Prior to this, migrant activism had mainly focused on issues such as underpayment, excessive working hours, and unsuitable accommodations for domestic workers. However, with the founding of migrant organizations devoted to LGBT rights, such grassroots activism began to pitch the problems of capitalist exploitation as sharing a set of challenges faced by LGBT people within the larger framework of human rights.

When gender and sexual politics served as the common denominator, Hong Kong and Southeast Asian activists came together to develop strategies for deepening transnational LGBT solidarity in this British postcolony. The difference between Hong Kongers and Southeast Asian workers is of course racialized (whether we consider skin color as a superficial phenotypical marker or language as a normative code of culture), but the point is that in the context of migrant labor activism, the line may very well be drawn across class lines. This exposes the artificiality of how abject/abnormal bodies are made within resistant movements to capitalist globalization. A queer of color critique in the context of the Sinophone Pacific enriches the dialogues about queers of color that have typically emanated from the West.

ŞAHİN: It is quite challenging to cogitate on queer of color critique as an analytic without simultaneously pondering the question of the Global South. I am particularly interested in interrogating how the Global South, which, in Roderick A. Ferguson's (2015) words, provided the invisible ink for Aberrations and indeed did constitute the unread genealogy of queer of color critique, has continued to be instrumentalized and deployed as an alibi in certain strands of queer scholarship to preserve the international division of knowledge production. The political economy of this queer instrumentalization has, I argue, substantially manufactured the asymmetrical financialization of the globe on an epistemic level. The Global North has crystallized as the fountain of episteme and theorem while the Global South has been transformed into a rich and productive reservoir of case studies and raw materials. The upshot of this hegemonic arrangement has not been limited, unsurprisingly, to the cementing of the assumed universality of the Global North's epistemic macrocosm. The economic and ideological attachments as well as biases of that universe, the secular being one of the principal ones, have also been exported, concealing the polymorphous workings of capital in both engendering regimes of normalcy/deviancy and legitimating acceptable patterns of knowing and representing. At this juncture, I should clarify that the intention of my abovementioned characterization is not to portray the Global North or the Global South as a monolith, nor is it to ascribe a perennial and culturalist subalternity/indigeneity to the Global South. It is, I maintain, precisely the very unpredictable formations that emerge from those complex convergences that queer of color critique should grapple with while being attentive to the North/South entanglements. If, for instance, capital is not secular and if formations of capital cannot be comprehended independently of religion, how did their historically contingent co-formations precipitate certain structures of truth and normative frames of bodily intelligibility in Ottoman empire and post-imperial Turkey? Such inquiry enabled by queer of color critique as an analytic would exhume the imperial commingling of religious and racial difference in configuring somatic valuation. It would also disinter an associated postimperial and national historiography within which capital weaponized ethno-religious alterity in administrative and bureaucratic layers as well as visual and textual media not only to ungender certain bodies/communities but also to rationalize wealth transfer, economic dispossession, and political disenfranchisement.

DEBANUJ: Queer of color critique develops an analytics of how the creation of racial surplus is simultaneously a gendered and sexualized process. It is arguably a US-centric project, since the field interrogates how US liberalism is formed through the displacement of indigenous communities, slavery, and ongoing displacement of migrant workers. The undocumented drag queen, Muslim migrant is rendered as a perverse figure within the normative politics of LGBT recognition, and often left to die at the gates of the US nation-state. Queer of color critique appeared as an important and timely intervention during the consolidation of the national security state in the

US; however, it falls short to rethink the formation of abject and abnormal bodies in a context other than the US. Yet, thinking about racialization and sexualization through both the analytical and hermeneutic strands within continental philosophy is a very important epistemological project. In our introductions to *Queering Digital India* Rohit Dasgupta and I lay out how queer of color critique provides a framework for bringing together post-colonial thinkers (such as the Subaltern Studies school, as well as Membe and Fanon) with continental philosophy.

Decriminalization of sodomy and trans/gender recognition projects in South Asia take on sexual modernity in assuming that "I," as an individual, is legible to the state as a rights-deserving subject. I find scholars such as Marquis Bey's argument about how cisgender as the binary opposite of trans/gender is a project of white supremacy very helpful in thinking through questions of caste, indigeneity, and gender identity in India. Certain bodies (such as Dalit/Adivasi bodies) are not ascribed gender historically. Adivasi (or those marked as tribal in the Indian census) were considered criminal tribes under British colonialism and so were "Hijras." Thus diverse gender expressions and the "tribal body" were the savage, criminal bodies in need of arrest, containment, and reform. The question of LGBTQ recognition in India has taken a very upper-class Hindu framework of recognition from the family and the nation-state. The Indian nation-state occupies and terrorizes people in Kashmir and many of the North-Eastern tribal communities. Surely, the North-Eastern communities are not seeking inclusion or recognition but rather seeking freedom from military occupation. Queer of color critique, especially scholarship that thinks through the biopolitics of surveillance, control, and settler colonialism, remains vital in writing about communities living under military occupation in India.

JOAO: A queer of color analysis can enrich understanding of the power structures produced by capitalist modernity, showing how "homosexuality," as a category and signifier, is now the language of North/South conflicts. Numerous works by queer thinkers of color such as Paola Bacchetta (2017), Fatima El Tayeb (2012), Jin Haritaworn (2015), and Jasbir Puar (2013) have shown historical and present-day uses of "homosexuality" as a way to differentiate the human from the nonhuman, the white from the non-white, the lives that deserve or not to be lived with dignity.

Queer of color critique's usefulness resides in the fact that it can question the heterosexual dimension of these racist and imperialist processes. However, French decolonial intellectual and political circles (to speak of a context that I know) reduce sexual imperialism to homonationalism. Heterosexual modernity, when it is mentioned, does not at all give rise to an analysis as rigorous as that to which these circles subject minority sexual identities.

Heterosexuality as it is experienced today in the West, by whites and people of color, even in a differentiated and of course hierarchical way, is also a product of the so-called capitalist modernity: the number of children one has, the age at which one has them, the hegemony of a romantic conception of love, the transformations of the labor market and the changes concerning the place of women in the productive sphere, the multiplication of divorces, new procreation techniques (not accessible to all of course), the effect of migration . . . These transformations are of course not uniform according to race and class, but they affect all social groups. The rise of sexual minorities as social groups (whether culturally or politically) is a by-product of these transformations. Yet, these sexual minorities are specifically designated as symbols of whiteness, even in radical circles, which seems to refuse to challenge this perception.

We must remember one essential thing: heterosexuality does not need to be named or to be self-claimed as an identity to be hegemonic, because it is set as a norm. For sexual imperialism in its homosexual version to work, one must declare oneself homo pro homo, because homosexuality as the transgression needs to be explicitly legible. For instance, threaten such African countries with sanctions if they do not change their laws on homos, or use LGBT flags in Qatar, etc. On the other hand, imperialism in its heterosexual version does not need to announce itself loudly as heterosexual. It suffices for instance to say, among other examples, "African women must have fewer children." Because reproduction has always been an issue in colonialism; we have repeated episodes in different places of colonialism of forced sterilizations on African, Caribbean, or indigenous women. This is heteronationalism—the need to transform the Global South population to fit new labor regimes and consumer markets. But many decolonial thinkers will fail to see this as part sexual imperialism.

Sexual imperialism in the hetero version is also, again without having to say it as such, the imposition of shopping centers in the major African capitals, which transform consumption patterns, create desires assimilated to forms of life associated with the West, transform the relationships between families, men and women. This extension of the capitalist market is the most powerful vector for the assimilation of the populations of the South to Western family models, mostly heterosexual, and then homosexual. Euro-American culturalist documentaries on the South, if they include more and more the figure of homos oppressed by so-called backward cultures, already included long before the idea that "the young" (read: straight), can't love each other freely, marry whoever they want, "over there."

CHRIS:

"¡Ni Una Menos!" (Not one [woman or travesti] less!)

"¡Nos Queremos Vivas!" (We want ourselves alive!)

"¡Vivas y desendeudadas nos queremos!" (We want ourselves alive and unindebted!)

These are some of the slogans that have appeared on protest signs in Argentina and throughout the Spanish-speaking Américas at Ni Una Menos protests. The movement has gained considerable momentum in its confrontation with the often fatal violence resulting in what have been called "femicides" and "travesticides," or the classed, racialized, sexualized, and gendered targeting of women and *travestis*.

The first Ni Una Menos demonstration took place in Argentina in 2015, in response to the discovery of a pregnant teenager who was murdered by her boyfriend in the province of Santa Fe. The movement quickly proliferated to other regions, with feminists from Chile, México, Brazil, Perú, Uruguay, Guatemala, and El Salvador joining ranks. The Marea Verde (or Green Tide) movement soon expanded its demands beyond an end to gendered violence, asserting support for bodily autonomy, economic freedom, and the elimination of debt.

Following the threads that link assassination with indebtedness also requires following those that link feminist anti-violence with feminist anti-capitalism, anti-racism, anti-colonialism, and anti-imperialism. Queer of color critique, in its refusals to isolate paradigms of sexualization and gendering from those of racial and national formation, offers capacious analytic terrain. Alongside Marea Verde feminists' own geopolitically expansive reflections on and refusals of abjection, such an approach might partially guide us toward questions that investigate the material conditions of the production of subordinated difference in a transnational register.

Argentine feminists and Marea Verde activists Lucí Cavallero and Verónica Gago open their 2021 treatise *A Feminist Reading of Debt*, with an introductory chapter entitled "Taking Debt Out of the Closet." For them, this means amplifying the tangible and everyday effects of what they call the "financial terror" of global finance and structural adjustment policies (2021:

13). However, it also means engaging the private debt incurred by those—whether waged, informally paid, or unpaid—who have borne the brunt of neoliberalism's more forward-facing extractions. Marea Verde feminists dwell in the intricacies of how women, trans people, and travestis navigate the subordinating relationships between husband and wife, banker and borrower, sex worker and john, factory worker and boss, owner and renter, police and subject of surveillance. These relations are thoroughly heterogenous, and differentially formed in the crucible of colonial invasion, populist nationalism, the persistent reach of the Washington Consensus, and broader economies of extraction. After all, "capital is a formation constituted by discourses of race, gender, and sexuality" (Ferguson 2013: 11). Examining individual and national debt through these discourses lays bare how "the creation of categories of value and valuelessness underpins contemporary racialized necropolitical regulation" (Hong and Ferguson 2011, 16).

DURBA: In *Aberrations in Black* (2003), Rod Ferguson sets an ambitious agenda for queer of color critique to center the history of knowledge in the study of queer life and denaturalize disciplinary norms that shape the study of our social worlds. As he shows, the history of knowledge about the excluded, abject, and the abnormal is always racialized and racial subjection is constituted through sexual abjection, and it is this twinned process of racial queering that makes possible capitalist institutions of the family and the state. In my work, I build on these insights from queer of color critique alongside women of color feminisms to demonstrate how the project of modern social knowledge is made possible through the control of feminized sexuality, produced by and through colonial racial subjection and neocolonial structures of knowledge that undermine the radical project of decolonization. The modern study of social life—the basis of social policy, law, policing, economics, institutions like marriage—is built on the queer, the abject, the abnormal. Queer and trans of color critiques are at their core, to me, about the undoing of knowledge and rethinking the categories we inherit in how we write our social worlds.

When I reflect on Howard Chiang's important intervention on the peculiar spaces of Taiwan and Hong Kong in thinking belonging and coloniality and Christoph Hanssmann's invocation of the total abjection of indebtedness, I feel that we must think with the methods of queer of color critique to understand the violent exclusion of subjects like workers whose abjection is rendered invisible. Migrant workers, sex workers, urban workers, they are rendered powerless in systems of economic dependency. To be queer, abnormal, abject is to live in conditions of impossibility where people must migrate under difficult conditions, far abroad, or locally move from rural spaces to the city, now because of climate crises. People are incarcerated as stateless subjects in the lands that they travel to for labor, from Dubai to Singapore to streets of a city. Their passports are taken, they are locked in tenement housing, marked as diseased vectors. Queer, gender nonconforming, and trans people are harassed and locked up by the police for their gender presentation, for loitering, for trespassing; they are harassed just for existing. It is a set of conditions that will soon affect much of the world more and all of us, as Sunil Amrith (2022) reminds us that, to be a migrant is to be simultaneously moving and incarcerated in a place that is not home. Queer of theory critique may offer powerful methods to critically assess our current conundrum of the simultaneity of forced migration and forcible capture in an increasingly uninhabitable world.

EVREN AND RANA: *To what extent does positioning queer and trans of color critique as methods objects and subjects, "beyond identity politics" or even "the Human," alleviate or otherwise reconfigure these issues?*

CHRIS: For the last decade, I've followed trans depathologization, or the efforts that trans people undertake to access gender-affirming care affordably and without undue scrutiny or barriers to care. Depathologization activists resist varying rules, laws, and guidelines defining sex/gender non-normativity as pathological. These differentially but persistently structure gender-affirming care, requiring psychiatric diagnoses and coercive assessments to access hormone prescriptions, surgeries, or other treatments and procedures. In their search to bring about what some have called "care without pathology," activists instead insist that they can assess their own needs, and that sex/gender non-normativity is not equivalent to unwellness—mental or otherwise.

During my fieldwork in Buenos Aires, one of the respondents with whom I spoke recounted his experience at a presentation on depathologizing health care to a group of officials. This longtime trans activist, who also had disabilities, described listening to a fellow activist beseech the audience about the need for depathologization by forcefully asserting that she was not ill, but was rather a human being. He laughed at her stark disavowal of disability, as well as her audacious insinuation that people with illness—himself included—were disqualified from humanity.

Disqualifications from humanity, in Sylvia Wynter's terms, spring from the imperialist and universalizing currents of Western epistemology.

Wynter's (2003) account of "Man-as-human" is a particular project of colonial erasure and domination masquerading as universal truth. In it, a bevy of self-replicating systems install, rationalize, and reproduce colonial knowledge to define who counts as human (and more pointedly, who does not). Walter Mignolo (2015: 122) is drawn to what he sees as Wynter's decolonial insistence that those who are excluded from humanity need not insist upon admittance within the terms of these systems, but must instead ask, "What does it mean to be human?"

From this perspective, trans disavowals of illness might be a frantic bid for admittance (see also Awkward-Rich 2022). Starting instead with what it means to be trans and/or Human might provide a more capacious approach to the problem of pathologization. Wynter's decolonial theorizing might inspire a shift away from appeals to wellness on medicine's own terms, and instead toward questions about how pathologization instantiates across regimes of colonization, racialization, or racial capitalism.

The multilayered and imbricated accounts of pathologization also underscore the nuances and asymmetries of colonization and capital accumulation, within which ascriptions of illness, abjection, criminality, and abnormality stick to different bodies in different ways, at different times, and in different sites.

DURBA: It seems to me that the field of transnational queer studies is essential for understanding rising authoritarianisms and forms of state violence that define our present. I believe that the best, most internationalist queer and trans of color critique offer theories of living: living in spite of, living with, living uncomfortably, sometimes the painful impossibility of living. We exist in a time of alarming authoritarianisms around the world, enacted again and again through the violent control and disappearance of women of color, queers, and trans people.

In thinking about queer of color thought as a resource against authoritarianism, I see Neferti Tadiar's (2022) theory of human dispensability and the life that is made outside of the calculus of economic productivity most profound. People in much of the world, seen only as laborers, seek to survive and thrive. They again and again seek the possibility of what Tadiar calls "becoming-human" against a global economic and political order that wages a "war to be human" in the violent paradigms of modern perpetual war in the form of policing and privatized war. These are the wars that are taken up on behalf of the select few who get to be human, for a supremacist vision of "freedom" and "democracy" in the aftermath of 9/11. These wars are waged by the police and military in America, Nigeria, India, Brazil, and around the world that render poor people, migrants, women, religious minorities, and queer, gender-nonconforming, and trans communities as outside of the domain of humanity. They are uncounted casualties, targets for drones, justified deaths, people "eliminated" because of their threat to public order. Sylvia Wynter (1994) so brilliantly theorized the urgency of the violence around the exclusionary category of the human, to undo the narrative status of dispensability through the LAPD's designation of N.H.I.: "No Humans Involved." Despite these narrative condemnations, the most marginalized people in the world engage in ongoing projects of living. They work, create art, and find community in impossible conditions of displacement and exploitation.

In my current work on the history of Third World feminism and anti-authoritarian thought, I analyze how the feminist study of social and political life in the decolonizing world has shaped a complicated postcolonial economy of knowledge in the form of everything from NGO reports to radical manifestos, diverse genres that shape how we write and argue for the rights of women, queer, and trans people. These critical theories—Third World feminisms, abolitionist and anti-carceral thought, and queer of color and transnational queer and trans studies—are resources for understanding the limits and possibilities of projects of dissent and how we might envision sustained movements against authoritarianism in our times.

JOAO: To move beyond a purely identity-based approach, through a queer and trans of color critique, I think that questioning the place of queer and trans people in production relations is crucial.

Are queer and trans people a "class"? The answer would be a priori no, since the social relationship that opposes them to heterosexuals or cisgender people is not strictly speaking a direct exploitative relationship in the same way as a boss who exploits a worker, but takes more the form of oppression: stigmatization, attacks, discrimination, etc. This does not mean that there are no economic consequences to the oppressions of gender and sexuality, but that we cannot speak of a "heterosexual class" in the face of a "non-heterosexual class," or from a "cisgender class" to a "trans class." But, how can we then understand this economic dimension?

The interest of materialist thought, unlike a purely identity-based approach, is to understand that this situation meets the needs of capitalism and is not the simple result of an anti-trans ideology that is corrected by speeches, even punching actions against transphobia. Jules Gill-Peterson (2018) invites us for instance to think about the economic dimension of the

US-based current anti-trans politics. Clearly, as long as capitalism needs to rely on this gendered, binary, and hierarchical principle in its functioning, transitioning will pose a problem. This does not mean that we should not fight against transphobia in particular, but that we must succeed in understanding the economic bases of transphobic oppression.

This reality of the economic consequences of transphobia combines with those of racism, which is why it is non-white trans people (including men) who are highly represented in the category of "marginal" condemned to the parallel economy whether it is prostitution (especially for women), the sale of drugs, or other forms of illegal and criminalized work. Analyzing homophobia, and especially transphobia, in its relation to capitalism forces us to understand why a question that supposedly only refers to a small number of people, is actually at the core of social and economic orders.

ŞAHIN: Since queer and trans identities, when they circulate transnationally as modern technologies of self-identification, always carry the risk of becoming complicit in the teleological and neoliberal reordering of the incommensurable, such identitarian transplantation is also very likely, as trans and queer of color scholarship has showcased, to eventuate in the racist reproduction of sexological violence and the concurrent act of locating the genesis in the medical archive sanitized of its secular, pecuniary, geopolitical, and necropolitical attachments. How would it be possible, for example, to talk about a trans historiography predicated on the black eunuchs of the Ottoman empire without such strategic positioning? How would it be imaginable for a trans or queer historiography to start with race and/or religion instead of gender? One might no doubt ask myriad analogous questions contingent on discrete geographic spaces and histories. When it comes to positioning queer and trans of color critique beyond the Human, however, I have some reservations not because I do not see its value or urgency but because I also would like to remain wary of its potential hegemonic deployments/consequences. On the one hand, I concur with queer and trans of color scholars such as José Esteban Muñoz (2015), who, in his theorization of the sense of brownness in the world, underscores the importance of thinking incommensurate queer inhumanity to not only unsettle conventional anthropocentric formations of knowledge production deemed universal but also "attune oneself to the potential and actual vastness of being-with." I recognize its conspicuousness and cruciality within the conceptual framework of my own work on slavery as well when I reflect on how the inhabited land, territorial proximity to the empire, and geographic situatedness intersected with racial and religious difference to create conditions of enslavement and violence. These insights and interpretations only become conceivable through an analytical reckoning with the inhuman/nonhuman. On the other hand, despite the significance of both identifying anthropomorphism as a colonial/capitalist/extractivist project and moving beyond the Human, I find the critical interventions of scholars such as Zakiyyah Iman Jackson (2015, 2020) and Jinthana Haritaworn (2015) invaluable as they remind us how the desire to move beyond the human may indeed betray the desire to move beyond race and reproduce the Eurocentric transcendentalism unless this desire is simultaneously invested in decolonizing the interconnected and persistent processes of dehumanization and racialization.

Overall, all of these substantial engagements with the potential implications of positioning queer and trans of color critique "beyond" categories accentuate the necessity to be in conversation with as well as learn from critical race studies, religious studies, and indigenous studies.

HOWARD: When scholars such as Lisa Lowe note the displacement of the African slave by the Chinese coolie in the 19th-century Atlantic world, they have documented a conceptual eclipse in the modern emergence of liberal humanism in which the fraught racialized division of labor re-justifies—and thus reconceals—itself through a seemingly "post-slavery" rhetoric. If we work with this definition of (modern) humanism, queer and trans of color critique offers methods, objects, and subjects that further trouble "the secular European tradition of liberal philosophy that narrates political emancipation through citizenship in the state, that declares economic freedom in the development of wage labor and an exchange market, and that confers civilization to the human person educated in aesthetic and national culture, in each case unifying particularity, difference, or locality through universal concepts of reason and community" (Lowe 2006: 192) The point that Şahin makes about bringing the black eunuchs of the Ottoman empire into a dialogue about "the global itinerary of racial capitalism" exemplifies such a possibility. Another congruent "subject," which has not been elaborated in this conversation yet, is the hijras of South Asia. The fact that race is decisively implicated across these various exemplars of "eunuchs," including the Chinese eunuch I discussed earlier, suggests that the critique of modern humanism can be strengthened when "intimacy"—in the way Lowe invokes it—becomes a queered modality of investigation in a transcultural framework.

What is at stake concerns the origins of definitions, whether around particular sets of identity or assemblages of the human, as well as the challenge to route theory and critique beyond binary constructions, including the West and the Rest, male and female, black and white, and so forth. That the instability of gender and sexual configurations provide an axial approach to rethink the accrued value of identity and the human questions the enduring labor performed by conceptual attachments to these constructs from the start. In my book *Transtopia in the Sinophone Pacific* (2021), I genealogize a Chinese category of trans inhumanism, *renyao* ("human-monster"), which squarely places geopolitics at the heart of trans history. From the viewpoint of Western trans studies, the *renyao* figure is explicitly othered and racialized in relation to the canon of trans historiography. Thus, the positioning of queer and trans of color critique demands a space of post-identitarian and post-humanisitic thinking, which would otherwise be similarly "eclipsed" by a persistent obsession with identities and humanisms defined around the tradition of European liberalism. Let me be absolutely clear: "European" here does not automatically stand for whiteness. Yet the implicitly racialized construct of the "European," perhaps standing more for the proper human, has been imitated across the Pacific, such as when the Japanese sought to lead a definition of the pan-Asian race in the early twentieth century or when the Han Chinese claim Han-ness as a property through capitalist accumulation.

References

Amin, Kadji. 2018. "Glands, Eugenics, and Rejuvenation in *Man into Woman*: A Biopolitical Genealogy of Transsexuality." *TSQ: Transgender Studies Quarterly* 5, no. 4: 589–605.

Amrith, Sunil. 2022. "Life, Moving: Notes from a Small Island" talk delivered at the Mahindra Center for the Humanities, Harvard University, November 28.

Arondekar, Anjali. 2009. *For the Record: On Sexuality and the Colonial Archive in India.* Durham, NC: Duke University Press.

Awkward-Rich, Cameron. 2022. *The Terrible We: Thinking with Trans Maladjustment.* Durham, NC: Duke University Press.

Bacchetta, Paola. 2017. "Murderous Conditions and LQT POC Decolonial-Anti Capitalist Life Imaginings in France." In double special issue on "Postcolonial Queers in Europe," *Lambda Nordica.* 22, nos. 2–3 :153–73.

Beauchamp, Toby. 2013. "The Substance of Borders: Transgender Politics, Mobility, and US State Regulation of Testosterone." *GLQ,* 19, no. 1: 57–78.

Bhattacharya, Tithi. 2017. *Social Reproduction t\Theory: Remapping Class, Recentering Oppression.* London: Pluto Press.

Bhattacharyya, Gargi. 2018. *Rethinking Racial Capitalism.* London; Lanham: Rowman and Littlefield International.

Brickell, K., and Datta, A. 2016. *Translocal Geographies: Spaces, Places, Connections.* Burlington, VT : Ashgate Publishing.

Cavallero, Lucí, and Verónica Gago. 2010. *A Feminist Reading of Debt.* London: Pluto Press. Translated by Liz Mason-Deese.

Charmaz, Kathy. 2003. "Grounded Theory: Objectivist and Constructivist Methods." In Norm. K. Denzin and Yvonna S. Lincoln (Eds.), *Strategies for Qualitative Inquiry* 2nd ed., 249–91. Thousand Oaks, CA: Sage.

Chatterjee, Indrani. 2002. *Gender, Slavery and Law in Colonial India.* London: Oxford University Press.

Chiang, Howard. 2021. *Transtopia in the Sinophone Pacific.* New York: Columbia University Press.

DasGupta, Rohit, and Debanuj DasGupta. 2018. *Queering Digital India: Activism, Identities and Subjectivities.* Edinburgh: Edinburgh University Press.

Davis, Angela Yvonne. 1983. *Women, Race, and Class.* New York: Vintage.

Davis, Muriam Haleh. 2022. *Markets of Civilization: Islam and Racial Capitalism in Algeria.* Durham, NC: Duke University Press.

El Tayeb, Fatima. 2012. "'Gays who cannot properly be gay': Queer Muslims in the Neoliberal European City." *European Journal of Women's Studies*, 19, no. 1: 79–95.

Ferguson, Roderick A. 2003. *Aberrations in Black: Toward a Queer of Color Critique.* Minneapolis: University of Minnesota Press.

Ferguson, Roderick A. 2015. "Queer of Color Critique and the Question of the Global South." In *The Global Trajectories of Queerness*, edited by Ashley Tellis and Sruti Bala, 49–56. Leiden: Brill.

Gill-Peterson, Jules. 2018. *Histories of the Transgender Child.* Minneapolis: University of Minnesota Press.

Hanssmann, Christoph. 2023. *Care Without Pathology: How Trans- Health Activists Are Changing Medicine.* Minneapolis: University of Minnesota Press.

Haritaworn, Jin. 2015. "Decolonizing the Non/Human." *GLQ* 21, nos. 2–3: 210–13.

Haritaworn, Jinthana. 2015. *Queer Lovers and Hateful Others: Regenerating Violent Times and Places.* London: Pluto Press.

Hong, Grace Kyungwon, and Roderick Ferguson. 2011. *Strange Affinities: The Gender and Sexual Politics of Comparative Racialization.* Durham, NC: Duke University Press.

Jaaware, Aniket. 2018. *Practicing Caste: On Touching and Not Touching.* New York: Fordham University Press.

Jackson, Zakiyyah Iman. 2015. "Outer Worlds: The Persistence of Race in Movement 'Beyond the Human.'" *GLQ* 21, nos. 2–3: 215–18.

Jackson, Zakiyyah Iman. 2020. *Becoming Human: Matter and Meaning in an Antiblack World.* New York: New York University Press.

Lowe, Lisa. 2006. "The Intimacies of Four Continents." In *Haunted by Empire: Geographies of Intimacy in North American History*, edited by Ann Laura Stoler, 191–212. Durham, NC: Duke University Press.

Lowe, Lisa. 2015. *The Intimacies of Four Continents.* Durham, NC: Duke University Press.

Machado, P. 2015. *Ocean of Trade: South Asian Merchants, Africa and the Indian Ocean. C.1750– 1850.* Cambridge: Cambridge University Press.

Mitra, Durba. 2021. "'Surplus Woman': Female Sexuality and the Concept of Endogamy." *Journal of Asian Studies* 80, no. 1: 3–26.

Mitra, Durba. 2020. *Indian Sex Life: Sexuality and the Colonial Origins of Modern Social Thought.* Princeton, NJ: Princeton University Press.

Morgan, Jennifer L. 2021. *Reckoning with slavery: Gender, kinship, and capitalism in the early black Atlantic.* Durham, NC: Duke University Press.

Muñoz, José Esteban. 2015. "Theorizing Queer Inhumanisms: The Sense of Brownness." *GLQ* 21, nos. 2–3: 209–10.

Ong, A., and Ray, A. 2011. *Worlding Cities: Asian Experiments and the Art of Being Global.* Chichester, UK: Wiley-Blackwell.

Patel, Geeta. 2006. "Risky Subjects: Insurance, Sexuality, and Capital," *Social Text* 24, no. 4 (89): 25–65.

Pierce, Joseph M., María Amelia Viteri, Diego Falconí Trávez, Salvador Vidal-Ortiz, and Lourdes Martínez-Echazábal. 2021. "Introduction: *Cuir*/Queer Américas: Translation, Decoloniality, and the Incommensurable." *GLQ* 27, no. 3: 321–27.

Puar, Jasbir. 2013. "Rethinking Homonationalism" *International Journal of Middle East Studies* 45, no. 2: 336–39.

Rifkin, Mark. 2010. *When Did Indians Become Straight? Kinship, the History of Sexuality, and Native Sovereignty.* Oxford, UK: Oxford University Press.

Rizki, Cole. 2020. "No State Apparatus Goes to Bed Genocidal Then Wakes Up Democratic": Fascist Ideology and Transgender Politics in Post-dictatorship Argentina." *Radical History Review* 138: 82–107.

Robinson, Cedric J. 2020. *Black Marxism: The making of the black radical tradition.* Chapel Hill: University of North Carolina Press.

Rothman, Roger. 2020. "Anarchism and the Hermeneutics of Faith." *Modernism/modernity* 27: 429–45.

Sacchi, Duen, Dana Galán/David Aruquipa, Ochy Curiel, Marlene Wayar, John Michael Hughson. 2021. "Disobedient Epistemologies and Decolonial Histories: A Forum on Latin American Praxis." *GLQ* 27, no. 3: 329–4.

Sanchez, Melissa E. 2019. *Queer Faith: Reading Promiscuity and Race in the Secular Love Tradition.* New York: New York University Press.

Santos, Boaventura de Sousa. 2014. *Epistemologies of the South: Justice Against Epistemicide.* New York: Routledge.

Sosa Villada, Camila. 2019. *Las Malas.* Buenos Aires: Tusquets Editores S. A.

Spillers, Hortense. 2018. "To the Bone: Some Speculations on Touch" lecture delivered March 23 at Studium Generale Rietveld Academie, Amsterdam, The Netherlands. Viewed on April 30, 2023. https://youtu.be/AvL4wUKIfpo.

Strassfeld, Max, and Henderson-Espinoza, R. 2019. "Introduction: Mapping Trans Studies in Religion." *Transgender Studies Quarterly* 6, no.3: 283–96.

Tadiar, Neferti XM. 2022. *Remaindered Life.* Durham, NC: Duke University Press.

TallBear, Kim. 2013. *Native American DNA: Tribal belonging and the false promise of genetic science.* Minneapolis: University of Minnesota Press.

Toledano, Ehud R. 1998. *Slavery and Abolition in the Ottoman Middle East.* Seattle: University of Washington Press.

Wang, Thelma. 2022. "Becoming with Hormones: DIY Feminizing Hormone Therapy of Trans People in China." Unpublished manuscript for Thinking Gender Conference workshop, UCLA.

Wynter, Sylvia. 2003. "Unsettling the Coloniality of Being/Power/Truth/Freedom Towards the Human, after Man, Its Overrepresentation—An Argument." *CR: The New Centennial Review* 3, no. 3: 257–337.

Wynter, Sylvia. 1994. "No Humans Involved: An Open Letter to My Colleagues." *Forum N.H.I.: Knowledge for the 21st Century* 1, no. 1.

Critical Event and Political Subjectivation through Chile's Social Uprising

Angel Aedo, Oriana Bernasconi,
Damián Omar Martínez, Alicia Olivari,
Fernando Pairican, Juan Porma, Editors

Angel Aedo, Oriana Bernasconi, Damián Omar Martínez, Alicia Olivari, Fernando Pairican, Juan Porma

Introduction: Widening the Space of Politics

The largest cycle of protests Chile has seen in the past thirty years began on October 18, 2019, preceded by sporadic actions of civil disobedience, including massive fare evasion by high school students in Santiago's subway system. That day, mobilizations diversified and spread across the country's capital, halting millions of commuters and city residents in their tracks. Some of the actions drew on a repertoire familiar from traditions of national protest: street barricades, *cacerolazos*,[1] performances, marches, and mass gatherings. Other actions included looting, the deliberate burning of metro stations and city buses, destruction of monuments and churches, and a profusion of graffiti-style inscriptions on the city's walls and infrastructure, demanding profound social change. These actions soon spilled over, becoming city-wide in scale.

The protests spread to all the country's major cities, creating an extraordinary scene of nationwide agitation. TV and social media showed image after image of convulsion in every corner of a country only recently described, by its then president, as a supposed "oasis" of stability and prosperity. Placards appeared declaring, "Neoliberalism was born here, and here it will die." Every day for the first few weeks thousands of actors from a wide range of origins and ages gathered, after work, in Baquedano Square, which protesters renamed "Dignity Square" (*Plaza Dignidad*). Members of social movements and organizations, students, workers, and whole families congregated in this ground zero zone. Multitudinous crowds gathered every Friday at various key points around Santiago and around the country, testament to the

The South Atlantic Quarterly 123:1, January 2024
DOI 10.1215/00382876-10920705 © 2024 Duke University Press

nationwide nature of the movement. The march of Friday, October 25, was the largest ever in the country's history.[2] Alongside the marches, self-convened assemblies in different neighborhoods drew up collective petitions and debated proposals for a new constitution. Thirty years after the transition toward democracy had begun, they hoped to finally replace the extant constitution, imposed during a cruel dictatorship.

The government, led by a right-wing coalition, responded from the outset by criminalizing the protest. A constitutional state of emergency was decreed, whose terms included a nighttime curfew. In some parts of the country soldiers were deployed in the streets over a ten-day period, leading to scenes last seen under the dictatorship. The army used live rounds, killing three people in engagements during protests (Amnesty International 2020: 4). A prolonged period of police repression likewise deployed weapons, using anti-riot shotguns, launching tear gas canisters directly at protesters, firing pistols with lethal intent, and driving motorized vehicles directly into crowds. According to Amnesty International the police inflicted deliberate harm on protesters with punitive intent, either intentionally or recklessly, using untraceable ammunition to enhance institutional impunity (4–5).

Cross-party negotiations between all political parties represented in congress produced an institutional exit route from the crisis. On November 15 the parties signed the Accord for Social Peace and the New Constitution, seeking to reassure mobilized citizens' groups that the constitutional replacement they were demanding in the streets was going to happen. Although protests continued, they began to lose impetus due both to the signing of the accord and the risks involved in exposure to the police response. Street actions resolved into something akin to a conflict between two regular combat forces. One of these was the so-called Front Line,[3] which had emerged as a self-defense force with an internal structure—complete with roles, rules, planning, and distribution of tasks—to resist police sorties. The militarized police response meanwhile continued to unleash repressive force, resulting in the detention of more than twenty-three thousand people by March 2020. By that same date, the government had brought formal criminal complaints against over three thousand citizens for alleged offenses ranging from public disorder and arson to attacks on police officers or soldiers (Rojas 2022: 1000–1001).

Summer vacation season, in January and February, further lessened the intensity of the protests. The process that was to lead to a constitutional assembly was also set in train, absorbing some of the media attention previously focused on the protests. The March 2020 Covid lockdown finally brought the protests to an end. Thousands of complaints had been registered over human rights violations occurring during those five months. The Office of the Public Prosecutor counted 5,500 individual victims of institutional violence, with most injuries caused by use of kinetic impact projectiles (Amnesty International 2020: 5). According to the Ministry of the Interior 347 people had received eye wounds; five were left permanently blinded (Senado de Chile 2020). During the first month alone, the Office of the Public Prosecutor reported twenty-six investigations into "people who have died in the context of social protests" (OHCHR 2019: 10).

Various subsequent studies have explored the causes of the deep disquiet that underlay the protests: dissatisfaction over profound social inequalities, the reduction of life to monetary transactions, a crisis of political representation, and a range of sector-specific demands (e.g., Araujo 2019; Garcés 2019; Gonzalez and Morán 2020; Rojas 2022; Somma et al. 2021). Acknowledging these contributions, this dossier approaches Chile's social uprising as a critical event of political subjectivation. In particular it explores how the uprising enhanced the political subjectivation of sectors of Chilean society with no previous background of (contentious) political action. By tracing the lived experiences of subjects who inhabited the social uprising, we show how the analytically separated categories of critical event and subjectivation in fact overlap and enrich one another.

The Critical Event and Political Subjectivation

The concepts of event and political subjectivation lie at the root of the issues problematized in this dossier. By event we refer to an irruption, disturbance, shock wave, dislocation, or unpredictable rupture, one that unfolds with a force or potency that renders it both total and impossible to apprehend. Within an individual, such an event summons, upsets, saturates, and reorients the multiple meanings of the world and of oneself. When an individual "is happened to," they have no choice but to notice the event, and let it happen to them (Romano 2008). In relation to the event, we understand the process of subjectivation as an unanticipated displacement, "the formation of a one" as "relation of a self to an other" (Rancière 1992: 60). This is an inescapably incarnated, situated, and relational process. By linking event and political subjectivation, we problematize the activation of the agency of excluded individuals. In the essays that make up this dossier, we will see how the uprising as an event offers its protagonists the space to become actors, provoking unprecedented processes of political subjectivation and opening the field of action and influence to subjects who had been kept on the margins of the construction of a pretended national history.

The three essays allow the reader to identify various critical dimensions in these processes of political subjectivation in times of social uprising. A first critical sense resides in the capacity of the uprising to disturb everyday time while joining the present, in tension, to previous contentious events—such as the preceding dictatorship—and to long-accrued relations of colonial duress (Stoler 2016). The Chilean uprising thereby weaves together heterogenous temporalities, challenges the histories and memory of ordinary subjects, and pushes them to become substantively involved. For example, the first essay shows how the time of state terrorism and the memory of resistance to the Pinochet dictatorship (Bernasconi 2019) offered Ricardo a historical referent for the political and ethical tipping point that pushed him to join the uprising, becoming part of the history of the present (Revel 2015). In parallel, the social uprising activated the time of student protests and working-class neighborhood struggles in the early post-Pinochet era (Olivari and Badilla forthcoming), a time that presaged a space in which subjects who had been left out of Chile's pacted transition to democracy would appear (Osorio and Gaudichaud 2018). The protests also conjured up subterranean and rebellious temporalities. This is reflected in the experiences of Marta and Juan (essay two), and Mauricio Lepin (essay three). Marta and Juan's practices of resistance foregrounded the "erased time" (Bradley 2019) of homeless children, families pushed into precariousness, and *pobladores*⁴ criminalized after the 1990 return to democracy (Aedo and Faba 2022). Mauricio's performance in the heart of the Chilean capital, at the height of the most multitudinous moment of the uprising, made present the long period of resistance by the Mapuche people to colonial domination and state violence directed against them (Pairican 2022). Taken together, these essays make clear the power of social uprising to produce critical effects by shattering the homogeneous time of domination (Rancière 2012) and by subverting a present from which none of the protagonists emerges intact or untransformed.

Another critical sense of this social uprising stems from its disruptive force regarding the self. Hundreds of individuals invested themselves in a sustained way in the uprising, through the insistent and stubborn occupation of space, the collective, affective, and expressive gathering together of bodies and signs, the production of sociality, and the crafting of rules, norms, and ways to withstand repression. They did so inspired by the desire to be a part of the uprising, recognizing their own historicity. The event emplaces, disrupts, and precipitates the production of meaning and connects with previous historical conflicts and relations of subordination, encouraging sustained engagement with the struggle and with the social and political space of uprising. At such a juncture, the critical attitude of the subject—which Foucault (2003) has tended to locate at the level of the individual—revealed itself to be part of a collective, plural assemblage. The protesters brought the protest to life, at the same time as it enabled them to appear before themselves and others challenging the order of things, while recognizing and embracing the value of their diversity (Butler 2015) and the political potency of keeping alive the gathering that allowed them to claim the power previously denied to them. The statement "Chile has awoken" (*Chile despertó*) appeared everywhere—on walls, placards, and social media, in press analysis, and in intellectual discussion. It denotes a pluralistic attitude and the desire of a people (*demos*)—left out of the distribution of the sensible (Rancière 2004)—to question the inevitability of the capitalist order and awaken the desire for a different form of life in common.

The coproduction of event and subjectivation confronted its participants with issues that would require political and ethical decisions both in everyday living and in street protest. In response they deployed counter-conducts against the intolerable. These counter-conducts ranged from Marta's creating a home with six local young people living in a situation of extreme precariousness, to Ricardo's total commitment and his caring for protesters wounded by the police. They include the extraordinary transformation of Juan, who was inspired by Marta's care and by witnessing a people taking to the streets to himself become a social activist in an impoverished Santiago neighborhood. They also include Mauricio Lepin's sudden decolonial act, affirming the sovereign self-determination of an indigenous people in the very epicenter of the nation that has for so long denied it.

At the level of the domestic, the uprising politicizes the *oikos*, that space supposedly reserved for the intimacy of the private sphere, beyond the reach of public deliberation. This dossier, especially its second essay, shows how, through the uprising, the home became an arena of experimentation and struggle. This is possible because transformations that are crucial for subjects and collectivities take place in the domestic sphere, such as the emergence of a genuine politics of care that goes beyond kinship to meet the community in the street and the neighborhood.

The social uprising, however, also challenged the entangled relationship between police and politics as developed by Rancière. The revolt, as an event made of acts disobedience, converged against the police order and the instituted political economy. The political aspect of this event, its critical force, resides in the fact that it makes dissent appear, manifesting the presence of other worlds in one. As the essays in this dossier show, the political nature of this event resonates simultaneously through processes of subjectivation that redefine the terms and modes of acting politically, by challenging public perception or the "manner of partitioning the sensible" (Rancière 2004: 6). The history of the present in which the experiences studied in this dossier are inscribed shows that the social uprising in Chile widened and reconfigured the space of politics, bringing in actors historically kept on the margins. Their voices called for justice, contested the normalized violence of inequality, and expanded the space for struggle and creation of a common world.

Methods

This dossier was prepared over a ten-month period by an interdisciplinary team affiliated with Chile's Millennium Institute for Research into Violence and Democracy. Three years had elapsed since the beginning of Chile's social uprising, and the project took as its starting point field material that was being produced with various protesters involved in it. The dossier format allowed us to select participants for an analytical exercise that we set ourselves the task of addressing collectively by identifying a shared problem. For the exploration we drew on the team's disciplines of origin (history, anthropology, sociology, psychology, and philosophy) and areas of research specialism (colonial violence, political violence, security and illegalism, social memory, and urban studies) combined with our interest in experiencing ways of coming together to problematize and collectively communicate some aspect of Chile's social uprising.

The cases chosen deploy different methodologies, converging around the biographical narrative format. Ricardo's case is based on an unstructured in-depth interview about his involvement in the protests, carried out in June 2022. Juan and Marta's story combines two unstructured in-depth interviews carried out in December 2021 and November 2022 as part of an audiovisual ethnography comprising a succession of encounters and episodic conversations in the field. The case study of Mauricio Lepin was produced for the dossier as oral history: an extensive life history was taken over two encounters in August 2022. Interviews were carried out by anthropologists and sociologists (Ricardo, and Juan and Marta) or by two Mapuche historians (Mauricio Lepin).[5]

Our participants have quite varied vital trajectories, allowing us to bring territorial, ethnic, class, gender, and generational insights to the analysis. This in turn allowed us to interrogate the biographical space, to identify and examine the repertoire of affects and actions with the power to constitute political subjectivation. Given the bounded scope of the exercise, we prioritized intersectionality rather than aspiring to representativeness. In terms of difference, the cases engage subjects who had hitherto seen the history of their own society pass them by. Workshops discussing the transcripts of each conversation enabled the team to define the arguments that would appear in each essay. We then undertook a collective writing process, commissioning an illustration for each essay that acts as a cartographical tool helping communicate local places, moments, and events for a global readership.

—*Translated by Cath Collins*

Notes

This work was funded by ANID—Millennium Science Initiative Program—ICS2019_025, ANID/FONDECYT 1212047, ANID/FONDECYT 1190834, ANID/FONDECYT 3220446 and ANID/BECA DOCTORADO NACIONAL 21191269, CIIR/FONDAP15110006, European Union–NextGenerationEU (Program for the Requalification of the Spanish University System [2021-2023] of the Spanish Ministry of Universities, modality "María Zambrano," University of Murcia) and German Research Foundation (Collaborative Research Center 923 "Bedrohte Ordnungen," University of Tübingen, Germany).

The order of authors in this article is alphabetical and does not indicate a hierarchical relationship among them. They all contributed equally to the conceptualization, data analysis, and writing of the introduction and the three articles in this dossier and should be considered co-first authors.

1   A non-violent way of showing discontent or solidarity with a cause. It involves concerted beating of pots and pans with kitchen implements, creating a noise through which participants recognize one another in a common sensory expression.
2   According to official estimates 1,200,000 1.2 million people took part.
3   The term *front line* or *first line* (*primera linea*) was coined to refer to the group of people who headed up any march or gathering. Their task was to take on the police, using stones and improvised home-made weapons, to allow other participants to demonstrate.
4   Residents of poor neighborhoods.
5   In accordance with the terms of confidentiality agreed with participants, only Mauricio Lepin appears under his real name.

References

Aedo, Angel, and Paulina Faba. 2022. "Rethinking Prevention as a Reactive Force to Contain Dangerous Classes." *Anthropological Theory* 22, no. 3: 338–61.

Amnesty International. 2020. *Eyes on Chile. Police Violence and Command Responsibility During the Period of Social Urest*. https://www.amnesty.org/en/wp-content/uploads/2021/05/AMR2231332020ENGLISH.pdf.

Araujo, Kathia. ed. 2019. *Hilos tensados. Para leer el octubre chileno* (*Tense Threads. Reading the Chilean October*). Santiago de Chile. Usach.

Bernasconi, Oriana. ed. 2019. *Resistance to Political Violence in Latin America: Documenting Atrocity.* London: Palgrave Macmillan.

Bradley, Arthur. 2019. *Unbearable Life: A Genealogy of Political Erasure.* New York: Columbia University Press.

Butler, Judith. 2018. *Notes Toward a Performative Theory of Assembly: The Mary Flexner Lectures of Bryn Mawr College.* Cambridge, MA: Harvard University Press.

Foucault Michel.(2003. "What Is critique?" In *The Essential Foucault,* edited by Paul Rabinow and Nikolas Rose, 263–78. New York: The New Press.

Garcés, Mario. 2019. "October 2019: Social Uprising in Neoliberal Chile." *Journal of Latin American Cultural Studies* 28, no. 3: 483–91.

Gonzalez, Ricardo, and Carmen le Foulon Morán. 2020. "The 2019–2020 Chilean Protests: A First Look at Their Causes and Participants." *International Journal of Sociology* 50, no. 3: 227–35.

OHCHR. 2019. *Report of the Mission to Chile from 30 October to 22 November 2019.* The Office of the High Commissioner for Human Rights, https://www.ohchr.org/en/documents/country-reports/report-mission-chile-30-october-22-november-2019.

Olivari, Alicia, and Manuela Badilla. Forthcoming. "The 2019–2020 Chilean protests. The emergence of a movement of urban memories." In *Handbook on Urban Social Movements,* edited by Anna Domaradzka and Pierre Hamel. Northampton, UK: Edward Elgar.

Osorio, Sebastián, and Franck Gaudichaud. 2018. "¿La democratización en contra de los trabajadores? La CUT, el movimiento sindical y el dilema de la transición pactada en Chile" ("Democratization against Workers? The CUT, the Trade Union Movement and the Dilemma of the Agreed Transition in Chile"). *Les Cahiers de Framespa. e-STORIA* 27. http://journals.openedition.org/framespa/4763 (accessed May 14, 2023).

Pairican, Fernando. 2022. *La vía política Mapuche: apuntes para un Estado Plurinacional (The Mapuche Political Way: Notes for a Plurinational State).* Santiago de Chile: Paidós.

Rancière, Jacques. 1992. "Politics, Identification, and Subjectivization." *October* no. 61: 58–64.

Rancière, Jacques. 2004. "The Distribution of the Sensible: Politics and Aesthetics." In *The Politics of Aesthetics The Distribution of the Sensible,* 12–9. New York: Continuum.

Rancière, Jacques. 2012. "In What Time Do We Live?" In *The State of Things,* edited by Marta Kuzma, Pablo Lafuente, and Peter Osborne, 11–38. London: Koenig.

Revel, Judith. 2015. "'What Are We at the Present Time?' Foucault and the Question of the Present." In Fuggle, Lanci, and Tazzioli 2015: 13–25.

Rojas, Hugo. 2022. "Chile at the Crossroads: From the 2019 Social Explosion to a New Constitution." *Seattle Journal for Social Justice* 20, no. 4: 981–1017.

Romano, Claude. 2008. *Lo posible y el acontecimiento (The Possible and the Event).* Santiago: Universidad Alberto Hurtado.

Senado de Chile. 2020. "Comisión de DD.H.H. revisa cifras a un año del estallido social." https://www.senado.cl/noticias/carabineros/comision-de-dd-h-h-revisa-cifras-a-un-ano-del-estallido-social .

Somma, Nicolas M., Matías Bargsted, Rodolfo Disi Pavlic, and Rodrigo M. Medel. 2021. "No Water in the Oasis: The Chilean Spring of 2019–2020." *Social Movement Studies* 20, no. 4: 495–502.

Stoler, Ann Laura. 2016. *Duress: Imperial Durabilities in Our Times.* Durham, NC: Duke University Press.

Angel Aedo, Oriana Bernasconi, Damián Omar Martínez, Alicia Olivari, Fernando Pairican, Juan Porma

Multitude and Memory in the Chilean Social Uprising

Ricardo is a thirty-eight-year-old emergency medical technician from Santiago. During the 2019 social uprising, he lived in a central neighborhood close to the epicenter of the protests. He worked at a local clinic attached to a public university, where student protests and clashes between masked demonstrators and police were common. Ricardo comes from a right-wing family: only he and his sister have left-wing leanings. He has never been a member of a political party, group, or organization, and in fact he expresses mistrust of them, and of Chilean politics in general. However, the neighborhood he lived in as a child bordered on another, *Villa Francia*, which has a long history of political and community organizing and is considered a combative place. Ricardo used to go there to get involved in protests on emblematic days.[1] A few years ago, he began to take part on and off in a musical troupe that often appears at popular street events and commemorations of September 11, the date of Pinochet's coup d'état.

In Ricardo's account, two main hermeneutical and agential phenomena configured the uprising as a critical event with the capacity for political subjectivation.[2] First, Ricardo's identification of the revolt as a historical event from his own lifetime, as he drew parallels between the social uprising and the 1973–90 dictatorship, the biggest sociopolitical catastrophe of Chile's recent history. Second, the power of the masses in public demonstrations, which activated Ricardo's desire and spurred him on to a total and systematic immersion in the front line of the protests,[3] evoking memories of the

The South Atlantic Quarterly 123:1, January 2024
DOI 10.1215/00382876-10920714　© 2024 Duke University Press

urban street fights he knew in his childhood. Once the dictatorship was over, Ricardo and his friends had repeatedly asked themselves, "What would I have done if I'd been there?" Faced with the social uprising, at first an unintelligible event, Ricardo returns to, and brings into the present, that generation-specific question: "Where am I going to be now?" His response rose to the occasion: an extraordinary level of immersion in, and by means of, street combat. The memory of the anti-dictatorship movement, the power of the spontaneous masses, and the street as a place of encounter and struggle will activate Ricardo's political subjectivation, and the configuration of the uprising as a critical event, one that he interprets in the light of the past.

Some academic accounts of Chile's social uprising refer to the "irruption of memories" through this protest cycle. These may be long-standing memories—such as of the violence visited on the Mapuche people[4] by the Chilean state—memories of the feminist or neighborhood movements, and/or memories of the recent dictatorship (Angelcos and Pérez 2017; Vivaldi and Sepúlveda 2021; Garcés 2019; Han 2012). Certainly, the repressive policing of the protests, and the decreeing of "states of exception" revived memories of the dictatorship the length and breadth of the country. The protests became places of commemoration and homage to victims of dictatorship-era violence, and spaces in which to denounce remaining gaps in truth and justice.

The demands that inspired the uprising also referred back to the period of the political transition (1990s), which had first denounced the legacy of the neoliberal societal model imposed at gunpoint under the military regime. The relationship between these memorialization practices and new processes of political subjectivation however remains unexplored, above all among actors who do not belong to political and protest movements such as the student, feminist, or environmental movements (Bravo and Pérez 2022). In this context, Ricardo's case demonstrates the intergenerational staying power of certain subterranean memories in the trajectories of people who either did not live through the dictatorship or lived it as children and do not have a history of activism or involvement in social organizations. Decades later, during the social uprising, memories of resistance to the dictatorship evoked an ethical imperative in this ordinary citizen. Ricardo experiences this as a form of duty to his time and to his own history. This experience blurs the analytical boundaries between ethics and politics, as it becomes the engine of mobilization and a desire for social transformation not through political militancy or trajectories, but rather in unexpected and sudden awakenings and agency arrangements.

The Construction of the Event

Many firsthand testimonies about the Chilean dictatorship begin by narrating the events of September 11, 1973. Similarly, Ricardo starts his account of his experience of the social uprising by talking about "the day it all began." A succession of scenes evokes the sensation of the disruption of the everyday that ensued when street protests spread across the city over the course of October 18, 2019 (see fig. 1). The surprise at what was unfolding, and the stream of images recalled, demonstrate how critical and historic this event was for Ricardo and for the country as a whole:

> I remember the day it all started. It was October 18, 2019. I was working at the University and I was on a late shift, due to finish at 9 p.m. I'd been planning to go on to a venue just a bit up the road and see a band . . . . But as the afternoon wore on, I started hearing news about what was going on with the subway, the students . . . people were doing mass fare evasion in the subway and there were protests, demonstrations starting up.
>
> I didn't really understand much at that stage. . . . Once I left [work] there were loads of people in the street, outside the subway stations and . . . after a while, I set off home and the whole way there I could see people on every street corner. I went down Santa Rosa [Avenue] and the water company offices had been set on fire; there were barricades on every corner. By then, it was around 10 p.m. I went through *Plaza Italia*⁵ and along that whole stretch of the *Alameda*⁶ by bike; it looked like a battlefield. I cycled the length of the Alameda and you know, I felt, it was as though bombs had fallen and you had to swerve around all the debris from barricades. It was unbelievable, unbelievable. I got to the *Brasil* neighborhood and there was a whole contingent of police. I tried to go round them and one of them tried to grab me. I got away and kept going. I got home and with my flatmate we were like, "Look, this is what's going on." We put the radio on. [They announced] that the soldiers (*milicos*) were being sent out onto the streets so we thought, "Fuck, it's actually happening," you know? This, what we'd been waiting for so long, an uprising; it was happening.

This event gradually takes shape in Ricardo's account, as it did in the experience of many people who were out and about in Santiago that day, seeing firsthand how protest practices sprang up all over the city. After work, on an improvised urban tour, Ricardo confirmed and augmented the information he'd picked up during the day from the radio, which had described acts of civil disobedience led by high school students: a "total" event, including buildings in flames, barricades, and groups protesting outside subway stations. In Ricardo's description his initial incredulity modulates into sur-

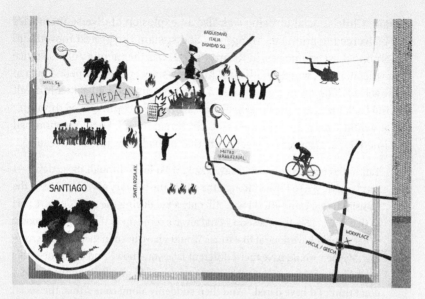

Figure 1. Ricardo's trajectory on October 18, 2019. Illustration by Francisca Yáñez.

prise—"it looked like a battlefield"; "it was like something out of a film"—and finally into a political emotion that sweeps over him when he becomes convinced that the "popular revolt" that he has been awaiting for years is finally happening on a national scale.

During the first few days of the social uprising, Ricardo's daily routine—like that of most of the rest of the population—was turned upside down. His narrative refers to three elements that make the event so earth-shattering. First, its strength and magnitude: this uprising is nationwide, making it different from previous cycles of contention such as the student protests of 2011. Second, the massive levels of direct participation. This disrupted the routine of every large city and activated national history. Third, its capacity to challenge subjects, their bodies, their emotions, their memories, and to make them seek within themselves for repertoires that allowed them to project forms of immersion that would transform them into agents of history.

The Action of Anti-dictatorship Memory in a Biographical Key

Memory can be defined as the work of constructing meanings about the past in order to act in the present and project future horizons (Halbwachs 1992). Understood in this way, it is a key element of subjectivation in general (Deleuze 2015), and political subjectivation in particular (Madhok 2018). As we said, Chile's social uprising was also an explosion of diverse memories that converged to animate, strengthen, and sustain the protest movement. Key among these memories, in Ricardo's case, was the memory of resistance to the dictatorship, which challenged him as a subject and compelled him to get involved. The event (re)activated a question that he had asked himself looking back toward "a previous historical era that the country lived through": "what would I have done in the same circumstances?" Such question had remained open, a source of uncertainty that he had been unable to resolve.

> Talking to friends you would say, "Look, if I'd lived through those days"—I was born in '83, so I lived through the end of the military government and the transition that came after; I was still only a kid during the most decisive part of that era. . . . So, the question would always come up in those conversations: What would I have done at that time? Would I have been in there, in the struggle? Maybe I would have met a different fate, you know? And everyone—this is all when you're among friends—everyone would give their opinion: "No, I don't think I'd have dared." And then suddenly along comes this, the social uprising, and it was like, "Fuck, now you have to see whether you are going to be part of it or not, you know?"

The uprising offers Ricardo the chance to revisit this question and transform the hypothetical scenario into a real, present, and urgent question. It pushes him to make a decision despite the possibility of facing the same fate as so many of those who resisted the dictatorship and were exiled, tortured, or killed. While this is a decision for the present moment, it is inseparable from a nostalgic vantage point on the past. The density of this affective and moral linkage is precisely what impels Ricardo to become an agent of the "history of the present" (Scott 2011).

The role memory plays in Ricardo's political activation contrasts with the role it has played in other cycles of contention. For example, those linked to the youthful protagonists of the 2011 student protests, whose emergent political subjectivity has as one of its key components a post-memory of the 1990s democratic transition that is particularly critical of its unfulfilled promises (Paredes, Ortiz, and Araya 2018). One of the keys to reading Ricardo's account is an understanding of his generational position. Born five years before the electoral defeat of Pinochet that began the transition toward democracy, his generation occupies a grey zone between a generation that lived through the dictatorship and took a position on it while it was still ongoing, and a generation that is the protagonist of the present day. This latter is a generation born in democracy, which has crafted new discourses and struggles in the transitional era and has been considered the key generational protagonist of the 2019 social uprising (Ganter 2022). This intermediate position is most evident among people who self-identify as on the political left, appearing as the 1980s generation, clearly set apart from those who did not live through the dictatorship at all, but equally not having lived through it fully themselves (Reyes et al. 2015).

The uprising as a new social event offers Ricardo an opening, a space to act "for and in common with," a unique invitation to feel part of history in the making. Ricardo takes to heart the question about his position regarding the historical event and makes a commitment to the ethical and political project associated with the uprising. His commitment traces back to a relationship with a past that shapes him even though he was not an active part of it. That relationship left him with a feeling of having been found wanting, but did not render him completely helpless. His ethical relationship with the uprising contains both nostalgic and future-oriented components, insofar as Ricardo says he joined the struggle seeking transformation not for his own benefit but for the sake of his daughter and eventually his grandchildren.

From Peripheral Participation to Total Involvement: The Role of the Street

The uprising awakened an ethical impulse in Ricardo to be part of something, which he lived out by participating actively in the protests during the months when they were at their height. His objective became "to uphold these social transformations, keep them alive," "to prevent this from dying down," and "to make it lead to something." To that end, he got involved in a range of spaces of struggle and "trenches" that the day, and the rituals emerging around the uprising, provided. He engaged in demonstrations and marches on most days, often joining the front line to allow the multitude to gather, letting participants express themselves and stay together while occupying the street.

> My participation was to go up as close to the front as possible, where the confrontations with the police were happening. I was on the front line. I would be with a friend or an acquaintance, then you might meet up with someone else there, but it wasn't, like, planned. It was more that you would go with a couple of friends, and once you got there, spontaneously everyone would go up to the front to protest. And by "protest" I mean throwing stones at the police, tear gas flying this way, Molotovs that way . . . . And basically you did it because it was containment, containing [them] so that the masses could be in the demo, so the police wouldn't overrun us and shut down the whole protest. It was a way of being there, you had to be there and hold the line.

Once a week Ricardo would alternate "holding the line" with providing first aid. Wearing his white coat and carrying medical supplies, he would attend to people wounded by police repression. Back in his home neighborhood, he would also take part in *cacerolazos*. The roles and functions that Ricardo takes on in the protest are connected to repertoires of collective action, political reference points, and emblems of resistance that appear in his personal history. He noted that the university where he works

> is a place where there are constant protests, they're a way of showing discontent . . . so helping someone who's been hit in the head by a tear gas canister during the uprising wasn't a new thing for me, I'd already done that here at the university and also, when I was a boy I lived near *Villa Francia*. I used to take part in the protests that happened there: sometimes just being around, other times maybe going to the gas station to fetch gas so that the guys could make Molotovs, you know?

These activities became part of his repertoire of action, allowing him to become an activist (*luchador*) who took part in street protests by directly confronting the police, defending and protecting the multitude involved in the demonstrations, and healing the wounded, putting into practice a kind of practical ethics (fig. 2).

For Ricardo, the struggle of the dispossessed against the police amounts to an act of disobedience that makes this mass of people part of history, in a new chapter of the age-old class struggle:

> The cops, the military, they work protecting the interests of the few, the powerful people in this country. So when we went out to fight, to throw stones at the police, it was standing up to that, that armed wing of the elite, the businesspeople and those with power in the country. Yes, that's how I see it, that's how I saw it back then.

Over the course of subsequent months certain more formally organized spaces opened up, including territorial assemblies where demands could be pooled and actions channeled. Ricardo nonetheless continued to opt for the street as the place for his own participation, a place where he could make his own decision to act, and practice protest repertoires learned over the course of his life. In the street he encountered "the masses," the vector for his action, the source of his strength, and a resource offering protection and the means to implement struggle:

> It's the tool you have, because you're fighting [with] stones against tear gas, against rubber bullets, you know? It's unequal, so [being part of] "the

Figure 2. Health volunteers under police attack. Santiago de Chile, December 20, 2019. Courtesy of GrosbyGroup.

masses" is what kind of puts you back on an equal footing. So, yeah, the protection of the masses is what gave me courage and strength, to be there every time I had to be there.

The masses out in the street brought together a whole range of people who joined in, autonomously, spontaneously, and sometimes only fleetingly. Being part of this multitude involved "shouting, jumping, singing, taking a rest, cleaning yourself up, drinking some water, getting your strength back, and losing your fear." One could "leave" the masses to "go to the front and defend [the multitude]," or to provide first aid and assistance for people who were hurt defending it. The power of the multitude was reflected not only in its size, but also in the way it served as a resource transforming many people into protesters and activists. The masses lent courage, provided tokens of solidarity, and gave witness to participation in a shared struggle with common meaning. This potential was what allowed Ricardo to immerse himself fully: "If you were taking part, you had to be clear that you were in it with everything you'd got, whatever happened. If you were needed over here or over there, if you had to face a whole contingent of cops, that's what you had to do, you couldn't be halfhearted about it, d'you see?"

This event also happens to subjects, it challenges them to take positions, pushing them to risk their lives to take part in a protest. Ricardo eventually reduced the intensity of his participation in the protests, under the combined weight of news about his partner's pregnancy, a change of neighborhood, and being hit by shotgun pellets fired by the police: two of the three pellets that injured him have still not been removed. Nonetheless, he is still visibly moved when he acknowledges that he placed himself on a particular side of history,

> to have dared to do it, when the time came. I don't think of myself as very brave, but in the moment you took courage, bravery that made you be there, made you go up to the front. . . . It was a big deal, and I think often you would take the risk without really thinking about what could happen. You could arrive home blinded in one eye, or you could be killed. So that's how it was . . . it was beautiful, and really striking. While I don't want to romanticize the protests, I think that those of us who lived it, at least in my case, it moves me because I feel that when you had to be there, I was there.

Final Reflections

Chile's social uprising was also a "graphic dispute" made up of inscriptions and erasures (Campos and Bernasconi 2021). Murals, posters, and other acts of public inscription—such as graffiti, tags, spray painted slogans—spread the protesters' demands across walls and urban infrastructure, assisting the production of territories in dispute. Many of the slogans and demands are testament to the range of memories that found a place in these events: "History is not repeating itself: This time we won't be silenced!"; "#Chilehasawakened"; "Where Are They?[7] Truth and Justice"; "Today, like yesterday, the dictatorship continues"; "Fight like a Mapuche."

The political subjectivation of a citizen like Ricardo, with no history of militancy in parties or formal associations, relies less on ideological discourse than on memories of the struggle against the dictatorship. In the face of the critical juncture, an embodied memory of bygone years' protest actions awaken, allowing Ricardo to take on roles in the new cycle of protests. That memory becomes an ethical imperative to be part of a possibility for societal change. The force of the multitude in the center of the city lends more potency to this imperative. The masses provide "shelter," allowing Ricardo to deploy resources for street struggle and care that are already part of his life story, making him suddenly an agent of history. This event affects Ricardo not only at the level of ideology—insofar as he sees certain causes as close to his heart—but above all in his body, his affect, and his ethics, all of which come together to inspire the final words of his interview: "it moves me because . . . when you had to be there, I was there." Ricardo became the embodiment of an activist (*luchador*) during the months following the uprising, before falling back into his everyday space of peripheral participation.

—Translated by Cath Collins

Notes

This work was funded by ANID—Millennium Science Initiative Program—ICS2019_025, ANID/FONDECYT 1212047, ANID/FONDECYT 1190834, ANID/FONDECYT 3220446 and ANID/BECA DOCTORADO NACIONAL 21191269, CIIR/FONDAP15110006, European Union–NextGenerationEU (Program for the Requalification of the Spanish University System [2021-2023] of the Spanish Ministry of Universities, modality "María Zambrano," University of Murcia) and German Research Foundation (Collaborative Research Center 923 "Bedrohte Ordnungen," University of Tübingen, Germany).

The order of authors in this article is alphabetical and does not indicate a hierarchical relationship among them. They all contributed equally to the conceptualization, data analysis, and writing of the introduction and the three articles in this dossier and should be considered co-first authors.

1 Dates associated with notorious repressive episodes.
2 We carried out an in-depth interview with Ricardo in June 2022. For details see the introduction to this dossier.
3 *Front line or first line (primera línea)* refers to a group of protesters at the forefront of confrontations with the police, facing them with stones and improvised homemade weapons.
4 Chile's largest First Nation, engaged in a historical struggle with the Chilean state.
5 The main city square and intersection, separating uptown from downtown, that would later become the Ground Zero of the protests.
6 The major city thoroughfare.
7 In context, this refers to those disappeared by dictatorship-era repression.

References

Angelcos, Nicolás, and Miguel Pérez. 2017. "De la desaparición a la reemergencia. Continuidades y rupturas del movimiento de pobladores en Chile" ("From Disappearance to Re-emergence: Continuities and Ruptures in the Chilean Squatters' Movement"). *Latin American Research Review* 52, no. 1: 94–109.

Bravo, Viviana, and Claudio Pérez. 2022. "La lucha de calles y la revuelta de octubre de 2019" ("Street Struggle and Revolt in October 2019"). In *Huelgas, marchas y revueltas. Historias de la protesta popular en Chile, 1870–2019 (Strikes, Demonstrations and Revolts: Histories of Popular Protest in Chile, 1870–2019)*, edited by Viviana Bravo y Claudio Pérez, 437–58. Santiago de Chile: FCE.

Campos-Medina, Luis, and Oriana Bernasconi. 2021. "Ciudad, estallido social y disputa gráfica" ("City, Social Uprising and Graphic Dispute"). *Atenea* no. 524: 111–28.

Deleuze, Gilles. 2015. *La subjetivación. Curso sobre Foucault (Subjectivation: A Course on Foucault).* Buenos Aires: Cactus.

Ganter, Rodrigo. 2022. "Subjetivación política y revuelta de los que sobran. Digresiones en torno a la dimensión generacional del 18-O en Chile" ("Political Subjectivation and Revolt of Those Who Are Left Over: Digressions on the Generational Dimension of the 18-O in Chile"). In *El despertar chileno. Revuelta y subjetividad política (The Chilean Awakening: Revolt and Political Subjectivity),* edited by Rodrigo Ganter et al., 87–130. Buenos Aires: CLACSO.

Garcés, Mario. 2019. *Pan, trabajo, justicia y libertad. Las luchas de los pobladores en dictadura (1973–1990) (Bread, Work, Justice, and Freedom: Squatters' Struggles under Dictatorship [1973–1990]).* Santiago: LOM Ediciones.

Halbwachs, Maurice. (1941) 1992. *On Collective Memory.* Chicago: University of Chicago Press.

Han, Clara. 2012. *Life in Debt: Times of Care and Violence in Neoliberal Chile.* Berkeley: University of California Press.

Madhok, Sumi. 2018. "Coloniality, Political Subjectivation and the Gendered Politics of Protest in a 'State of Exception.'" *Feminist Review* 119, no. 1: 56–71.

Paredes, Juan Pablo, Nicolás Ortiz, and Camila Araya. 2018. "Conflicto social y subjetivación política: performance, militancias y memoria en la movilización estudiantil post 2011" ("Social Conflict and Political Subjectivation: Performance, Militancy, Memory in the post-2011 Student Mobilization"). *Persona y Sociedad* 32, no 2: 122–49.

Reyes, María José, Marcela Cornejo, María Angélica Cruz, Constanza Carrillo, and Patricio Caviedes. 2015. "Dialogía intergeneracional en la construcción de memorias acerca de la dictadura militar chilena" ("Intergenerational Dialogue in the Construction of Memories of the Chilean Military Dictatorship"). *Universitas Psychologica* 14, no 1: 255–70.

Scott, Joan. 2011. "Introducing History of the Present." *History of the Present* 1, no. 1: 1–4.

Vivaldi, Lieta, and Bárbara Sepúlveda. 2021. "Feminist Revolution: A Fight for Recognition, Redistribution, and a More Just World." *Social Identities* 27, no. 5: 567–78.

Angel Aedo, Oriana Bernasconi, Damián Omar Martínez,
Alicia Olivari, Fernando Pairican, Juan Porma

A Politics of Care from the Margins
of Chile's Social Uprising

This essay examines Chile's social uprising through the eyes of Juan (thirty-six) and Marta (fifty-nine),[1] a couple who live in *La Bastida*, a low-income neighborhood on the periphery of Santiago. Despite a lack of previous experience in social and political organizations, Juan and Marta got involved in one of the many territorial expressions of the critical event that the uprising represented. Through Juan and Marta, we explore how the powerful nature of the uprising drove acts of contention on the urban margins. We also encounter the repressive response of the police-prison apparatus of a state at a loss about how to deal with an event that appeared, at least to some authority figures, of almost otherworldly origin (Dammert and Sazo 2021). The critical force of the uprising resides precisely in this entry into the political space of actors whose presence was unforeseen, and, by some, undesired. To do so, we explore the ethical and biographical dispositions that encouraged Juan and Marta to become politicized as the uprising went on.

As in the case of Mauricio Lepin, also discussed in this dossier, Juan's and Marta's experiences allow us to appreciate the shift of two people who began as "othered"—stigmatized as *flaites*[2]—and became activists (*luchadores sociales*). This shift, which served as a mode of subjectivation, takes place as a critical attitude unfolds in them, one that finds expression in public interventions in defense of equality and social justice, and in acts of community and neighborhood solidarity.

The South Atlantic Quarterly 123:1, January 2024
DOI 10.1215/00382876-10920732 © 2024 Duke University Press

The case study that we present throws light on a dimension of social upheaval that is rarely explored: the ways in which certain actors live out this critical event collectively, via a politics of care that serves as a bridge between the intimate sphere and the political sphere, the *oikos* and the *polis*. This politics of care is not built on an explicit body of discourse, nor does it spring from principles enunciated by the protagonists of our story. Care is an inherently relational activity that generates ties and bonds. When care relationships give rise to bonds that fall outside of the conventions considered proper to policing the family (Donzelot 1984) and come up against state institutions (Ziv 2017), they can become critical for the subjects living them out.

The sections of this essay follow a spatial sequence of concentric circles, with the uprising as a crosscutting event. The center and point of origin is the "home" as domestic space. This *oikos* is placed under internal tension by a "micropolitics" (Deleuze and Guattari [1987] 2005) that turns it into a place of care and hospitality for homeless young people. The essay next moves out into the "street," place of struggle and of political "appearance" (Arendt [1963] 1990; Butler 2015). In the "street," the essay expands its frame of reference to allow in the uprising as a local critical event, via the occupation of a piece of land adjoining *La Bastida,* the *población*³ where Juan and Marta live. Next, "prison" is the circle that literally and politically suspends the couple's space for expression when their lives collide with state-administered security and punishment (see fig. 1).

The Home

Marta was born in the 1960s in one of Santiago's most emblematic *poblaciones*. Her life has been hard: she lived on the street for several years and suffered abuse and violence. However, she turned her traumatic experiences into an ethical sensibility for solidarity and care, spurring her on to first welcome Juan into her life and then take in a series of young people living in circumstances of precarity. The couple met for the first time in 2015 on social media, although they subsequently fell out of touch. Sometime later, Juan sought Marta out again at a time when he was in the throes of severe addiction, cancer, and depression. "And we've been inseparable ever since," declared Juan. "She's a great woman. She got me off drugs. . . . She was the one who got me up out of my sickbed when I had cancer. She wouldn't let me just lay down and die." The relationship is not one of dependence, though, but of a caring for the other that triggered self-care. When the uprising began, this same predisposition in Marta led her to temporarily take in a group of precarious young people:

Figure 1. Home, street, prison, critical event. Illustration by Francisca Yañez.

I lived on the streets for three years. I know what abuse is, I know what it's like to be cold and hungry. And Juan told me about some kids that had nowhere to live. So, seeing as I've got a spare room upstairs, I told him: "Juan, tell them they can come and stay here."

Marta shared a roof and a table with the young people. She drew up rotations for chores, with everyone taking turns at cleaning, and showed care and concern by setting limits on the time people were to be home at night and even enforcing bedtimes. When someone didn't come home on time, Marta would suffer. On one occasion Eduardo, one of the young people, left the household and ended up sleeping on the street. Marta refused to give up until he was found and brought home. "When he got here I hugged him and told him 'That's the last time you sleep out on the street. If you're somewhere and they throw you out, you come and knock on the back window here and I'll get out of bed to let you in. But I never want to see you out on the street again.'" The affection that was cultivated in this shared household created a sense of family that both Marta and Juan referred to repeatedly in their interviews. Some of the young people came to acknowledge and reciprocate the feelings, treating the pair "like we were their mom and dad." In this way, in the heat of the uprising, Marta brought them all together and acted as the head of this assembled, provisional household, proudly ensuring that "no one ever went without" even when they were obliged to resort to one of the many *ollas communes* (soup kitchens) that sprang up during the Covid pandemic. This same identity was the one Marta would appeal to time and time again when the public prosecution service subsequently accused them of constituting an organized group that had supposedly come together for the purpose of attacking a local police station, and its occupants, with incendiary devices and firearms. She counters with "Here, we were a family."

The space of care that Marta created grew from a series of everyday affects that circulated in the background of various political subjects entangled in this event. An ethical awareness rooted in her own history predisposed Marta to be part of the whole, to protect the weak, to rebel against neoliberal individualism, and to transform her home into a space that was as hospitable as it was politicizing, and where all would radically participate. Care, responsibility, rows, and comradeship were all part of community life in Marta and Juan's spontaneous home, demolishing the boundaries that usually separate public from private, care from politicization. This politics of care started to take shape before it was articulated as a properly political discourse. As we will see, however, it was in the force field galvanized by the social uprising that the commitment binding Marta and Juan's household together was interpreted, by the state's security apparatus, as a sign of insurrectionary intent.

The Street

Prior to October 2019 Juan had taken part in protests each September 11, commemorating the 1973 coup d'état led by General Pinochet. Other than this, however, he had no history or habit of participating in social or political organizations. The social uprising accordingly marked a turning point in his attitude to the political, although his own biographical narrative indicated two events that predisposed him to get involved in a large-scale event such as the uprising and emerge from it as an activist. The first event was having been the subject of Marta's care, as we mentioned above. This care allowed Juan to transform his relationship with himself and move toward becoming "the person I am now, an activist [*un luchador social*]."

A second event is connected to his membership in *La Garra Blanca* (literally, White Claw), an association of soccer fans (known in Chile as *barras bravas*).[4] *La Garra Blanca* is made up of supporters of Colo-Colo, one of the country's most popular soccer clubs, which has a large following in *poblaciones* (Aguilar 2023). Belonging to *La Garra* gave Juan a community *pathos* that combines a love of soccer with explicit support for the struggles of the Mapuche indigenous people, and an anti-fascist, anti-system ethic that plays out in regular confrontations between *La Garra Blanca* and the police: "I'm a Garra member, a fighter," Juan said. "The antifas of the *Colo* [Colo], we're all anti-cop. We fight for the rights of the Wallmapu,⁵ . . . it's not only about the social context of around here [i.e., of urban Santiago]."

When the uprising came along, Juan translated the sense of community that he had forged in the *barra brava* into a conception of neighborhood, of commitment to his area and his *población*, to "the street." This reached the point where he stopped attending to the calls that came from the *Garra* fans, to stay alive to the struggle of the moment, which he saw as the one happening in his own neighborhood:

> They would say "let's head to the stadium." [But] No; my time is in the street, the street's here, the people who need me are here in the *población*. The stadium can wait, the struggle there will always be there waiting for me, but the people here in the *población*, they're the ones fighting for their homes, their rights, decent health care and education, they're here.

The history of *La Bastida* fed that incipient neighborhood identity due to its own traditions, including social struggles for housing and historical resistance to fascism and to the Pinochet dictatorship, articulated through grassroots organizations.

The uprising triggered something vital in Juan, which he identified with his experiences of commonality in *La Garra Blanca*. But it went further: it gave him "more strength," bringing out in him something that, he says, "I never knew existed" but "I had inside of me": his "essence" as an activist "who can fight every day on others' behalf." Juan, then, moved in a direction that led him to describe himself as an activist (*luchador social*). Marta, on the other hand, does not identify herself in this way. This should not be mistaken for a lack of politicization on her part: it simply represents a different form of subjectivation. The uprising also produced a shift in her, in how she understands politics and the importance of protest: "If people told me to go out and protest," says Marta, "I'd do it. . . . If there's a need to go and march, I'll get out there and march."

A Critical Event

Some weeks after the uprising began, a large group of low-income families occupied an area of land belonging to a family from the Chilean high elite, bordering on the northern limit of *La Bastida*. The aim of the occupation was to highlight the problem of overcrowding on the urban margins of Santiago, in housing districts that often originate in land squatting and self-construction, characteristic of what Teresa Caldeira (2017) has called "peripheral urbanization." The police response was repressive and the situation escalated into levels of violence that had not been seen since the 1990s, when the Pinochet dictatorship ended. *La Bastida* was surrounded by police for over a week, with daily confrontations between police and demonstrators. The Inter-American Commission on Human Rights produced a report detailing raids and destruction, tear gas launched into homes and health centers and close to educational institutions, deliberate running over of protesters with police vehicles, arbitrary detentions, and torture committed inside police stations.

Groups of residents demolished an emblematic boundary wall separating *La Bastida* from the occupied land, leaving a long thoroughfare full of rubble and burning barricades. The police station was attacked on various occasions with fire and stones. Avenida Bogotá, a street close to Marta and Juan's house, became the material and symbolic center of this territorial expression of the social uprising in *La Bastida*. It was a site of intense conflict over various months, even after the Covid pandemic arrived.

A certain sense of vertigo can be detected in the way Juan and Marta talk about this encounter with the multitude. There seems to be a sense of *déjà vu*, where the same actions and people are repeated day after day: "Shit. It's the same thing all over again," says Juan. "We're always the same people who turn up. You see the same faces every day." But then the adrenaline kicks in: Juan, who knows other active protesters, feels an inexplicable attraction for "the street": "I started to get a taste for following along, getting out there; the adrenaline rush, it's like the street was calling me, like the street was saying 'come on, we need you out here.' So there were a couple of weeks after that when I was basically out in the street the whole time." His references to the magnetism of the street, to adrenaline, and to seeing the same familiar faces, is reminiscent of Durkheim's (1984) "collective consciousness" or Randall Collins's (2009) "emotional energy," which contributes to generating a sense of belonging to a group. Juan recalls that "here [Avenida Bogotá] was full of people, if you came here someday at nighttime, you could easily count five hundred, six hundred people." This collective consciousness, expressed in asphalt and a multitude of familiar faces, was what grabbed Juan and Marta and "wouldn't let them go." This sense of vertigo is the same one with which Juan and Marta speak with a certain nostalgia about Avenida Bogotá, no longer full of protesters. Only the black asphalt remains as a visible reminder of what went on: "For me, what makes me nostalgic is seeing that we used to gather there, we protested there and went out to fight for others, and to see the street empty now, the night empty . . . and nothing."

When Juan and Marta speak about their involvement in the uprising, they do not craft a discourse in the way community leaders often do. Their discourse always refers to actions and experiences, to what the event really did "in and through" them. When their words seek to explain the reasons behind their lived experience, they tend, however, to reach for conventional formulas. The truth value of these statements is perhaps less important than what they reveal about the overabundance of meaning that this event had in their lives, their ways of recognizing one another, and their ways of being in relation to others. When Juan is asked about the reasons that led him to protest, his voice abandons the personal register to personify a collective subject: "We didn't go out to fight for our own benefit, but for the good of the whole country, for the sake of the *población*." He adopts as his own, a reason that belongs to an "us:" "because we want more dignified lives in this country, we don't want more injustice, we don't want any more human rights violations." His testimony about his own experience fluctuates, sometimes situating Juan and Marta inside the event, as protagonists of the uprising, and at other times outside, as casual observers of the urban periphery who end up swept along by the adrenaline created by the situation. Looking at Juan during the interview, Marta told him:

> One day I told you "Let's go for a look," and we went to look and I enjoyed running away from the cops; seeing how they set fires; and then we started going for a look . . . we went out to have a cigarette on Avenida Bogotá . . . and we stayed at the protest, watching, because there were so many people there already. Why would you go home and sit indoors when you were there seeing how people were running away from the cops and all that? . . . And if the cops were on their way, you weren't going to stand idly by . . . for the cops to pick you up . . . obviously you had to run away, right?

Prison

"Quick! Get dressed, get dressed!" were the first words Marta heard very early one apparently ordinary morning in October 2020. She had been awakened shortly before, by noise on the galvanized steel roof. "Suddenly," she says, "I hear the door being opened. And there's a cop standing there." In the course of an ongoing investigation that the public prosecutor's office had begun some months earlier, the police had come to raid Marta and Juan's house looking for evidence against them and the young people they had fostered. Marta grows visibly agitated as she recounts the details, as though it had all happened only yesterday: the violence visited on them, the destruction of their belongings. After an exchange of words, one police officer said to Marta: "Look, *hueona*,[6] look me in the eye and tell me where the gun is." Marta looked him straight in the eye and said, "Look, *hueón* . . . you won't find—look me in the eye, then, you look me in the eye the same way I'm looking at you—you're not going to find any damn thing here. There's nothing here. You're not going to find anything, anything, anything." "And it was true," Marta concludes, "he didn't find anything." They were all arrested and held on remand, accused of criminal association, making and launching incendiary devices, and possession of firearms. Juan and Marta were accused of leading the group in an attack on the local police station. After five months, in Marta's case, and eight months in Juan's case, they were released. Some of the young people were kept in jail for longer. At time of writing only one was still detained.

Even once out of preventive detention, Juan's conditions of release include a five-year suspension of his right to vote. He is currently on parole. Marta must report to a police station once a month, for the next three years. They reflect that the state may have got what it wanted when locking up them and other protesters: to intimidate people and put an end to the social uprising. "People were so scared that they never went out to protest again. Who wouldn't be scared if they smashed up your house?" asks Marta. Their close encounter with police repression and, finally, with incarceration are the modes by which state coercion affected their lives. The message sent to these poor, politically unaffiliated *pobladores*[7] was clear: if you dare to show your discontent in the streets, and seek to join your voice to that of the multitude, you will be met by violence from the state. The traces repression left on Juan and Marta, however, led to something more than simple paralysis through fear. They awoke a consciousness and a desire to assist comrades and neighbors still in detention, through neighborhood solidarity activities and the creation of a Political Prisoners' Support Group in *La Bastida*. Both became key actors organizing collections, bingo nights, and solidarity events to provide food and toiletries for young people still in prison. This shift reveals how a total event such as the social uprising continues in less spectacular forms, requiring ethical-political gestures (Foucault 1997) of solidarity and fraternity. This takes Juan and Marta out of the circuit of care practices limited to the private sphere, into a public arena whose importance they want to accentuate.

Closure

Autonomous care practices that emerge from below and are not subordinated to a governmental rationality, such as those we see through Marta and then through Juan, create bonds, construct loyalties, and allow for the development of new forms of social participation. But care is also affected by events: acts of care happen and are also called forth by other events. Marta and Juan's entry into the October 2019 revolt made their (hospitable) care practices necessary and pushed them to develop fraternal relationships with people imprisoned as a result of the uprising. As an event, the Chilean uprising shone a spotlight on care practices that took on a political character in Juan and Marta's lives, through awakening the couple's solidarity with the oppressed, and through motivating them to engage in counter-behaviors that became, for the state, reasons to denounce, condemn, and punish them.

State security and punishment comes into the lives of Marta and Juan, erupting into their home in the form of a police raid that put them on a collision course with the criminal justice system and with prison. The pandemic that hit Chile six months after the uprising began led to the introduction of biosecurity quarantine measures that closed down impoverished urban areas, accentuating existing enclosure and socio-spatial margination of *poblaciones* like the one where Marta and Juan reside. The Chilean uprising, however, left a crucial and exceptional legacy: it triggered changes in the nature of *población* altruism as practiced by Marta, and in the openness to community experiences associated with Juan's membership in the *Garra Blanca*. The reach of these changes, which over the course of this essay we have treated as amounting to shifts, is evidence of their incorporation of the event as a critical instance of subjectivation via the politicization of care, and the domestication of politics.

The uprising broadened the ambit of action of care relationships, causing Marta and Juan to enter into a political arena that was for them unprecedented. Care turned out to be subversive as it began to erase the frontiers between the private and the public, transforming the meaning and practices of creating a family and turning the street from a mere space for circulation into a "space of appearances" (Arendt [1963] 1990; Butler 2015). In this appearance, Marta and Juan re-encountered one another while performing roles they had never before taken on. In the process, they came to question the social order that favors the few while marginalizing the majority. The raid on their home and their subsequent incarceration revealed, in part, the disruptive force unleashed during the uprising by this couple who counted for little in the eyes of the Chilean state. The social uprising that spread through

Chile's major cities ran parallel to processes of subjectivation that should be understood as inherent with the revolt, as Juan and Marta's experience shows. By becoming political subjects, they created a space of action for a community, breaking down the barriers between *oikos* and *polis* (Arendt [1958] 1998).

—Translated by Cath Collins

Notes

This work was funded by ANID—Millennium Science Initiative Program—ICS2019_025, ANID/FONDECYT 1212047, ANID/FONDECYT 1190834, ANID/FONDECYT 3220446 and ANID/BECA DOCTORADO NACIONAL 21191269, CIIR/FONDAP15110006, European Union–NextGenerationEU (Program for the Requalification of the Spanish University System [2021-2023] of the Spanish Ministry of Universities, modality "María Zambrano," University of Murcia) and German Research Foundation (Collaborative Research Center 923 "Bedrohte Ordnungen," University of Tübingen, Germany).

    The order of authors in this article is alphabetical and does not indicate a hierarchical relationship among them. They all contributed equally to the conceptualization, data analysis, and writing of the introduction and the three articles in this dossier and should be considered co-first authors.

1   Names of people and places have been changed to protect anonymity. The couple was interviewed in December 2021 and November 2022, using audiovisual ethnographic techniques.

2   Pejorative term used in Chile to refer to people with low levels of formal education who live in low-income neighborhoods, associating them with violent or criminal behavior. Reasonably close analogies might include the term "chav," as used in the UK.

3   The term *población* in Chile refers, strictly speaking, to low-income neighborhoods, but it retains a series of political, historical, and symbolic connotations that enrich the concept beyond a literal rendering. Given the importance the term has as used by our protagonists, we have chosen to retain the original Spanish-language usage. *Población* dwellers are referred to as *pobladores*.

4   *Barras bravas* are groups of soccer fans who use the space around fandom as a place to create and affirm an identity. In the case of the Colo-Colo soccer club, that identity pays homage to a wise indigenous community leader (*longko*) of the sixteenth century, who defended the Mapuche during the wars of colonization of Chile's southern Araucanía.

5   Mapuche term for their own ancestral lands, located in the south of Chile.

6   A vulgar way of addressing someone, in context clearly intended to be offensive.

References

Aguilar, Felipe. 2023. "Aliento, violencia y un fenómeno social: La historia detrás de la Garra Blanca, barra oficial de Colo-Colo" ("Cheering, Violence, and a Social Phenomenon: The Story behind Garra Blanca, Colo-Colo's Official Soccer Club"). *Sentimiento Popular (Popular Sentiment).* May 4, 2023, https://sentimientopopular.cl/2023/05/04/aliento -violencia-y-un-fenomeno-social-la-historia-detras-de-la-garra-blanca-barra-oficial-de -colo-colo/.

Arendt, Hannah. (1958) 1998. *The Human Condition*. Chicago: The University of Chicago Press.

Arendt, Hannah. (1963) 1990. *On Revolution*. London: Penguin Books.

Butler, Judith. 2015. *Notes Towards a Performative Theory of Assembly*. Cambridge, MA: Harvard University Press.

Caldeira, Teresa. 2017. "Peripheral Urbanization: Autoconstruction, Transversal Logics, and Politics in Cities of the Global South." *Environment and Planning D: Society and Space* 35, no. 1: 3–20.

Collins, Randall. 2009. *Interaction Ritual Chains*. Princeton, NJ: Princeton University Press.

Dammert, Lucía, and Diego Sazo. 2021. "La teoría del complot en el Estallido chileno: un examen crítico" ("The Theory of the Plot in the Chilean Uprising: A Critical Examination"). *Ciper*. March 20, https://www.ciperchile.cl/2021/03/20/la-teoria-del-complot -en-el-estallido-chileno-un-examen-critico/.

Deleuze, Giles, and Felix Guattari. (1987) 2005. *A Thousand Plateaus: Capitalism and Schizophrenia*. Minneapolis: University of Minnesota Press.

Donzelot, Jacques. 1984. *The Policing of Families*. New York: Pantheon.

Durkheim, Émile. 1984. *The Division of Labour in Society*. London: Macmillan.

Foucault, Michel. 1997 "What Is Enlightenment?" In *Ethics, Subjectivity and Truth. Essential Works of Michel Foucault*, edited by Paul Rabinow and James D. Faubion, 303–19. New York: The New Press.

Ziv Tali. 2017. "'It be hard just existing': Institutional Surveillance and Precarious Objects in the Northeast Rustbelt." *Ethnography* 18, no. 2: 153–74.

Angel Aedo, Oriana Bernasconi, Damián Omar Martínez, Alicia Olivari, Fernando Pairican, Juan Porma

Mapuche Anticolonial Politics and Chile's Social Uprising

Mauricio Lepin was twenty-six years old when Chile's social uprising began in 2019. [1] He was born in 1992, the year that marked the five hundredth anniversary of the arrival of Christopher Columbus to what is now the Americas and, thus, the year in which began mobilizations by indigenous peoples repudiating this event in history. Lepin recalls that the flag he wore on his back during the months of mobilizations in Santiago in 2019 drew attention and comment: "What a beautiful flag!" "What do those colors represent?" The flag's design was first presented in October 1992, by the Mapuche organization Council of All the Lands, at a mobilization in the city of Temuco (the capital of Chile's *Araucania* region; see fig. 1). One of the flag's creators explains its meaning: "The black and white colors represent the balance or duality between night and day, sun and rain, the tangible and the intangible. The blue represents the purity of the universe; the green represents our *mapu* (lands), Wallmapuche, the lands that are the seat of our nation. The red stands for strength, power, the blood of our ancestors, that was spilled. In the middle of the flag is the *kultrung* [a ritual drum] . . . and on the top and bottom borders of the flag you have a representation of the *kon*" (Cayuqueo 2010). [2]

Lepin joined the social uprising together with some friends after receiving a call to join via social media: "everyone came along after they got out of work" to a designated meeting point that had been suggested. This was outside the main campus building of the Universidad de Chile on the Alameda, Santiago's main city thoroughfare, very close to the epicenter of the protests. "We never thought it would be so big," he recalls. In the first

The South Atlantic Quarterly 123:1, January 2024
DOI 10.1215/00382876-10924623   © 2024 Duke University Press

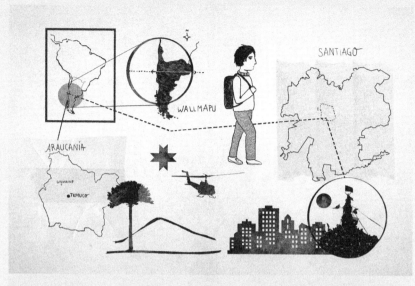

Figure 1. Mauricio Lepin. From Mapuche Territory to the Chilean Capital. Illustration by Francisca Yañez.

days of the mobilization, various businesses temporarily ceased operations, through fear of coming under attack. The firm Mauricio worked for was one of them, and Mauricio made the most of the opportunity to become a full-time participant in the social uprising.

As the days wore on, Lepin saw the uniformed police shooting kinetic impact projectiles at women, children, and older people and came to accept that his role would be to join with others to create space "allowing people to march." The only way to generate that space, he declares, was "through confrontation." From that time on, as soon as his working day was over Lepin would often join the protest's Front Line, a group that came together spontaneously to defend and protect other protesters by engaging with the forces of state repression.

On 25 October, seven days after the protests began, 1.2 million people—in a city with fewer than 6 million inhabitants—filled all the main highways around the capital's Plaza Baquedano square, which the protesters renamed Dignity Square. Lepin walked toward the square, the epicenter of the protests, with his flag tied around his neck (see fig. 2). He knew it would likely be difficult to get close to the monument at the center of the square:[3] its access points were being guarded by members of Chile's *barras*, working-class organizations of soccer fans:[4] "I just held the flag out. It wasn't a

Figure 2. *Re-evolución*. Courtesy of Susana Hidalgo.

planned thing I saw I was up there, I had the flag around my neck, I opened it out. It was maybe ten seconds, or even less, I don't know."

In this photograph, Lepin appears stripped to the waist, arms outstretched, looking westward in the direction of the setting sun. He stands atop the statue, just in front of the sculpted face of General Manuel Baquedano. If Lepin's objective had been to make the Mapuche presence felt and denounce the injustices that they have been subjected to for over five hundred years, he partly achieved his aim: the photo became a global icon of the Chilean social uprising.

This essay draws on Lepin's experience to explore the anti-colonial character of the social uprising, as a fundamental dimension of an event that became critical through subjects exercising a politics of presence. This politics of presence does not only assert the plural right to appear (Arendt [1958] 1998; Butler 2015) but also promotes sovereign self-determination as the underlying principle of a critical emancipation (Simpson 2020). The social mobilization awoke temporalities that were unevenly laid down or sedimented, in territories and population "ruined" by a colonial duress that continues to act (Stoler 2016). The vigor with which the social uprising spoke to and challenged Mauricio Lepin, leading him to decide to play a role in it, can be traced to those same temporalities: a long history of Mapuche dispossession and resistance interwoven with a biography containing social marginalization, political exclusion, and economic precariousness, a history he shares with the majority of both Mapuche and non-Mapuche young people in Chile. A young life full of timelines that were truncated by movement and enforced relocations spills into a present that explodes, allowing Mauricio to rediscover himself as a political actor among the multitude in the struggle. At the end of the day of October 25, against a backdrop of agitation that looked like a battlefield, for a few seconds his body and his flag subverted colonial domination. They did so before thousands of witnesses, on the pinnacle of the monument at the center of the most massive demonstration seen since Chile's 1990 return to democracy. This triumphant gesture draws together places and moments that Mauricio has had to go through and projects them into the future, almost as if they had been unwittingly preparing him for political subjectivation in newly agitated times.

Ancestral Memory in the Multitude

Mauricio Lepin is the son of a domestic servant, who found herself unable to bring up a child at the same time as holding down her job as a live-in maid.

So, at six months of age, Mauricio was sent to live with his grandparents in the *Pelantaro* community in Galvarino, in Chile's southern Araucanía region. He grew up in a rural household, following Mapuche cultural traditions as promoted by Domingo Aniñir and Malvina Nain, his grandparents on his mother's side. They taught him Mapuche culture and history, and Mapuche ways of being. His grandfather was a *Longko*[5] who inculcated respect for others, taught Mauricio how to address other people, and encouraged him to be a decent person while also standing up against racism: "never to bow your head to anyone." It was a sheltered childhood, but it came to a premature end. When Mauricio was eight, his grandfather died. Seven years later, he also lost his grandmother. This double loss left him "rudderless: I lost all my childhood. Everything about me that was still a child."

Against the backdrop of Mapuche demands for restitution of their ancestral lands, Mauricio's community took part in practices of the recuperation of land,[6] which meant he grew up suffering constant harassment from the police. "That was an important feature of my childhood: we were always being raided, because the estate under recuperation was very close by." Domingo Aniñir had played an active role in land recuperation under Chile's agrarian reform process between 1962 and 1973.[7] During the subsequent counter-reform that happened under the dictatorship, he suffered political persecution. Being descended from a *Longko* was part of the ancestry of the Lepin family, and in fact Domingo's father before him had also been the community's *Longko*. Lepin remembers his grandfather telling him that he, Mauricio, would also be a *Longko* one day, because he had an innate gift for leadership even as a boy.

Despite his grandfather's best efforts to protect Mauricio from the effects of his own political activism and the political dynamics of the community, these traditions and memories inspired Mauricio to take part in the Mapuche movement, which by the time Lepin entered adolescence had declared itself to be a movement of national liberation.

Another formative influence on Mauricio came from his grandmother and her own community of origin, Fortín Ñielol. Malvina Nain was acknowledged in her community as a *lawentuchefe*, a term for people who are skilled in medicine and the healing arts without being *Machi*.[8] "She avoided accepting becoming a *Machi*. It would have been a role with a lot of responsibility and would have meant not being able to take care of us." In practice, Malvina represented in Mauricio's life something "much better than the mother who gave birth to me: to me, my only mother and father are my grandmother and grandfather."

Lepin had just started at the renowned Pablo Neruda High School in Temuco when his grandmother died of stomach cancer. Mauricio was transformed by his stay at this prestigious high school, which brought together young Mapuche from different communities. He felt not only the weight of academic expectations in a demanding school but also distinctions of class and race. "There was a lot of discrimination. A dark-skinned young man would arrive and speak a word or two of *mapuzungun* [the Mapuche language], and you'd be told 'oh the Indian's arrived.'" In those years the more radical wing of the Mapuche movement stepped up its sabotage actions, which included burning lorries and, to a lesser extent, setting fire to homes belonging to large-scale farmers. In the Araucanía region, racism took on new forms: Maupches were referred to as "lorry burners" or "forest burners." Or it would be said, in "hostile" phrases that Lepin remembers hearing, "watch out for them, they might set you on fire." Far from being cowed, Mauricio was spurred on to a greater desire to take part in Mapuche mobilizations for the liberation of prisoners, or in protest against the raids that were inflicted on communities linked to the Mapuche movement. At this point, in 2009, Jaime Mendoza Collío was killed. Mendoza was a member of the Requem Pillan indigenous community, in the Ercilla district of the Araucanía. His murder proved to be a tipping point toward more open activism. Lepin allied himself with those communities that resisted the securitization tactics imposed successively by all of the post-dictatorship government administrations. "I went on all the marches. I even led movements. We created a youth movement called New Force (*We Che Newen*)." This organization aimed to pay renewed attention to cultural aspects of the Mapuche people's identity, such as the teaching of their language or of traditional ceremonies. "We built up a really great group, we got *Machi* and *Longko* to come along. It was a new thing for the high school, and they supported us to take part in other events."

The politicization of Mauricio's identity coincided with a doubling down on state securitization policies. This came to a head in 2010, the year that marked the bicentenary of the Chilean republic and in which the Mapuche chose to carry out one of the longest hunger strikes in their history, an action that produced gestures of solidarity from the Chilean people. Lepin took part in these mobilizations, which contributed the following year to the creation of a nationwide Mapuche students' union, the *Federación de Estudiantes Mapuche*. Mauricio became an active member. "It was a way of showing our discontent. I started to understand the injustices I saw being committed against the Mapuche people, the discrimination, and to get into politics proper." First the loss of his grandparents, then Mapuche mobilization in the

Araucanía and state repression of it began to open the eyes of this young man who would go on to fly the Mapuche flag during the social uprising.

Some Mapuche connected to organizations began to distance themselves from political activism for fear of being harassed, arrested, and questioned by the police. Lepin experienced this firsthand when he was detained and interrogated twice by the detective police. "They showed us photos taken in various places, in communities or in Temuco, [saying] "We know that's you.'" They would list the nicknames or aliases by which friends or fellow activists were known, and threatened him: "We'll lock you up and your family won't know where you are." Lepin decided to leave Temuco and travel to Santiago in search of study and work opportunities. Like many of his fellow activists, on arriving in the capital he kept a certain distance from activism: "I preferred not to carry on."

Returning to Politics: The Uprising as a Moment of Plurality and Horizontality

Mauricio moved to Santiago in 2011, but he did not completely lose sight of developments in Mapuche politics in the South of the country. He studied to become a technician in logistics, in a private technical training school, working to finance his studies and pay for his keep. Once his son was born things became even more challenging, as he had family responsibilities to think about. At this time he started to experience what has been termed *mapurbidad*,"[9] a variegated identity in which Mapuche communitarian traditions vie with the experience of margination on the urban periphery (Aniñir [2005] 2018). A *mapurbe* is a subject who lives in the city yet is conscious of belonging to a Mapuche movement that has defined itself as being one of national liberation.

Lepin was disturbed by the absence of justice for the Mapuche people, and the impunity that police enjoyed in cases connected to the movement for Mapuche autonomy. His sense of injustice was augmented by the death of Camilo Catrillanca in 2018,[10] but above all by the trail of false evidence that the police created around it while trying to disguise the fatal shooting as the product of an exchange of gunfire. The resulting outrage found expressions including a hunger strike the following year, by Mapuche political prisoners. For Lepin, "the whole of Chile saw that we Mapuche are always being painted as criminals for no reason, just to silence our leaders."

By the time of the social uprising Mauricio's childhood with his grandparents, his student activism, and his experiences of securitization in the

Araucanía made up a set of life experiences that found echoes in the slogans of the social mobilization, in the phrases in *mapuzungun* sprayed onto walls and in the incorporation of the Mapuche flag into this new cycle of popular mobilizations. There was something of the history of his ancestors at stake in the Santiago protests: "I kept on seeing the same injustices, absolutely nothing had changed. And I compared. . . . The injustice we were living through there as an indigenous people . . . was like the injustice inflicted on any ordinary Chilean person, any worker, wage worker. And unfortunately I saw that those people didn't realize the injustices that were being visited on them, because they were kept down in a submissive world, where you go to work at 8 and get out at 6 p.m. That, more than anything, was what led me to get involved in the movement again."

Moving from observer to participant, from spontaneous actor to reflexive one, and from being a defender of the mobilizations to becoming a frontline warrior, Lepin's history once again was joined to that of the dozens of people who were demonstrating for a better way of life. As part of the front line he was hit by shotgun pellets various times: "I got about ten in my back, one in my head and three in my legs. The biggest [thing I got hit by] was in my leg, because a tear gas canister exploded just a couple of meters away." This projectile was shot from three meters away, when police violence escalated after various days of confrontations: "The police officer aimed at my leg and shot the tear gas at me."

Mauricio recalls the fraternal atmosphere and sense of commonality between the protesters of the front line and members of the soccer fans' organization: "I think a good coming together happened there. That's what's missing from politics today, to support whoever's beside you without looking to see what party they're from. Say the fans from the Católica [club] are the posh ones [*los más cuicos*], and the fans from the U[niversidad de Chile] and Colo[-Colo clubs] are the most working class; that day, everyone came together."

Final Reflections

Chile's social uprising was a dispute over historical memory. Lepin's decision to carry the Mapuche flag on his body, and incorporate it into a mobilization that acquired plural dimensions, is indicative of how ethnicity fed class to generate a new kind of mobilization. The same was seen in some parts of the *Wallmapu*, where monuments signifying the history of state violence against the Mapuche people were pulled down. From quite early on the mobilizations produced graffiti in *mapuzungun*, and a group of Mapuche installed a *chemamul*[11] in the Plaza de la Dignidad alongside two other statues representing indigenous peoples. Thirty-nine Mapuche people later put themselves forward as candidates for the 155-person constituent assembly that was to draft a new Chilean constitution. The creation of the citizens' assembly, one of the outcomes of the uprising, was approved by national plebiscite in 2020. A quota of seventeen seats was set aside for indigenous peoples, and in 2021, Mauricio Lepin was one of the Mapuche representatives who stood for election. He received 1.1 percent of the total votes cast for indigenous delegates. Lepin stood on a platform of working toward a plurinational, intercultural, communitarian, and democratic state that would establish mechanisms for autonomy for First Nations and would recognize self-determination for the Wallmapu, with separate constitutional charters and restitution of Mapuche territory.

The subjectivation of Mauricio Lepin is a process undertaken by a citizen with an ethnic identity rooted in his family, ancestors, and a community named after Pelantaro, one of the principal military leaders in Mapuche history. In the intense days of the revolt, the experiences of having taken part in the Mapuche movement and having suffered state police persecution triggered Lepin's decision to take part in the mobilization, first as an observer, then as an activist. The social uprising brought to mind the pro-autonomy Mapuche movement that he had known in the Araucanía. This experience equipped him with tools for taking on roles in the situation created by the uprising, tools further honed by drawing strength from the multitude during the protests. His people's long history of dispossession and resistance, and his own experiences of social marginalization, political exclusion, and being rendered economically precarious in a life marked by movements and enforced relocations, all converge into a gesture that subverted centuries-long colonial domination. Through this gesture, a *Mapurban* youth made his entry into the recent political history of Chile.

"We were there all day, so that they wouldn't do anything to other people." This ethical sentiment could proceed from his lineage as a *Longko*, something that his grandparents had identified in him, and that he lives out through helping and defending those who could be considered weaker than him. But it also intersects with his personal history of experiencing coercion as a Mapuche activist, and in precarious work settings in Santiago. The social uprising—or, as it was seen by indigenous peoples, the anti-colonial revolt—brought about a subjectivation in Mapuche citizens in Chile's major cities, expressed in the de-throning of figures who represent political violence unleashed on the Mapuche people from the time of the Spanish colonization through to the present. Perhaps these are the reasons that led Mauricio to take part in the later constituent assembly process: although he was not elected, he felt that he could make a contribution to the needs of his people: "I wanted to make the people who live in the Araucanía visible, because I've seen how lands are stolen, the forestry companies . . . how most of our people these days are left without access to water, connectivity for everyone, education, that's still precarious today. There are schools in the Araucanía that don't have an electricity supply, and no one sees it. There are rural schools that don't have decent plumbing in their bathrooms. And that's what I wanted to make visible, to have brought into the discussion in the [Constituent] assembly. As we know, if no one else sees [these things], or if it's only seen by someone like me, no one believes it."

For Mauricio Lepin, the critical nature of the uprising lay less in a revaluing of the project of the Mapuche movement than in its revelation of a political system in crisis, a crisis brought about by the lack of incorporation of Chile's indigenous peoples into the distribution of power and wealth. The uprising also meant reliving, and feeling anew, a period of violence that Mauricio and his family have suffered. The exhaustion due to the lack of consideration from the political system toward the Mapuche people that was evidenced by Mauricio's entering into the October revolt did not mean that Mapuche resistance to current forms of colonial domination tired or weakened. On the contrary, it raised serious questions about the cunning nature of the politics of cultural recognition (Povinelli 2002), which aim at political demobilization and the commodification of indigenous culture. Standing proud, bare-chested, and raising the Mapuche flag before the image of Baquedano, one of the generals who led the nineteenth-century expansion of Chilean territory into *Wallmapu*, Mauricio's gesture transcended the ethnic frontiers of one people, bringing into play political signifiers beyond mere discourse. Lepin's action represented a corporal collective presence that expressed itself through the defiant declamation "We're still here!" (Antileo 2020), addressing the multitude of singularities that in the social uprising refused to sink into the shadows of public life.

—Translated by Cath Collins

Notes

This work was funded by ANID—Millennium Science Initiative Program—ICS2019_025, ANID/FONDECYT 1212047, ANID/FONDECYT 1190834, ANID/FONDECYT 3220446 and ANID/BECA DOCTORADO NACIONAL 21191269, CIIR/FONDAP15110006, European Union–NextGenerationEU (Program for the Requalification of the Spanish University System [2021-2023] of the Spanish Ministry of Universities, modality "María Zambrano," University of Murcia) and German Research Foundation (Collaborative Research Center 923 "Bedrohte Ordnungen," University of Tübingen, Germany).

The order of authors in this article is alphabetical and does not indicate a hierarchical relationship among them. They all contributed equally to the conceptualization, data analysis, and writing of the introduction and the 3 three articles in this dossier and should be considered co-first authors.

1   Countervailing that generates balance through reciprocity.
2   A statue to General Baquedano.
3   See discussion of the *barras bravas* in the second essay of this dossier.
4   A traditional authority, political leader of a group of Mapuche territories.
5   During the 1990s the Mapuche carried out a series of land occupations. These were initially (1990–94) symbolic in nature, i.e. temporary, and voluntarily (peacefully) discontinued when the police arrived. In a later, more active, phase effective control was asserted over territory (1998 to the present). Some occupations were of mixed type.
6   The Mapuche made use of the agrarian reform years as a way of recovering lands that had been usurped by the Chilean State during the process of installation of indigenous communities within designated, delimited territories.
7   A traditional Mapuche authority who makes contact with the gods in order to heal illnesses and preside over ceremonies.
8   A compound term coined by combining "Mapuche" with "urban-ness" (*urbanidad*).
9   Camilo Catrillanca was a Mapuche community member killed by the police on community lands. The investigation into his death revealed that police officers had concealed evidence and given false statements.
10 A Mapuche wooden statue, linked to funeral rites, that represents communication between our dimension, which is in the middle, and the other dimensions below ground, and in the sky.

References

Antileo, Enrique. 2020. ¡Aquí estamos todavía! Anticolonialismo y emancipación en los pensamientos políticos mapuche y aymara (Chile-Bolivia, 1990–2006) (*We Are Still Here! Anticolonialism and Emancipation in Mapuche and Aymara Political Thought [Chile-Bolivia, 1990–2006]*). Santiago de Chile: Pehuén.

Aniñir, David. (2005) 2018. *Mapurbe. Venganza a raíz* (*Mapurbe: Revenge at the Roots*). Santiago de Chile: Pehuén.

Arendt, Hannah. (1958) 1998. *The Human Condition*. Chicago: The University of Chicago Press.

Butler, Judith. 2015. *Notes Towards a Performative Theory of Assembly*. Cambridge, MA: Harvard University Press.

Cayuqueo, Pedro. 2010. "La bandera es un símbolo de liberación, de auto reconocimiento como nación" (The Flag Is a Symbol of Liberation, of Self-recognition as a Nation). *Azkintuwe* [Place from where you can see]. March 7, https://web.archive.org/web/2010 1028030327/http://azkintuwe.org/may134.htm.

Povinelli, Elizabeth. 2002. *The Cunning of Recognition. Indigenous Alterities and the Making of Australian Multiculturalism*. Durham, NC: Duke University Press.

Simpson, Audra. 2020. "The Sovereignty of Critique." *South Atlantic Quarterly* 119, no. 4: 685–99.

Stoler, Ann Laura. 2016. *Duress: Imperial Durabilities in Our Times*. Durham, NC: Duke University Press.

Notes on Contributors

Şahin Açıkgöz is assistant professor of Islam, gender, and sexuality in the Department for the Study of Religion and a member of the executive committee of the Middle East and Islamic Studies Program at the University of California, Riverside. They were a Chancellor's Postdoctoral Fellow in Religious Studies at UCR from 2020 to 2022. They received their PhD in comparative literature and LGBTQ studies from the University of Michigan, Ann Arbor, where they cofounded the Transnational Gender and Sexuality Studies Rackham Interdisciplinary Workshop and were the Mary Fair Croushore Graduate Fellow at the Institute for the Humanities. They were also the recipient of the 2019 Sarah Pettit Doctoral Fellowship in LGBT Studies at Yale University and the Holstein Dissertation Fellowship in Queer and Transgender Studies in Religion at UC Riverside. Their research areas are queer and trans studies in Islam; slavery, gender, and sexuality in Islamicate societies; trans of color critique; the Global South; transnational feminisms; and gender politics in the Middle East.

Neda Atanasoski is professor and chair of the Harriet Tubman Department of Women, Gender and Sexuality Studies at the University of Maryland, College Park. She is the author of *Humanitarian Violence: The U.S. Deployment of Diversity* (2013), coauthor of *Surrogate Humanity: Race, Robots, and the Politics of Technological Futures* (2019), and coeditor of *Postsocialist Politics and the Ends of Revolution* (2022), (the latter two with Kalindi Vora). She is currently the coeditor of the journal *Critical Ethnic Studies*. Previously, she was a professor and founding codirector of the Center for Racial Justice at UC Santa Cruz.

Angel Aedo is associate professor in anthropology at Pontificia Universidad Católica de Chile and alternate director at the Millennium Institute on Violence and Democracy Research. His research interests concern destabilizing difference, anthropology of security, prison society, (il)legalities, critical migration and border studies, policing, affects, aesthetics, and politics. His work has recently appeared in *Anthropological Theory, Security Dialogue, Critique of Anthropology, Social Anthropology (Anthropologie Sociale), Anthropological Forum, Journal of Material Culture, Journal des Anthropologues, Antípoda, and Revista de Estudios Sociales*. Among his published books are *Experts et Technologies de Gouvernement: Une Généalogie des Think Tanks au Chili (Experts and Technologies of Government: A Genealogy of Think Tanks in Chile)* (2012) and *La Dimensión más Oscura de la Existencia: Indagaciones en Torno al Kieri de los Huicholes (The Darkest Dimension of Existence: An Inquiry into the Kieri of the Huichols)* (2011). Email address: jaedog@uc.cl.

Oriana Bernasconi is professor of sociology at Alberto Hurtado University, where she also serves as codirector of the Interdisciplinary Research Program on Memory and Human Rights. She is an associate researcher at the Millenium Institute on Violence and Democracy Research. Her work examines contemporary subjects and subjectivities and how societies confront state violence and its legacies. Recently she edited the books *Sujetos y subjetividades: Aproximaciones empíricas en tiempos actuales* (*Subjects and Subjectivities: Empirical Approaches in Current Times*) (2022) and *Resistance to Political Violence in Latin America: Documenting Atrocity* (2019) (*Documentar la Atrocidad: Resistir el Terrorismo de Estado* [2021]). Her latest articles appear in *Subjectivity, Discourse and Society, International Journal of Transitional Justice, Colombia Internacional, Antipoda,* and *Boletín de Estética.* Email address: obernasc@uahurtado.cl.

Howard Chiang is Lai Ho and Wu Cho-liu Endowed Chair in Taiwan cultural studies, professor of East Asian languages and cultural studies, and director of the Center for Taiwan Studies at the University of California, Santa Barbara. He is the author of two prize-wining monographs: *After Eunuchs: Science, Medicine, and the Transformation of Sex in Modern China* (2018) and *Transtopia in the Sinophone Pacific* (2021). Between 2019 and 2022, he served as the founding chair of the Society of Sinophone Studies.

Debanuj DasGupta is assistant professor of feminist studies at University of California, Santa Barbara. Debanuj's research and teaching focuses on racialized regulation of space, immigration detention, queer migrations, and the global governance of migration, sexuality, and HIV. Debanuj's scholarly work has been published in journals such as *GLQ, Journal of Human Rights, Human Geography, Women's Studies in Communication, Disability Studies Quarterly, Contemporary South Asia, SEXUALITIES, Gender, Place and Culture,* and *the Scholar and the Feminist (S and F online).* She is the coeditor of *Queer Then and Now: The David R. Kessler Lectures 2002–2020; Friendship as Social Justice Activism: Critical Solidarities in Global Perspective,* and *Queering Digital India: Activisms, Identities and Subjectivities.* Debanuj served as board cochair of the Center for LGBTQ Studies (CLAGS) at the City University of New York between 2017 and 2022. Prior to joining academia, Debanuj worked for over twenty years in movements for sexual liberation and migrant justice in both the US and India.

Joao Gabriel is a Guadeloupean writer, panafricanist, and PhD student in history. He is the author of *Le Blog de Joao,* which addresses issues regarding colonialism, gender, and the African diaspora, especially in the Caribbean.

He is currently working on the history of prison in relation to the French abolition of slavery in the nineteenth century.

Christoph Hanssmann is assistant professor of gender, sexuality, and women's studies at the University of California, Davis. He studies the politics of health, science, and medicine, focusing on relationships between biomedicine and social movements. His first book, *Care without Pathology: How Trans- Health Activists are Changing Medicine* (2023) examines trans- health as a transnationally emergent field and public good, and analyses social movement–driven depathologization in health care. He works collaboratively with researchers and activists in feminist, queer and transfeminist health and justice, and has published articles in *Transgender Studies Quarterly, Medical Anthropology Quarterly,* and *Social Science and Medicine.*

Rana M. Jaleel is an associate professor in the Department of Gender, Sexuality, and Women's Studies and the Department of Asian American Studies at the University of California, Davis, where she chairs the Graduate Group in Cultural Studies and is a Dean's Faculty Fellow as well as a Chancellor's Fellow. Her work examines the politics of evidence: how concepts like labor, sex/gender, race, and property are sustained or transformed through the recognition, narration, and redress of harm. Her book, *The Work of Rape* (2021), received a 2021 Duke University Press Scholars of Color First Book Award and was cowinner of the 2022 Gloria E. Anzaldúa Prize from the National Women's Studies Association. Other academic work has been published in places like *Amerasia, Critical Ethnic Studies, Social Text: Periscope, Cultural Studies, Syndicate,* and *The Brooklyn Law Review.* Dr. Jaleel is part of the *Critical Ethnic Studies* journal's editorial collective. A longtime member of the American Association of University Professors, she presently serves on the Committee on Academic Freedom and Tenure.

Petrus Liu is associate professor of Chinese and comparative literature and of women's, gender, and sexuality studies at Boston University. He is the author of *The Specter of Materialism: Queer Theory and Marxism in the Age of the Beijing Consensus* (2023); *Queer Marxism in Two Chinas* (2015); and *Stateless Subjects: Chinese Martial Arts Literature and Postcolonial History* (2011).

Damián Omar Martínez is postdoctoral researcher "María Zambrano" at the Department of Sociology, University of Murcia (Spain), and Research Fellow at the *Viodemos* Institute on Violence and Democracy Research (Chile). With a background in philosophy and social theory, he works at the ethnographic intersection between anthropology and qualitative sociology. He has conducted ethnographic research in Murcia and Santiago de Chile, on topics like urban diversity, ethics, politics and morality, temporality, and more recently, environmental future-making in Mar Menor, Spain. He has published in journals such as *Social Anthropology* (*Anthropologie Sociale*) *and Anthropological Journal of European Cultures*. Email address: doma@um.es

Durba Mitra is the Richard B. Wolf Associate Professor of Women, Gender, and Sexuality at Harvard University. Mitra works at the intersection of feminist and queer studies. She is the author of *Indian Sex Life: Sexuality and the Colonial Origins of Modern Social Thought* (2020). Mitra's current book, *The Future That Was* (under contract with Princeton University Press), analyzes Third World feminist thought as anti-authoritarianism.

Alicia Olivari is postdoctoral researcher at the School of Anthropology of the Pontificia Universidad Católica de Chile and the Millennium Institute on Violence and Democracy Research. Her main lines of research are the construction of collective memories and their sociopolitical effects, intergenerational transmission, political violence, and collective action. She has published in *Psicologia and Sociedade, Clepsidra, Bitácora Urbano Territorial, Revista de Antropología Social*, and *Endoxa*. Email address: aliciaolivariv@gmail.com

Fernando Pairican holds a PhD in history from the University of Santiago. He is lecturer at the Pontificia Universidad Católica de Chile and researcher at the Millennium Institute on Violence and Democracy Research. His research has focused on the history of the Mapuche movement, the uses of colonial violence, Mapuche political organizations, and their contributions to democracy. Among his recent books are *Nueva Constitución y Pueblos indígenas* (*New Constitution and Indigenous Peoples*) (2016); *Wallmapu: Plurinacionalidad y Nueva Constitución* (*Wallmapu: Plurinationality and New Constitution*) (2020); *Küme Mongen, Suma Qamaña, Mo Ora Riva Riva: Ensayos y propuestas para una Constitución Plurinacional* (*Küme Mongen, Suma Qamaña, Mo Ora Riva Riva: Essays and proposals for a Plurinational Constitution*) (2021); and *Malon: la rebelión del movimiento mapuche 1990–2013* (*Malon. The Rebellion of the Mapuche Movement 1990-2013*) (2014). Email address: fernandopairican@gmail.com.

Juan Porma is a history teacher, holds a master's in applied social sciences, and is a PhD candidate in history at the Pontificia Universidad Católica de Chile. He has worked on the history of Mapuche communities with an emphasis on readings of colonial violence. His recent work focuses on the study of Mapuche politicians in the mid-twentieth century and the transition of the contemporary Mapuche political movement that uses violence as a means of resistance. Email address: juanporma01@gmail.com.

Rahul Rao is reader in international political thought at the University of St Andrews. He is the author of *Out of Time: The Queer Politics of Postcoloniality* (2020) and *Third World Protest: Between Home and the World* (2010).

Evren Savcı is assistant professor of women's, gender, and sexuality studies at Yale University. Her first book, *Queer in Translation: Sexual Politics under Neoliberal Islam* (2021), analyzes sexual politics under contemporary Turkey's AKP regime with an eye to the travel and translation of sexual political vocabulary. Her work on the intersections of language, knowledge, sexual politics, neoliberalism, and religion has appeared in the *Journal of Marriage and the Family, Ethnography, Sexualities, Political Power and Social Theory, Theory and Event, Journal of Feminist Studies in Religion,* and *GLQ.* She received her PhD in sociology from the University of Southern California. Following her PhD, she was a postdoctoral fellow at The Sexualities Project at Northwestern (SPAN).

Svati P. Shah is associate professor of women, gender, sexuality studies at the University of Massachusetts, Amherst. They are also a research associate in the Department of Anthropology, Archaeology and Development Studies at the University of Pretoria and are affiliated to the Centre for Women's and Gender Studies (SKOK) and the Global Research Programme on Inequality (GRIP) at the University of Bergen. Their work has appeared in a range of scholarly journals, including *Gender and History, Cultural Dynamics* and *Antipode.* Their first book, *Street Corner Secrets: Sex, Work and Migration in the City of Mumbai* was published in 2014 by Duke University Press. Their second monograph, *Dissent in Queer Times* (forthcoming), is an ethnography of queer and transgender movements in India that emerged in the wake of autonomous feminist, civil liberties, and democratic rights movements after the Indian Emergency in the 1970s.

Hentyle Yapp is associate professor of performance studies in the Department of Theatre and Dance at UC San Diego. He is the author of *Minor China: Method, Materialisms, and the Aesthetic* (2021) and the coeditor of *Saturation: Race, Art, and the Circulation of Value* (2020).

DOI 10.1215/00382876-10937412

Keep up to date on new scholarship

Issue alerts are a great way to stay current on all the cutting-edge scholarship from your favorite Duke University Press journals. This free service delivers tables of contents directly to your inbox, informing you of the latest groundbreaking work as soon as it is published.

To sign up for issue alerts:

1. Visit **dukeu.press/register** and register for an account. You do not need to provide a customer number.

2. After registering, visit **dukeu.press/alerts**.

3. Go to "Latest Issue Alerts" and click on "Add Alerts."

4. Select as many publications as you would like from the pop-up window and click "Add Alerts."

Rana M. Jaleel and Evren Savcı

Transnational Queer Materialism

The introduction to this special issue takes up the narrations and values produced by the travels of words like *queer of color, race,* and *racial capitalism* to
both comobilize and retheorize queer of color critique and the content and
contours of global racial capitalism. With and beyond the story of US empire
and the transatlantic slave trade—from peripheral European engagements
with Africa to the circulation of caste in Africa via Indian Ocean worlds—in
this special issue the authors examine some of the histories and present
modes of capitalist accumulation that are relevant to telling global stories of
race and capitalism. A queer/trans lens keeps the authors' attention trained
as well on the arrangements and estrangements of the sex/gender systems
that power such narratives of race and capitalism. So positioned, the authors
enter ongoing debates on the geopolitics of queer studies, the import of queer
materialism, and theorizations of racial capitalism by asking (1) What is the
"racial" of racial capitalism?, and (2) What is the "of color" in queer/trans of
color critique? The questions form a method for thinking global racial capitalism and queer/trans of color study together—what the authors call transnational queer materialism.

Keywords   racial capitalism, transnational gender studies, queer materialisms, queer/trans of
color critique

Neda Atanasoski and Rana M. Jaleel

Reproducing Racial Capitalism:
Sexual Slavery and Islam at
the Edges of Queer of Color Critique

This article tracks contemporary debates surrounding human trafficking, sex slavery, and the slave trade, in which the specter of the Ottoman empire and its system of slavery—as well as other "Oriental" slave systems—emerge as templates for imagining the place of sex in slavery. At the same time, the authors highlight how Ottoman and "Oriental" slavery is largely considered irrelevant to the genealogy of present-day racial capitalism. By contrast, the authors argue that considering historically parallel and entangled slave systems is important not just to accounts of modern-day slavery but also for how we conceptualize the "racial" in racial capitalism and the "queer" and "of color" in queer of color critique. Building on Black feminist historiography on the transatlantic slave trade, the commitments of queer of color critique, and contemporary research concerning sexual violation and racial capitalism, the authors explore how interconnected struggles across the globe are partitioned by imagined frameworks of racial and sexual difference that isolate entangled systems of gendered and sexual enslavement.

Keywords   sexual slavery, racial capitalism, white slavery, Ottoman empire, human trafficking

Petrus Liu

Homonormativity's Racial Capitalism:
On the Differential Allocation of Grievability

This essay argues that racial capitalism in East Asia requires and reproduces a hierarchical reading of gender-nonconforming bodies and desires, while the rise of a homonormative discourse finds expression in racialized violence against Chinese-identified subjects. These entanglements preclude an analysis of Taiwan's geostrategic role in a US-led regime of capital accumulation and dispossession. Shifting the conversation from a celebratory view of Taiwan's LGBT legal and civic victories to homonationalism's complicities with racial capitalism, this essay considers memoirs of survivors of the Chinese Civil War as articulating an alternative and unintelligible order of queer kinship rooted in the differential allocation of grievability.

Keywords   racial capitalism, homonormativity, China, queer kinship, memoir

Rahul Rao

Is the Homo in Homocapitalism
the Caste in Caste Capitalism
and the Racial in Racial Capitalism

This article attempts to think through the relationship between homocapitalism, racial capitalism, and caste capitalism. It conceptualizes homocapitalism as immanent within the assemblage of homonationalism but also as becoming partially disembedded from it as a result of the shift in conjuncture from the "war on terror" to the "global financial crisis." Having made a case for the partial autonomy of homocapitalism from homonationalism, the article explores the relationship between homocapitalism, racial capitalism, and the emergent theoretical conceptualization of caste capitalism. The author demonstrates how the central analytical insight of racial and caste capitalism—namely, that capitalism mobilizes precapitalist social hierarchies as a means of furthering accumulation—throws open the field for a range of ideological approaches that seek emancipation from racial and caste oppression through varying relationships with capitalism. This allows the author to make a crucial distinction between analytics and ideologies, a distinction that has been unhelpfully blurred in discussions of homocapitalism. As ideology, homocapitalism intensifies and derives some of its purchase from its affinities with discourses of liberatory capitalism such as Black capitalism and Dalit capitalism. As analytic, homocapitalism illuminates the fractioning of queerness in terms of its potential (ability, willingness) to contribute to production and social reproduction. Central to the comparison around which this article is structured is the illumination of racialization as a technology for the extraction and attribution of value that operates across racial capitalism, caste capitalism, and homocapitalism.

Keywords homocapitalism, homonationalism, racial capitalism, caste capitalism

Svati P. Shah

Caste Capitalism and Queer Theory:
Beyond Identity Politics in India

This article uses "caste capitalism" as a framework for thinking through the entanglements of sexuality politics, caste, and capital in contemporary India. The author uses a queer hermeneutic of heritability and endogamy, drawing inspiration from Indian feminist, queer, anti-caste, and Marxist critiques, and from racial capitalism as theorized by Cedric Robinson. The author argues that caste capitalism, read through a queer hermeneutic, makes the historicity of caste rules clearer, showing how they are both enforced through violent social norms, and, at the same time, selectively or intermittently ignored, e.g., in spaces of non-normative sexuality and gender expression. The use of this hermeneutic emphasizes the normative functions of caste-based endogamy while undoing the idea of sexuality as a scientized aspect of the privatized and "private" self, which is understood here as an effect of conceiving the body as hived off from questions of land rights, economic autonomy, and historically contingent iterations of caste categories and relations. This use of caste capitalism contributes to countermanding Hindu nationalist deployments of homonationalist rhetoric that rely on the ahistoricity of caste as a central aspect of arguing for a timeless and territorially coherent religion and culture that must now be defended through violent and autocratic means.

Keywords   queer hermeneutics, caste, capital, India, homonationalism

Hentyle Yapp

The Ubiquity of Asia:
Cai Guo-Qiang's Fireworks
and Spectral Marxism

Asia is everywhere. Asia feels ubiquitous, from soft to hard power; from high to low culture; and from the Americas to Africa. In the American cycle of capital accumulation, under Giovanni Arrighi's schema, the overrepresentation of the United States was marked through representation-based and symbolic notions like Disneyfication (Jean Baudrillard) and "the ascendancy of whiteness" (Rey Chow). Under our contemporary Asian cycle of capital accumulation, this geographic area's affective ubiquity appears much like that of the US by saturating global public sentiment. However, considering that Asia's ubiquity emerges across sites like China, South Korea, India, and Japan, among others, what might we use to capture this sense of affective intensity and spread beyond representation-based frames? More specifically, how do we contend with geographic space within racial capital today, and how might we update our models for understanding race and capital so as to fully grapple with this transitional moment from American empire to Global Asia? Under the American cycle, representational frames like Orientalism and white supremacy emerged to understand Asian racialization. Can these frames still help explain the ubiquity of Asia today? This essay explores how we might discuss the subject beyond representation and in light of the ubiquity of Asia and what methods we deploy for Marxist analysis. This essay focuses less on Asian bodies and Asian spaces and turns toward aesthetic objects and practices that engage the affective sublime. More specifically, it examines the aesthetics of fireworks for what they might offer as a lexicon to contend with the transition in cycles of capital accumulation and changes in our ideas of space and race. The article thus turns to the artist Cai Guo-Qiang for insight on the subject amid contemporary racial capital and the methods available for critique.

Keywords   Marxism, aesthetics, race, global Asia, China

Şahin Açıkgöz, Howard Chiang, Debanuj DasGupta,
Joao Gabriel, Christoph Hanssmann, Rana M. Jaleel,
Durba Mitra, and Evren Savcı

Roundtable: Queer/Trans of Color Transits and
the Imaginaries of Racial Capitalism

In this roundtable, scholars respond to the following guiding questions of
the special issue: *Racial capitalism in US scholarship is necessarily and rightfully narrated through the Transatlantic slave trade. While this is a globally relevant history for understanding the past and the present of transnational racial
orders, what other histories and present modes of capitalist accumulation are
relevant to telling a global history of racial capitalism? How do queer hermeneutics reckon with global and transnational histories of social differentiation
that ground in other or additional intellectual traditions of what we might
expansively call "race"? How would queer of color critique as an analytic be
useful to question the very making of abject and abnormal bodies, the structures
of knowledge and regimes of truth that produce them, and the political economies that necessitate them? To what extent does positioning queer and trans of
color critique as methods objects and subjects, "beyond identity politics," or even
"the Human," alleviate or otherwise reconfigure these issues?*

Keywords   religion, Ottoman empire, East African slave trade, Turkey, Global South

Angel Aedo, Oriana Bernasconi, Damián Omar Martínez, Alicia Olivari, Fernando Pairican, Juan Porma

Introduction: Widening the Space of Politics

This dossier proposes to explore the uprising as a critical event provoking unprecedented processes of political subjectivation and opening the field of action and influence to subjects who had been kept on the margins of the construction of history. This introduction begins by describing the social uprising that occurred in Chile in 2019, the largest cycle of protests since the end of the Pinochet era. It then discusses the notions of critical event and political subjectivation and the methods followed with the research participants. Finally, drawing on the three essays, the introduction identifies four dimensions of the critical nature of this event and its entanglements with the production of political subjectivation, namely, time, oikos, police, and politics.

Keywords   event, critique, political subjectivation, Chile, uprising

Angel Aedo, Oriana Bernasconi, Damián Omar Martínez, Alicia Olivari, Fernando Pairican, Juan Porma

Multitude and Memory in the Chilean Social Uprising

Between October 2019 and March 2020 Chile experienced the most massive and heavily repressed cycle of social protests in its post-dictatorship (1973–90) history. This essay explores the social uprising as a critical event of political subjectivation through the story of Ricardo, an ordinary young medical technician with no background of political affiliation who fully immersed himself in the forefront of confrontation with the police in the ground zero protest zone while also providing first-aid assistance to those injured. Two vectors triggering Ricardo's unexpected and sudden transformation into an activist are identified: the intergenerational potency of antidictatorial memories and the power of the spontaneous multitude in demonstration. In recalling the dictatorship, Ricardo and his friends used to ask themselves, "What would I have done if I'd been there?" In the face of the social uprising, Ricardo brings to the present that generation-specific question and responds with total exposure, defending the multitude and healing the wounded. We argue that the event's critical nature is interpreted in the light of the past. Ricardo's involvement becomes an ethical imperative in his time and in his own history. This duty fuels his mobilization and desire for social transformation, blurring the analytical boundaries between ethics and politics.

Keywords Chile, political subjectivation, critical event, antidictatorial memory, generation

Angel Aedo, Oriana Bernasconi, Damián Omar Martínez, Alicia Olivari, Fernando Pairican, Juan Porma

A Politics of Care from the Margins of Chile's Social Uprising

This essay addresses the Chilean social uprising of 2019 through the experiences of Marta and Juan, two residents of the peripheries of Santiago, who became involved in this event despite having no previous experience of participation in social and political organizations. It explores this event's strength in triggering contentious actions on the urban margins, and repression by the police-criminal apparatus of the state. Delving into the ethical and biographical dispositions facilitating this couple's politicization during the course of the revolt, it argues that the critical force of this event lies precisely in the entry of unexpected—even unwanted—actors into the political space. Through a biographical narrative approach, it details the shift of its protagonists. By way of subjectivation, this shift unfolds in them a critical attitude embodied in public interventions demanding equality and social justice and in acts of community and neighborhood solidarity. The case sheds light on a rarely explored dimension of social revolts: the way certain actors collectively experience these critical events through a politics of care, bringing the polis into the domestic space, and from such politicization of the *oikos*, opens an unusual way of challenging the police order of their world.

Keywords Chile, political subjectivation, prison, care, critical event

**Angel Aedo, Oriana Bernasconi, Damián Omar Martínez,
Alicia Olivari, Fernando Pairican, Juan Porma**

Mapuche Anticolonial Politics
and Chile's Social Uprising

This essay examines milestones in the life history of one subject, Mauricio Lepin, and his involvement in the Chilean social uprising. By exploring the encounter of his trajectory with the uprising, the essay reveals under-explored dimensions of the anticolonial character of this critical event in Chile's history of the present. Lepin's case shows the entanglement of a long history of dispossession and resistance of the Mapuche people with a biographical story of social marginalization, political exclusion, and economic precariousness, shared with large majorities of Mapuche and non-Mapuche youth. It concludes by analyzing how, through the uprising, Lepin appears before himself as an actor among a multitude in struggle by putting into action the plural right to appear and the self-determination of a sovereign people.

Keywords   social uprising, political subjectivation, anti-colonial struggle, Mapuche, Chile

Printed and bound by CPI Group (UK) Ltd, Croydon, CR0 4YY

13/04/2025

14656470-0001